Revealing
King Arthur

REVEALING KING ARTHUR

SWORDS, STONES AND DIGGING FOR CAMELOT

CHRISTOPHER GIDLOW

For AVG and VJG

First published 2010

The History Press
The Mill, Brimscombe Port
Stroud, Gloucestershire, GL5 2QG
www.thehistorypress.co.uk

© Christopher Gidlow, 2010

The right of Christopher Gidlow to be identified as the Author
of this work has been asserted in accordance with the
Copyrights, Designs and Patents Act 1988.

British Library Cataloguing in Publication Data.
A catalogue record for this book is available from the British Library.

ISBN 978 0 7524 5507 5

Typesetting and origination by The History Press
Printed in Great Britain
Manufacturing managed by Jellyfish Print Solutions Ltd

CONTENTS

LIST OF MAPS

ACKNOWLEDGEMENTS

First and foremost I have to thank Mark Pluciennik, Simon James and Ruth Young, and the rest of the distance learning team at the University of Leicester School of Archaeology, without whom I would never have managed to get the research done for this book. Also my employer, Historic Royal Palaces, and especially John Barnes and David Souden, for supporting my studies.

Since publishing *The Reign of Arthur*, I've enjoyed a lively correspondence with readers of all sorts, which has helped generate some of the ideas you find here. Thanks to Terry Price for pushing me to review the chronology of the period. Howard Wiseman's very perceptive review was extremely helpful to me as have been his subsequent comments. Peter Field, Francis Pryor, Tom Green, Malin Holst, Vicky Dawson, the late Richard Avent of Cadw, Sarah Jackson of Centrescreen. Geoff Denford of Winchester City Museum and Lisa Hill of English Heritage have taken the time to answer my questions. Especial thanks to my most indefatigable correspondents Andy Derksen, Edwin Pace and Phil Hirst of PlanetX Television, who encouraged me to make up my mind on several key issues.

Apologies in advance to Ken Dark, Nick Higham and Tom Green. Along with Christopher Snyder, in another age they would be considered the vanguard of Arthurian scholarship. My use of their work in the service of a pro-Arthur position should not be taken as a reflection of their ideas, and my disagreements with Higham and Green in particular do not in any way diminish my respect for and enjoyment of their work.

Andrew Smith has once again been kind enough to correct my Latin and give me the benefit of his vast Arthurian knowledge and his library. I'm extremely grateful to Julie Hudson for her support and encouragement, and permission to use her super maps. Finally, I would never have written any of this had it not been for the influence of my parents, Alan Gidlow, whose digs on the Saxon Shore forts introduced me to archaeology from a very early age, and Valerie Gidlow, who read me all the stories about King Arthur and who made sure we spent every one of her 'Saturdays off' visiting historic sites.

The maps used in this book are copyright Julie Hudson and are used with permission. The quotations from Caxton's introduction to Malory's *Le Morte D'Arthur* is taken from Vinaver, A., Malory *Works* (OUP, 1971). It is reprinted by permission of Oxford University Press. Quotations from Gildas are reproduced by kind permission from Arthurian Period Sources, volume 7, *Gildas* (edited and translated by Michael Winterbottom), published in 1978 by Phillimore.

INTRODUCTION

'The Age of Arthur'

In the darkest of Dark Ages, Britain stood alone. Barbarian hordes assailed the island. From their beachheads on the eastern coasts they raged across the land. With battering rams they broke down the walls of the Roman cities. They heaped the bodies of the slaughtered Britons in the town squares, giving them no burial save in the bellies of the beasts.

Abandoning the cities, the British threw defences round the ancient forts of their ancestors. Withstanding the flood, they at last fought back against the invaders. Battles, sieges, a generation of campaigns and at last, victory! Though the lowlands had been lost, stable British kingdoms remained in the west and north, and in embattled enclaves amid the alien settlements. Long after, when the darkness lifts a little, we find sources naming their saviour in their darkest hour. Arthur.

This, at least, was the story the Britons told of the end of Roman Britain and the establishment of their Dark Age kingdoms. The poets sang of these realms of adventure, ruled by King Arthur and his knights. Behind these romances could be found legends; behind those, fragments of history. But what lay at their heart? Reality or just the wishful thinking of a later age?

Did King Arthur really exist? If this story is true, we would expect it to be confirmed not just in the written records but by archaeology. Forts and cities, battlefields and burial sites do not just disappear. Surely modern archaeologists would have no difficulty uncovering the truth about King Arthur?

In this volume we will be examining various attempts to pin down this mythical figure to reality. Twentieth-century archaeologists and historians generally thought they had the answer already. Up until the 1970s it was 'yes' and archaeology would provide the final definitive proof, or at least corroboration. Since then

i. KING ARTHUR'S BRITAIN

KEY

✗   Battle sites

Licat Anir   Wonders

the academics have answered 'no', and no amount of archaeological evidence could possibly alter this.

From the outside, the question is an odd one. Did Henry VIII exist? Did Queen Victoria? Do history books about them have to start by proving their existence? Arguably Arthur stands equally high in public knowledge of British history, one of the most well known of our monarchs, certainly the most well known of our 'medieval' ones, as the 2002 poll of the 'Greatest Britons' showed.

Imagine that you were invited to a costume party on the theme of King Arthur. Without much thought, men would dress up in cloak and crown, or more likely knitted 'chainmail' and plastic helmet. Women might opt for a long dress with exaggeratedly wide sleeves, a crown or perhaps a headdress like a tall cone with a veil hanging off it. More adventurous guests might choose a wizard's robe covered with stars and a pointed hat. Pushed for character names, Lancelot, Guinevere and Merlin might crop up. You can imagine that the host might provide a round table, punch mixed in a holy grail and the motif of a sword in a stone might inform the buffet food. Guests might contribute some themed banter about the air speed of a fully laden swallow or strange women lying in ponds distributing swords.

Imagine now that you were invited to a party on the theme of Henry II or Edward I. They were undeniably important monarchs in the medieval history of Britain, but difficult to place visually and without any associated images or themes to make such a party accessible. This is why the question is so emotive and why, outside the contemporary academic world, the answer is still likely to be given as 'yes'. Arthur is not just any 'medieval' monarch. He comes complete with a package of imagery and associations which are widely familiar and entertaining. It is no more conceivable that there wasn't a real King Arthur than there wasn't a real Henry VIII.

'But fained and fables'

It is surprising to realise that scepticism about King Arthur can be traced back to the medieval period with which he is most closely associated. At the very end of the middle ages, in the early 1480s, the first printer in England, William Caxton, was being coaxed into publishing a work on King Arthur. English material for an English market, rather than the classical or French material he had been translating. Caxton professed scepticism: 'divers men hold opinion that there was no such Arthur and that all such books as been made of him be but fained and fables, because that some chronicles make of him no mention ne remember him nothing.' Caxton knew that fine and inspiring tales of Arthur existed, tales which could attract and excite an audience, but he considered that their value as improving literature would be compromised if there were no factual basis to them. It is worth mentioning here that Caxton was suggesting that the Arthurian legends were less well founded than those of the Trojan War, the subject of his first book.

Against this, 'gentlemen' including 'one in special', usually assumed to be Arthurian enthusiast Anthony Woodville, Earl Rivers, argued that Arthur's existence was supported by ancient chronicles. Moreover there was much physical evidence to confirm his existence:

> first ye may see his sepulture in the monastery of Glastonbury ... in the abbey of Westminster, at St. Edward's shrine, remaineth the print of his seal in red wax, closed in beryl ... in the castle of Dover ye may see Gawain's skul and Cradok's mantle, at Winchester, the Round Table, in other places Lancelot's sword and many other things ... in Wales, in the town of Camelot, the great stones and marvellous works of iron lying under ground, and royal vaults which divers now living hath seen.

Caxton was convinced, or at least convinced that a viable market for Arthurian material existed – he was nothing if not a businessman. In July 1485, he published what would be one of his most celebrated works, the *Morte d'Arthur*, using translations, adaptations and new material composed by Sir Thomas Malory 14 years before.

Malory told the story of Arthur, according to him a fifth-century King of England, his conquests, the exploits of his knights and his death. Malory took pains to stress that the action took place in the real England, not in a mythical neverland as might be imagined from the French sources. He offered modern equivalents of the romance place names, Camelot was Winchester, Lancelot's castle Joyous Garde was Alnwick or Bamborough, Astolat was Guildford.

Essentially, these have been the grounds on which King Arthur has been debated ever since. He features in romances, of which the *Morte d'Arthur* is often seen as the 'authorised version', tales of chivalry and adventure, romance, wonder and tragedy which continue to inspire. The tales seem grounded in reality and this lends them an immediacy, an authenticity, beyond that of fantasy. Unfortunately, it remains true that some 'chronicles', particularly those historical works closest to the fifth century, make no mention of him, and those that do are steeped in fabulous material. Supporters of a historical Arthur still defend the historical material in which he does appear against these charges, using the supporting evidence of archaeology to confirm the written accounts.

Getting Medieval

The first point to note is the time period in which Arthur is placed. The popular image of King Arthur, informing our choices for the themed party, is that he was a 'medieval' monarch. England has a late date for the middle ages, starting in 1066 and ending in 1485 with the Battle of Bosworth, less than two months after the publication of *Morte d'Arthur*. For most of this period, Arthur was a popular figure in the romances, the upper-class fiction celebrating chivalry and courtly love. The romances, though often nominally set in the past, featured all the best parts of the contemporary lives of their readers and writers. The characters wore the same clothes, lived in the same sort of castles and enjoyed the same recreations as their modern day consumers. When illustrated versions of the tales became the vogue, in the second half of the thirteenth century, Arthur and his court were immortalised in visual form in the fashions of that age. It is from here that the image of knights in armour, flowing robes and pointy hats originated. This was common to all the romances, whether ostensibly about the Trojan War, Alexander the Great, Charlemagne or characters from the Old Testament. The difference with Arthur is that no competing 'historical' image was retrieved in the renaissance, leaving him stuck in the middle ages while other historical figures celebrated in romances are now visually assigned to their proper period.

In spite of the anachronism of their portrayals, there is no doubt in the medieval sources that Arthur was a hero from a much earlier epoch. The late thirteenth-century Arthurian enthusiasts Edward I and Eleanor of Castile, who in pictures look very much like archetypal 'Arthurian' monarchs, are in fact separated from him in time by seven centuries, as distant as they are from us.

Discovering King Arthur

My journey to uncover the reality of Arthurian Britain begins with the supposed discovery of King Arthur's body at Glastonbury in 1191. Most of the evidence, however, was found in the last 50 years, when Arthurian sites were subjected to new, scientific archaeology. These have yielded fascinating discoveries, but what they tell us about the legends is less than clear. Whether the evidence was used to confirm or refute the traditional narratives depended more on who uncovered them and when, rather than what they actually found. The historicity of Arthur was 'deeply contested across the twentieth century' (Higham 2002: 10). Thus archaeologists in the 1960s and 70s were eager to link the name of Arthur to the sites beneath their spades. These were men who had grown up during an age when war and defence against German invasion had been a commonplace. They interpreted their findings as confirming the written sources, which described the fifth and sixth centuries as a time of desperate warfare as beleaguered Britons resisted the invasion of German barbarians. This approach culminated in the self-proclaimed 'Quest for Camelot' – Leslie Alcock's excavations at South Cadbury hill fort.

Their rivals and successors led a backlash which swept all before it. They poured scorn on the suggestion there had ever been wars of conquest and resistance, let alone a King Arthur to play a leading part. By the 1980s Alcock was publicly repudiating his former beliefs. Tenured academics mocked the fanciful notions of their predecessors. Arthur's name vanished from the covers of academic literature. The long-awaited reports on Cadbury/Camelot dismissed him altogether. The result of the debate is that, in 1971, Leslie Alcock could entitle his book on British history and archaeology AD 367–634 *Arthur's Britain* (Alcock 1971). Thirty years later, Ken Dark, covering more or less the same subject in *Britain and the End of the Roman Empire* (Dark 2000), never uses the name Arthur at all.

Nothing in any published excavation had disproved the idea that a king called Arthur lived and led the Britons. It was textual criticism, combined with archaeological fashions and a changed perception of Britain as a place of cultural integration rather than a post-imperial power, which altered the way archaeologists interpreted our past.

The casualties in this war of words have been objectivity and engagement with the public. While the archaeologists of the 1960s were happy to link with popular culture, placing the names of Arthur and Camelot on the front of their best-selling books, those who followed them hid in the obscurity of academic periodicals. The public, they seemed to think, were irredeemably wedded to the fanciful notions of medieval romance and could never be persuaded of the new, anti-Arthurian orthodoxy, unable to shake the 'power of the search for the literal verification of myths and legends' (Fleming 2006: 64), symptomatic in Fleming's view of society's retreat into the reassurance of myth and irrationalism in general.

It is true that the public's belief in Arthur has not waned, and this conflict between public perception and current academic orthodoxy will be a continuing theme on the journey to 'reveal' King Arthur. There is a feeling that relics or 'proof' of King Arthur are the sorts of things archaeologists are expected to uncover. The completely un-Arthurian televised *Big Dig* was publicised with trailers 'which showed a woman going down into a pit and coming back waving Excalibur' (Smith 2003 quoted by Hale 2006: 257). The *Time Team Royal Special* was celebrated in the press as 'Time Team solves mystery of the Round Table' (Davies 2006).

It was the discovery of an inscribed stone at Tintagel, Arthur's fabled birthplace, that brought the archaeological debate back to the fore. Once again, tangible proof was emerging from beneath the ground confirming some important details of the Arthurian story. Yet the discoverers seemed to bend over backwards to deny the link.

The stifling of all academic debate about the connection between the written sources and the archaeological remains is every bit as counter-productive as the earlier unthinking acceptance of the traditional accounts. Can archaeology really tell the story of Arthurian Britain when the written records fail? Far from disproving the historical basis of the Arthurian legends, archaeologists have illuminated the context which gave rise to the myths and point towards a new history of the fifth and sixth centuries.

How Dark were the Dark Ages?

In my day job, I work as an interpretation manager. It is my responsibility to make the past accessible to the visitors who come to our sites, to make connections with what they already know as a means of exploring the complexities of the buildings and their stories. As we examine Arthurian sites you will find me perhaps unduly interested in how they are presented, by signs, audio-guides and such like. Similarly I am interested in how archaeologists publish their excavations, the language they use and the assumptions they make.

Francis Pryor (2004: 179) ridicules 'an 'expert' in 'interpretation'' for the use of the term 'Dark Age' throughout the English Heritage guide to Tintagel, instead of the archaeologist-preferred 'early Christian'. Here, I totally agree with the interpreter. 'Dark Age' at least conveys the right era and level of material culture and is very likely to be familiar to a visitor. 'Early Christian' makes me think of bearded men with robes out in the Holy Land, or perhaps martyrs being thrown to lions. In this precise case, arguing that Tintagel was a secular site not a monastic one, calling the sixth-century remains 'early Christian' could be rather confusing.

Other terms sometimes suggested for the period AD 400–600 are equally unhelpful: 'Late Antique' (grandfather clocks?), Brythonic (Conan the Barbarian?) Early Medieval (knights in armour?). They simply serve to obscure what the archaeologist is talking about from the general public.

The renaissance originators of the term 'the middle ages' used it to refer to the 1000 years which separated their own early fifteenth-century era of classical 'rebirth' from the fall of the Roman Empire in the West. Trying to revert to this wide definition is fighting a losing battle and, in the case of King Arthur, counter-productive. 'Medieval' means castles, knights in armour, heraldry, chivalry and the feudal system, all firmly connected with the legendary Arthur rather than the historical one. For this reason I am happy to use the term 'Dark Age' for the period in which the Western Roman Empire fell (in Britain 409/410) and barbarian kingdoms jostled for position in the wreckage. It ends with the establishment of recognisable modern states (England in the British Isles, from the tenth century at the earliest).

The era in British history assigned to King Arthur, somewhere between the mid-fifth and the mid-sixth centuries is, by most people's standards, a real dark age. Social systems which had endured 400 years disappeared, material culture declined catastrophically and equally importantly written sources all but dried up. This is not to deny that there was beauty, learning, perhaps a vibrant era of change and experimentation. But the fact a chieftain of the period might have worn magnificent jewellery (this has been inspiring 'Dark Age not so dark' headlines since the discovery of the Sutton Hoo treasure in 1939) should not override the fact that he and his people had no running water, no books, did not mint their own coins and that we often do not even know their names. They might as well have been living in prehistoric times.

I also make no apology for referring to the character we are looking for as 'King Arthur'. This is to distinguish him from any other 'Arthur' there might have been. It is sometimes argued that, though he might have existed he was not a king. It is questionable whether there was a difference between a 'real' king and a very powerful warlord in the Dark Ages. There are good examples from the period of warlords ending up as kings.

The focus of this book is the tangible physical remains which may or may not be linked to Arthur. Readers interested in the arguments over the written sources can follow these up in *The Reign of Arthur* (Gidlow 2004) where they are covered in depth. It was suggested in the 1970s that these were flawed and could not be accepted uncritically as true. That may well be so but hostile academics went far beyond this, insisting that that they must be rejected uncritically as false. This absurd overreaction had the effect of setting an agenda in which scepticism of the most blinkered kind was valued as 'more academic' than belief, no matter how circumspect. I completely reject the validity of this. I make no secret that I take a positivist view. It is possible that Arthur existed and I consider all evidence with that possibility in mind. There are two specific areas where we will need to look afresh at the written sources, however. One is to counter new and detailed arguments setting out to *prove* that Arthur was not a historical character. The other is to investigate the possibility of establishing a detailed chronology of the Arthurian period.

Unlike some other books which claim to reveal the secret of King Arthur, I do not intend to unmask him hiding behind some other name. Usually these 'real Arthurs' are insubstantial figures from genealogies or medieval texts of whom we know even less than we do about King Arthur. Neither do I intend to reveal, against all odds, that King Arthur 'shared my postcode'. I am originally from Kent, now living across the border in Sussex and I do not think Arthur lived in either county!

It is possible that proof of Arthur's existence may be found. Arthur lived in a literate society, albeit barely so, and until we find a monument to him, a coin minted by him or an object with his name upon it, we cannot be certain that we have 'revealed' him. True, such items have supposedly been found but are now lost, proven of later date or of such hopelessly poor provenance that no archaeologist will touch them. In the absence of such items, we cannot claim to have proved any particular theory. Instead, we will be looking at attempts by archaeologists to reveal him, sites which were taken as revealing him and, just as importantly, sites which would have been taken as revealing him had not archaeological fashions parted company from such ideas in the 1970s

We will journey through Arthur's Britain, from mythical Avalon and Arthur's 'birthplace' at Tintagel to the site of his final battle. We search for Camelot and the 'war-zone' where Arthur's Britons struggled for survival against invading Saxons. What have the archaeologists found at these sites of legend? Do they confirm or contradict the traditional accounts? And why have academics, keen to embrace Arthur in the 1960s and '70s, now turned so emphatically against him? We shall see what has really been revealed about the Britain later generations claimed King Arthur ruled.

1

THE ISLE OF AVALON

In our own lifetime Arthur's body was discovered at Glastonbury, although the legends had always encouraged us to believe that there was something otherworldly about his ending, that he had resisted death. (Gerald of Wales *De principis instructione*: I)

In 1191, the monks of Glastonbury Abbey dug a grave between two ancient 'pyramids' in the graveyard for one of their number who had recently died. There had been inscriptions on the pyramids, now illegible due to their 'barbarous character and worn state' (Ralph of Coggeshall *Chronicon Anglicanum*: 36).

The monks had to dig deep. According to the Margam chronicle (in Barber 1986: 131) they uncovered a woman's coffin, beneath which was a second, containing a man. Under these was a third, identified by an inscribed lead cross. This was probably a not untypical result of digging in a crowded graveyard beside an ancient church. The lowest coffin was 'an extremely old sarcophagus' (Ralph of Coggeshall: 36).

When Gerald of Wales visited Glastonbury soon afterwards, he was told of only a single coffin, a hollowed-out oak bole, divided two-thirds of the way along its length to include a man's body in the longer part and a woman's, identified by a tress of blond hair, in the shorter (Gerald of Wales *De principis instructione*: I).

Ralegh Radford's excavation in 1962 found what seems to have been the original hole, irregular in shape and filled in soon after opening, using refuse from the building works of 1184–89. The hole had destroyed two or three of the slab-lined graves belonging to the earliest stratum (Radford 1968: 107). There were no finds to securely date this level, except that it pre-dated the ninth century. Radford theorised they were part of the original church, in place before 688.

When the slab covering the final coffin was raised, the monks found a leaden cross fixed to the underside, with its inscribed face turned inwards towards the slab. Prising it off, they could read the name of the man buried beneath. Abbot Henry showed Gerald of Wales the very cross: Gerald examined it closely, tracing the inscription himself: 'Here lies buried the famous king Arthur with Guinevere his second wife in the Isle of Avalon' (Gerald of Wales *De principis instructione*: I). Others reported a shorter inscription, without mention of Guinevere (Ralph of Coggeshall: 36), but Gerald is adamant on the wording, recording his surprise that Arthur had two wives.

There is a picture in William Camden's *Britannia* (1610) of what purported to be the cross in his day. This has no mention of Guinevere and cannot be the object Gerald saw. Gerald insists that the entire inscription was on the inner side.

The blonde hair from the woman's grave disintegrated immediately when touched by a lustful monk (Gerald of Wales *De principis instructione*: I). However, Arthur's bones were available for inspection. The shin bone was three inches longer than that of the tallest man present. The skull was huge and marked with ten or more wounds. All were mended except the last gash, presumably the mortal one (Gerald of Wales *De principis instructione*: I).

Whodunit?

The sensational find was accepted as real by all contemporaries. There is nothing about the discovery which is obviously outlandish. The bones, while huge, were clearly human. Nevertheless, it is difficult to find any modern description of the discovery which does not include the word 'hoax' (Time Team website) and cast aspersions on the monks or King Henry II as perpetrators of some Piltdown Man-style deception. The details of the discovery are treated as clues in an armchair 'whodunit'. Rahtz (1993: 43, following Gransden 1976) suggests the monks deliberately buried two skeletons and the cross, then invited the famous writer Gerald of Wales to add credence to the proceedings.

The old church at Glastonbury had burnt down in 1184 and the need to pay for rebuilding provided a possible motive. Diversion of donations to the Crusade with the accession of Richard the Lionheart might have added to the financial imperative (Wood 1991: 276). However, no evidence of financial benefit to the abbey has ever been advanced (Ashe 2002: 249). The idea rests on a misunderstanding of how pilgrimages and donations worked. Pilgrims, although they had much in common with modern tourists (Selwyn 1996: 6), did not visit shrines nor part with their money without expecting something in return. This would be in the form of spiritual indulgences or miracles gained by the intercession of the saint. Previous examples of Glastonbury's 'form' included fraudulent claims to possess the relics of Saints Patrick, Brigit, Gildas and Dunstan (Wood 1991: 275). The tomb of King Arthur would provide no such relief. Abbeys always hoped to attract the rich and powerful to be buried in them. Burials would be accompanied by grants of land and other sources of income, which would allow masses to be said on behalf of the dead as long as the Abbey endured. Just finding a king's body at the site would not bring any of these benefits.

✂

Ecclesiastical forgery was rife in the twelfth century, it is true, but it did not work in this way. The wealth of an abbey like Glastonbury rested in is lands, not in its tourist income. Its estates were vast and had supported the already completed rebuilding. The origin of these grants dated back to immemorial antiquity, the accumulated result of bequests by long forgotten Britons and Saxons, buried in uninscribed graves around the site. This sort of explanation would not stand up to the acquisitiveness of Norman and Plantagenet conquerors. The new legalistic framework of government demanded written proof of ownership or the land could be seized.

Faced with this, many ecclesiastical foundations resorted to faking ancient charters or saints' *Lives* to justify the land holdings (Rahtz 1993: 31). Caradoc of Llancarvan's *Life of St Gildas* (*c.*1130) culminates in King Arthur and King Melvas of Somerset bequeathing lands to the abbey (in Wade-Evans 1944). Gerald was told that Arthur had been a generous patron, supporting the monks with many donations for which he was highly praised in the records (Gerald of Wales *De principis instructione*: I). None of this required the possession of Arthur's actual body.

Gerald unwittingly added another suspect for the armchair detectives. Although it is clear that the discovery of Arthur's tomb was completely unexpected, as no earlier source even hinted he was buried at Glastonbury, after the fact it was claimed that some had been in on the secret. Gerald mentions the abbey records, the letters carved on the pyramids and the visions of holy monks. Most importantly, an old British singer of stories had told King Henry II exactly where the body lay and the king had given the monks every encouragement to find it (Gerald of Wales *De principis instructione*: I).

This is taken as proving Henry II must have had a sinister motive in faking the burial of Arthur to demonstrate to his Welsh, Breton and Cornish foes that their hope for Arthur's return was vain. He would thus remove a dangerous potential rallying point (Barber 1986: 135, Time Team).

The Plantagenet conspiracy has not a shred of evidence to support it. Henry's knowledge of the site was only brought up after the discovery, to add credibility to the find. Henry died in 1189, so the discovery came too late for his purposes. Why he would have fixed on Glastonbury for his propaganda coup is baffling. With the whole of the Angevin Empire at his disposal, he could have chosen Camelford, Isle de Sein, Caerleon, London, Silchester or Stonehenge or any other location which actually featured in the work of Geoffrey of Monmouth, the definitive biographer of Arthur, rather than coming up with an entirely new one.

Neither Henry nor Richard the Lionheart made any political capital out of disproving Arthur's immortality. Henry's last wars were against his sons and the King of France. His own army (Diceto, quoted in Hallam 1986: 185) included Welsh and Bretons. The discovery of Arthur's body made no difference to the hope for his return, which Gerald reports as still current among credulous Britons in 1216 (Gerald of Wales *Speculum Ecclesiae*: IX). If the Plantagenets had an anti-Arthurian agenda, they had a strange way of conveying it, supporting writers like Layamon and Wace, whose English and French versions of Geoffrey of Monmouth brought the legend of Arthur's survival to an even wider audience. Richard's actual heir, Henry's grandson, was Arthur of Brittany, presumably named with the legends in mind.

With no proven ulterior motive, the most reasonable supposition is that the monks really did find an unexpected burial. The gigantic size of the bones would probably have suggested an identification with an ancient hero. Virgil (*Georgics:* I.497, quoted by Gerald of Wales *De principis instructione:* I), and the Bible (*Genesis* VI 4) supported the idea that the famous heroes of old had been giants. In the Welsh romance *The Dream of Rhonabwy*, a twelfth-century Welshman who travels to Arthur's court in a dream is laughed at for his puny size (Gantz 1976: 182). Perhaps if the discovery had been made earlier, the monks might have picked on some other hero, a famous Saxon for example, but in the atmosphere of 1191, it had to be Arthur.

There is no particular reason why it should not have been King Arthur. The man in the grave was apparently a Christian. He was buried in an east/west alignment without grave-goods in the context of a Christian graveyard. From the very earliest accounts of his career, Arthur is portrayed as a zealous Christian fighting pagan Saxons (HB 56 and AC: LXII). He is connected with south-east Wales and the Somerset area (Gidlow 2004: 57). Outside a very ancient church in Glastonbury is the sort of place where such a man might reasonably be supposed to be buried.

The major stumbling block is the leaden cross. The object drawn by Camden is not sixth-century; it is very different from the rounded inscriptions of the period, found on stones (Dark 2000: 157). Nor is it typical of the 1190s. A sixth-century cross might have called Arthur a king – the sixth-century writer Gildas uses the word of his contemporaries, in a fairly fluid way. His heirs might even have described him as 'famous'. The eighth-century Catamanus is described on his tombstone as 'the wisest and most renowned of kings' (Dark 2000: 157). The '*Hic iacet*' formula would be perfectly acceptable for a British tomb inscription of the period (Knight 1996: 111). The fact that it is almost a direct quotation from Geoffrey of Monmouth (HRB: XI.2) is one of the biggest reasons for suspecting it.

Avalon

The most suspect part of the inscription is the one which was to have the greatest impact on the modern perception of the site. It describes Arthur's burial place as being in the Isle of Avalon. Readers of Geoffrey's work, where the phrase originates, had last heard of Arthur *en route* for Avalon to be healed of his mortal wound. Geoffrey's later *Life of Merlin* gives details of this paradisiacal land where crops are produced without the need for farmers and people live for over 100 years. It is ruled by nine sisters, the leader of whom, Morgen, is the most beautiful, and a skilled healer and enchantress. It seems a faraway place, only reachable because the steersman knew the sea and stars (White 2004: 22). Geoffrey's description of Avalon is partly taken from the work of the first-century geographer Pomponius Mela, describing the Isle de Sein off the coast of Brittany (Lacy 1988: 33). Geoffrey, whose works show an interest in Brittany, may well have intended that exact location.

The place-name Avalon is derived from the Celtic word for apples (Bromwich 1978: 267). Gerald gives this etymology while rationalising Morgan as a noble cousin of Arthur who organised his burial (Gerald of Wales *Speculum Ecclesiae*: I.IX).'Avalon' was familiar to Gerald as the name of the continental birthplace of the famous St Hugh, the Bishop of Lincoln at the time of the discovery (Hallam 1986: 181). In Britain, Aballava, a related form, had been the name of the Roman fort at Brough-by-Sands (Rivet and Smith 1979: 238), but it had never been given as the name of Glastonbury. The suspicion has to be that this was a piece of interpretation by the monks specifically intended to answer the criticism that Arthur's grave should be in Avalon, not Glastonbury.

Glastonbury is presented to the modern visitor as 'Avalon', a mystic region where Arthurian concepts such as the Holy Grail mingle with neo-paganism and assertions of ancient pagan significance. A roadside notice even tells them they are entering the 'ancient Island of Avalon' (Rahtz 1993: 33). This image is presented in the shops which crowd the town and precede access to the abbey. Archaeologist Philip Rahtz characterises modern Glastonbury as a battleground in 'the struggle of the rational against the draw of the irrational', the first represented primarily by the 'archaeological establishment' and those who want a town free of tourists, cars, 'unnecessary shops' and supermarkets. Their opponents are a compendium of foes of Middle England; 'leyliners', 'druids', 'drug-abusers' and 'armed beggars' (Rahtz 1993: 132). A more balanced answer to Rahtz's question 'Whose Glastonbury is it?' can be found in Hutton's recent essay 'Glastonbury: Alternative Histories' (in Hutton 2003).

The only clearly fifth/sixth-century finds from Glastonbury come from Rahtz's excavations in 1964–66 on the Tor. It was an occupation site of high status. Rahtz, after considering all the options, interpreted the Tor as the stronghold of a local chief (Rahtz 1968: 120). Compared with rulers of sites like Cadbury, the chieftain who lived there was probably 'no Arthur but someone of lesser stature, though quite important at Glastonbury, and doubtless known to the denizens of Camelot' (Rahtz 1968: 120). 'If we wished to put a name to the chief of Glastonbury, it would be Melwas' (Rahtz 1968: 121), Arthur's adversary from Caradoc of Llancarfan's *Life of St Gildas*. Rahtz now clarifies that, while the Melwas story 'cannot be taken as true history, it is in keeping with the scenario suggested' (Rahtz 1993: 59).

The abbey is owned by the Church of England. Most of the interpretation of the site, not surprisingly, is about early Christianity in England, monastic life and the dissolution of the monasteries. The abbey site is undoubtedly beautiful, with a strong sense of atmosphere. As such, however, it is hardly unique. It is the Arthurian and attendant New Age connotations which have raised Glastonbury to the status of modern pilgrimage site (Rahtz 1993: 10). Rahtz even claims that the majority of those who live in Glastonbury or visit it believe in the existence of Arthur and his connection with the site (Rahtz 1993: 44). If so, and with their expectations stoked by the Avalonian emphasis of the town, they will find little to engage with in the interpretation of the Abbey site.

Interpretation boards in the visitor centre present a muddled version of Gerald of Wales's account of the discovery of Arthur's tomb. It states that visions and old manuscripts led the monks to search out the grave of Arthur. This is, up to a point, what Gerald wrote in *Speculum Ecclesiae* (I.VIII), though earlier accounts are clear it was actually fortuitous. Since the discovery, we are told, there has been debate over whether the burial was genuine. The person responsible for the sign has already made up their mind, suggesting it was a 'publicity stunt' following the 1184 fire, and that the 'publicity' brought in pilgrims 'and money'. The writer obviously gave up under the strain of trying to disentangle the story of Arthur from the large number of conflicting Arthurian sources: 'By the late fifteenth century the strands of Arthur, Guinevere, the Round Table, Joseph of Arimathea, the Quest for the Holy Grail, Excalibur, Mordred, the Pons Perilous, Avalon and Camelot had become so intertwined that it is now impossible to unravel Glastonbury's true part in the story.' There is not even an attempt to interpret the development of the legend or disentangle irrelevancies. The board (entitled *King Arthur*) ends in the abbey's comfort zone, the functions of the Saxon abbey and the concept of chantry chapels endowed by rich benefactors. It concludes with a plaintive list of 'some important burials', 'notably three Anglo-Saxon Kings – Edmund I (d.946), Edgar (d.975) and Edmund Ironside (d.1016).' This suggests that the abbey would prefer to have dealt with these 'real' royal burials but appreciated that no-one was going to read a board entitled 'King Edgar' or 'Chantry Chapels'. Without any interpretation of the historical context, the leap from Arthur to the (undated) 'Saxon period' is unexplained.

Two further Arthurian signs can be tracked down at the site. One marks the 'site of the ancient graveyard where in 1191 the monks dug to find the tombs of Arthur and Guinevere', a non-committal way of marking Radford's excavation site. Much more prominent is the sign and delineated rectangle on the ground, marking the 'Site of King Arthur's tomb' ('the only grave now recorded in the turfed area is, alas, that of "Arthur"', Rahtz laments (1993: 90)). This location was identified in 1931 (Ashe:1968: illustration 70) as the site of the imposing black marble tomb which housed the bones of Arthur and Guinevere until the dissolution of the abbey in 1539.

The sign explains that the bodies of 'King Arthur and his Queen' were said to have been discovered in 1191. In 1278, they were 'removed in the presence of King Edward I and Queen Eleanor to a black marble tomb on this site' which survived until the dissolution. Edward and Eleanor were Arthurian enthusiasts. (Prestwich 1988: 120). They reverently opened the tombs of their famous predecessors. Edward wrapped King Arthur's bones in precious silk while Eleanor wrapped those of Queen Guinevere. (Adam of Domerham in White 1997: 528).

Edward was the first king to take an interest in Arthur's tomb (Prestwich 1988: 120). Though he had a romantic streak, he was also a consummate politician. The previous year he had subdued Llewellyn, Prince of Wales, the last heir to the British dynasties of the sixth century. Later he was to use Arthurian material to bolster his claims over Scotland (Prestwich 1988: 492). A chronicler wrote that not even Arthur had possessed the realms of Britain as fully as Edward (in White 1997: 534).

By the end of the Middle Ages, the abbey's history was being interpreted to visitors by a large billboard covered with manuscripts of the stories of the shrines, including this new tomb (Rahtz 1993: 44). At modern Glastonbury the visitor can chose an audio-guide which adds more information to the sparse signage. Glastonbury is not the only site to opt for this method of interpreting legendary connections (Bath 1996: 160). Perhaps stories are seen as more suitable to this medium. There may also be an element of safety in consigning this material to an ephemeral medium, less likely to be challenged than written texts. The narrator recommends a visit to South Cadbury and that those interested in finding out more should read Geoffrey of Monmouth or the medieval romances. The Arthurian material is rounded off by posing the question was the discovery of Arthur's body the greatest 'fundraising stunt' or 'a genuine interpretation of the evidence uncovered?'

For a site which owed much of its fame to the archaeological confirmation of a myth, a myth still strong in the hearts of its visitors, the abbey is disappointing in its interpretive approach. Although it was the site of 34 seasons of excavation between the 1900s and the 1960s, none has been fully published (Hutton 2003: 75). After an early flirtation with the legend, Philip Rahtz turned against it. Whether this was warranted by the largely unpublished findings is unclear. Timber stakes from the cemetery area have yielded seventh-century dates, but with margins of error which could support a mid-sixth century date for those inclined to believe (Hutton 2003: 75). There is no attempt at Glastonbury Abbey to engage with the archaeological data nor to unpack the medieval legends. A lost opportunity, and by no means unique in that.

2

Ancient Books

The Glastonbury burial notwithstanding, King Arthur is a literary figure more than he is an archaeological one. It is not surprising therefore that the main battleground over his existence is the texts in which he appears or does not appear. Caxton tells us that the sceptics of his time started from the premise that various chronicles make no mention of him, as we saw. I don't want to go over old ground covered in *The Reign of Arthur*, but some of the written sources will soon become important as we consider the archaeological sites, so it is worth pausing here to consider the best of them.

My love for the Arthurian legends grew from the romances, the fictional accounts of Arthur and the Knights of the Round Table of which the *Morte d'Arthur* is the last great example. In the nineteenth, even the twentieth century these sources were examined for clues about the historical Arthur. Did Arthur lead heavily armoured cavalry? Did they go on quests for lost religious artefacts? When they met did they customarily sit at a circular piece of furniture? Generally effort spent in these activities was wasted. The romance writers had no interest in conveying historical truths to their audience. They wanted to entertain. They were as likely, more likely in fact, to draw on aspects of their contemporary society for inspiration rather than history, and added to the folklore and classical legends indiscriminately.

What the romancers did not generally do, however, was base their stories on completely fictional characters. Like Caxton, they assumed that the moral and entertaining messages in their tales would be less convincing, less appealing if they did not have some historical basis. Thus romances of the 'Matter of Rome' drew on the history or presumed history of the classical world, Alexander the Great and the Trojan War. The Matter of France took the deeds of Charlemagne and more recent European history. German material could take the era of Attila and Theodoric. The Matter of Britain used Arthur in the same way.

The romancers' conception of a historical Arthur derived from Geoffrey of Monmouth's *History of the Kings of Britain* (*Historia Regum Britanniae* – HRB).

ii. GILDAS'S BRITAIN

Geoffrey was a cleric (he ended his career as Bishop of St Asaph's in Wales). He wrote his history in the early 1130s in Latin prose, the normal language of historical writing. Romancers generally used their own native language and at first composed in verse. Prose romances like the _Morte d'Arthur_ only became the norm later.

Geoffrey's book is racy, exciting, full of pithy anecdotes and memorable incidents. This is an important reason for the success of his vision. He dramatised battles, enlivened political squabbles with personalities, explained the origins of contemporary customs and place names. _Historia Regum Britanniae_ is just the sort of book you would want on your bookshelf! Geoffrey covers the whole extent of British history from the arrival of Brutus the Trojan, who brings human colonists to the island formerly inhabited by giants and names it after himself (in about 1000 BC). He ends with the exile of King Cadwalader at the end of the seventh century AD, after which time the Britons are more or less confined to Wales and Brittany while the English dominate the island.

It is worth pausing here to explain the meaning of these terms. In Geoffrey's time writing the history of distinct peoples to explain their origins and how they came to inhabit their lands was commonplace. In the absence of a concept of 'pre-history' historians would link their stories back to the sources with the longest historical scope, the Bible and the legends of Classical Greeks and Romans. Brutus therefore carries a classical name, is of Trojan stock and comes to Britain from Italy, a milieu which Geoffrey knew from Virgil's _Aeneid_. Taking this aside, the idea of 'national' histories indelibly marked the way we think of the past and the way we define our identities.

For Geoffrey, Britain is the name for the whole island. The usage was common from the sixth century. Before that it had been used in more limited ways, such as for the Roman province whose northern border was defined by Hadrian's Wall. The Britons were the indigenous inhabitants of Britain. They were defined by their common heritage and their language.

These days the language of the Britons is defined as a Celtic language, with close affinities to the languages spoken in Gaul and other parts of Western Europe before the Roman conquests and, at a more distant remove, in Ireland. The Britons are therefore often described as 'Celts', though the validity of the modern label is frequently questioned. When Julius Caesar encountered the Britons he did find them similar to the Gauls he had been fighting, with similar speech and making common cause with the Gallic tribes. The Gallic religion was led by the Druids who had very close links with Britain. They often went to Britain to train.

Britain was conquered by the Romans and was ruled by them for nearly 400 years. Towards the end of that period we encounter in the historical record the Scots, who are Irish-speaking raiders from Ireland, and the Picts who lived north of the Firths of Forth and Clyde, where the most northerly version of the Roman frontier, the Antonine Wall, had been built. Geoffrey thought the Picts had also invaded from overseas. The modern view is that 'Pict' was a new overall identity for the tribes the Romans had already encountered in the north of Britain, like the powerful Caledones, some of whom spoke a Celtic language and some of whom did not.

After the end of Roman rule in the early fifth century, the Britons had a brief period of self-government during which new peoples established themselves in lowland Britain. The Britons called these newcomers 'Saxons'. The Saxons spoke a language which is now described as Germanic, with affinities to those spoken by many peoples who lived east of the Roman frontier on the Rhine. 'Germanic' peoples, like the Vandals, Goths and Franks in this same period, were making their presence felt throughout the western half of the Roman Empire. They settled, they conquered and they eventually overthrew the institutions of the Roman state in the lands they controlled.

The language of the Saxons is the ancestor of the English language we use now. Why this language is not called 'Saxon' is a question of how these people identified themselves. Although to the Britons they were all indiscriminately Saxons, we know that by the early eighth century they thought of themselves as deriving from distinct continental groups. Those in Kent, Hampshire and the Isle of Wight considered themselves as 'Jutes', with affinities to the inhabitants of Jutland. Other southern groups rigorously asserted their Saxon identity. Their kingdoms usually carried their tribal identity proudly: the South Saxons, the East Saxons, the West Saxons. Their lands are still called Sussex, Essex, Wessex and Middlesex to this day. They saw their homeland as being round the lower reaches of the Elbe, in 'Old Saxony'. The northern groups, however, saw themselves as Angles (from the Latin *Angli*) or English, coming from 'Old Anglia' or Engeln, in the southern part of the Jutland peninsula, between the lands of the Jutes and the Saxons. Some Angles used this tribal designation in the names of their kingdoms (the East Angles, for instance) but mostly they used geographical descriptions. Their largest kingdoms were Mercia ('the Border') and Northumbria (land north of the Humber estuary). The Angles covered geographically the largest area of lowland Britain and were the dominant political force in the early eighth century. They had a prominent place in the religious history of the island. When Pope Gregory the Great was told that the blond-haired, blue-eyed slaves he saw for sale in Rome were 'Angles' he had been moved to reply 'not Angles but Angels'. He had determined that these angelic barbarians should be converted to Christianity. His missionaries to Britain had come looking for Angles and more or less treated the Jutes and Saxons they encountered en route as subsets of a wider 'Anglian/English' people. Over time the Angles, Saxons and Jutes coalesced into a single identity of 'English' and their lands as 'England'. Sometimes they used the hybrid term 'Anglo-Saxon' to encompass their joint identity. I tend to favour 'Saxon' when I look at the evidence from the Britons, following their usage. I use Anglo-Saxon when looking at their archaeology specifically, and occasionally English or Angle when including the Saxons in northern material seems wrong.

British control of Britain was reduced to an ever-shrinking western highland zone. They too adopted a new identity in the period of Saxon expansion, calling themselves the Combrogi or 'fellow citizens'. The name survives in Cymru and Cumbria. The English heaped a final indignity on these native Britons by calling them the Welsh, or 'foreigners'.

So, to return to Geoffrey of Monmouth. When he wrote his *History of the Kings of Britain* he set out explicitly to chronicle the story of the British, from their origin to the time when control of the majority of the island was yielded to them. In spite of the epic 2000-year sweep of the history, half the book is concerned with the 100 years *c.*450–550 AD, the pivotal point after which the balance tipped decisively from the Britons to the English as rulers of the island. Within this period the outstanding figure is King Arthur.

Ideas which are first written down by Geoffrey – that Arthur was the King of Britain, married to an unfaithful Guinevere, wielded Excalibur and was carried off to the Isle of Avalon – are now integral to what 'King Arthur' means. His influence over later portrayals is undeniable. Apart from the formula '*hic iacet sepultus*' 'here lies buries', the inscription of the Arthur cross is taken almost word for word from his work. On the other hand much of Geoffrey's work is fictitious, often demonstrably false. His witness to events of the fifth/sixth centuries cannot be taken at face value. Geoffrey claimed that his primary source was a very ancient book in the British language. Nothing like this has ever been found and most historians doubt it existed. Instead we have to turn to other sources nearer in time to attempt to illuminate the darkness of the fifth and sixth centuries.

Most highly regarded is *The Ecclesiastical History of the English People*, by the Northumbrian writer and monk Bede, from 731. Referred to as HE – *Historia Ecclesiastica* – it is written in Latin, the official language of the Christian Church. Although this history is full of miracles and massive bias against the Britons and in favour of the Northumbrian Angles, this has in the past been forgiven. Bede comes across as a warm, human and level-headed author, deceptively modern especially in his use of the familiar AD dating system, which he popularised. To him we owe such details as the division between Angles, Saxons and Jutes, the names of some of the early leaders of the Saxons and so forth. He is understandably much less informed about their British adversaries. Older books tended to accept Bede uncritically, but as we shall see his version of history is open to dispute.

The basic framework set out by Bede was used for the Anglo-Saxon chronicle (*c.*891 then added to contemporaneously). Its lateness makes it more open to challenge than Bede, but it provides reassuring dates, battle names and details of the exploits of the early Saxons on whom Bede touched only lightly. It is actually written in 'Old English', as the Anglo-Saxon language is usually called, and is a series of year by year annals rather than a continuous narrative in the style of Bede.

These sources, whatever their value, are written long after the facts they relate. They are increasingly seen as products of their own time rather than impartial preservers of historical truth. Luckily we do have a one British work from the period, *On the Destruction of Britain (de Excidio Britanniae* DEB) by Gildas. Archaeologist Francis Pryor, who has no time for Gildas as we will see, calls him (Pryor 2004: 23) 'a shadowy figure of whom all we know is that he was a monk and that he died around 570 or 571'. In fact we don't even know that. Most experts would tend to place him or at least his writing earlier than this. He was a cleric, but not a priest or a bishop, which logically would place him in the third order, a deacon, but monastic writings which quote him suggest that he could have been a monk, though he himself never says this. Gildas was dismayed by the moral decline of his contemporary Britons. Although, 'by the will of God' their fathers and grandfathers had won a memorable victory over the Saxons, they had used the respite gained to turn to all manner of vice and especially civil war. After ten years of indecision, Gildas took it upon himself to admonish them and warn them, through many examples from the Bible, that if they carried on in this way they would soon face an even worse fate, destruction from their enemies. 'Before I make good my promise, I shall try, God willing, to say a little about the situation of Britain' (DEB 2).

Gildas provides a potted history of Britain up to his own time. He doesn't, he admits, have access to written sources, and his reconstruction of British history does include demonstrable errors. He is the initiator of the view of Picts as overseas invaders, and believes it was only their invasions which caused the northern walls to be built across the hitherto undivided island after the 380s (really the early second century). As we approach his own time, though, Gildas would be expected to be more accurate. He is writing of events of his own lifetime and of the grandparents and great-grandparents of his readers. His position as an eyewitness ought to be unassailable. He directly addresses five tyrants by name, admonishing them with detailed criticism of their conduct.

As we shall see, this is not at all how Gildas is used by the archaeologists. It is inconvenient for them to abandon a blank canvas of fashionable speculation to fit in with the rantings of a misguided cleric. There is a sense of annoyance that Gildas had not written the book they would have wanted him to have written. No doubt if Gildas had been aware that his book would be the only one to survive from the period, he would have written something different. As it was, he set out clearly his intentions and wrote the book he intended to write. Pryor quotes with approval Leslie Alcock's sentiment that Gildas is 'prolix, tedious and exasperating' (Pryor 2005:23, quoting Alcock 1971: 21). There is no accounting for taste, but Gildas is at least pithy, to the point and very short. The complete works of Gildas weigh in at 81 pages of translation, representing just 60 in the Latin, a fraction of the length of Pryor's *Britain AD* (244 + notes) or Alcock's *Arthur's Britain* (364 + notes). If Gildas's tale of invasions, murder, adultery and intrigue bore them, I wonder how they manage to stay awake through some of the reports their fellow archaeologists have produced! It is symptomatic of the attitude that plodding through Gildas is a bit of a chore which archaeologists would rather avoid.

Pryor never misses an opportunity to criticise the 'manifestly unreliable 'historical' version of Dark Age Britain provided by Gildas (Pryor 2004: 150). This is a completely wrong-headed approach. Gildas was actually living in the period in which we are interested. If he says certain features existed or did not exist in his own time we need to take him seriously. He needed to convince his errant contemporaries of his message and every mistake they could pick up on would surely weaken his case. Gildas needs to be read with care and attention, with a Biblical concordance at the ready to check the references he expects his readers to grasp. If this is done, *De Excidio Britanniae* is a very fertile source of information. Nick Higham, possibly the most diligent scholar working on Gildas, was able to write a whole book based primarily on the information it in (Higham 1994). Unfortunately most archaeologists give up at the first hurdle. Some do not read Gildas at all. Others, such as Pryor, unfortunately, read one paragraph, take against it and never get any further. He gives his view (2004: 233) that Gildas lacks all credibility 'when he suggests that cross-sea contact was a rare event: three boatfuls of Saxon warriors arrive on the coast and life in Britain … is changed forever'.

It is absolutely impossible to write this having read any more of Gildas that the paragraph Pryor quotes (DEB 23:3). The paragraph which immediately follows it reads 'the mother lioness [the Saxon homeland] learnt that her first contingent had prospered, and she sent a second and larger troop… It arrived by ship and joined up with the false units.' The narrative up to this point is awash with sea-borne contacts. Gildas opens with a description of how luxuries used to come up the main estuaries of the Severn and the Thames, brought by ship from overseas. The Romans come and go by sea several times in invasions, usurpations and rescue missions. Threats from the maritime Scots and Picts cause the Romans to build towers along the south coast to guard against them. The previous page (in my edition) tells how the Picts and Scots crossed the sea in their *curuci* (as with Saxons, Gildas's obvious interest in seafaring is signalled by his use of the name the invaders give their own ships) to invade and it is the rumour of a new invasion which leads to the Saxons being recruited. How this can be taken as demonstrating that Gildas thinks cross-sea contact is rare, and that he should therefore be dismissed altogether is beyond me, but Pryor's attitude is completely symptomatic of that of the contemporary archaeological community.

I use Gildas as the touchstone for any theory of the period. If an interpretation of archaeological remains is tenable with the evidence in Gildas, then it is worth considering. If it flies in the face of Gildas's contemporary testimony then I would argue it needs serious rethinking. Bede used Gildas as one of his primary sources, and this contributed to the Anglo-Saxon Chronicle's picture of the period. These sources followed Gildas in one particularly important way: none of them named Arthur.

This is sometimes given as a killer argument. It is certainly true that if Gildas had named Arthur, there would be rather less debate about his existence. There is nothing to be deduced from the contrary position, though. Hardly anybody is named by Gildas. Only eight Britons are named in the whole book: three martyrs killed in the great persecution and five contemporary tyrants. Nobody is named in Arthur's generation.

It is generally accept that the earliest reference to Arthur is in the poem *Y Gododdin* ('The Gododdin'). The poem is a series of elegies for the fallen warriors of the Gododdin, a British tribe from the Edinburgh area. They have died on an expedition to Catraeth, Catterick in Yorkshire, to fight the Saxons. One of the warriors, Guaurddur, is celebrated for his prowess and his generosity:

He brought down black crows to feed before the wall
Of the city, though he was no Arthur

The setting is supposed to be an expedition in the mid-sixth century, supposedly written by a survivor, the poet Neirin. These traditions are embodied in the poem as we now have it, in an early fourteenth-century manuscript. However, it is clear than some verses are much older than others, their language going back to the very origin of the Welsh tongue. It is now argued that these verses, including the one about Guaurddur, could date from as early as the 570s. Arthur features in other early Welsh poems too, but none dated as early as *The Gododdin*.

The first source to give Arthur a historical context is known as *Historia Brittonum* (*The History of the Britons* – HB). This was written in the 820s and seems very much a riposte to Bede. The Britons are shown clearly as the original inhabitants of the island. They fight valiantly against the Saxon invaders under heroic leaders, the greatest of whom is Arthur. Older works on *Historia Brittonum* describe it as the work of a monk called Nennius, who guilelessly made a heap of all the ancient sources he could find and presented them, loosely ordered but essentially unchanged in a historical scrapbook. The current editor of the *Historia*, David Dumville, is convinced this is not the case. The *Historia* exists in various different forms, grouped into families of manuscripts, called 'recensions'. The prologue naming the author as Nennius and giving his supposed methodology is not found in most, and not in the oldest. Following Dumville's scholarship, the work is now treated as anonymous. Dumville also argues that the work is actually quite carefully constructed with a strong authorial intent. The inference he draws from this is that the *Historia* is essentially fictitious. As we have been waiting for 30 years for him to produce his definitive edition we are not really in a position to judge.

In the oldest manuscript of *Historia Brittonum* there is a survey of various wonders of Britain, two of which, in south-east Wales (a miraculous tomb which cannot be measured and a footprint on a stone) are associated with 'Arthur the Soldier'. It is assumed that this is the same Arthur, the war leader, and that the author is the same or at least shares the same interests as the author of *Historia Brittonum*.

In addition in the same manuscript there is also another historical source, *Annales Cambriae* ('the Annals of Wales'). This is a sort of Anglo-Saxon Chronicle to *Historia Brittonum*'s Bede, listing events by date. It has two references to Arthur, in the sixth century. One has him as a warrior fighting at the Battle of Badon (called a memorable victory by Gildas and the culmination of Arthur's campaigns against the Saxons in *Historia Brittonum*) but with details which are different from but seem to corroborate the earlier references. The other is to Arthur's death at the strife of Camlan. The *Annales* were once seen as secure sources, compiled more or less contemporaneously. We now know this is not the case. Later writers took an existing framework of Ulster Annals, interweaving or replacing Irish entries with British ones. The whole work as we now have it was finished in the late tenth century, but earlier phases can be detected.

In *the Reign of Arthur* I treat Gildas, the *Historia Brittonum* and *Annales Cambriae* at some length. It is my view that together they give a plausible account of the British resistance to the Saxons, and the hypothesis of *Historia Brittonum* and *Annales Cambriae* that the leader of the Britons at the siege of Mount Badon, as Gildas calls it, was called Arthur. The focus of this book is on physical remains rather than literary ones, but we will find ourselves revisiting these works later as we examine how archaeologists have used or ignored them, and scholarly assaults on the hypothesis of a historical Arthur.

3

TINTAGEL AND THE 'ARTHUR STONE'

Clue to King Arthur discovered. An ancient stone bearing a sixth century inscription similar to the name Arthur has been unearthed at Tintagel Castle, the mythical birthplace of the legendary king. The discovery could prove that King Arthur had his headquarters at the site of ruined castle on the coast of north Cornwall. (BBC News)

It was 1998 and the headline I'd waited all my life to read. It was the modern equivalent of the discovery of Arthur's body at Glastonbury. It was also ringing alarm bells. What would constitute proof of the mythical birthplace of a legendary king? How similar could a name be to Arthur? Artorius, a Roman name from the second century often cited (Myres 1986: 16) as the original form? Arthurus maybe? Worse still, the facts that the inscription were supposed to prove – that Arthur had been born in Tintagel and had his headquarters there – had never been claimed by any Dark Age or medieval writer. They were products of nineteenth-century imagination.

Tintagel Castle is presented by English Heritage, the government organisation which manages it, as its Arthurian site *par excellence*. It is a popular tourist destination, with about 250,000 visitors a year (Thomas 1993: 9). Although the site is spectacular and unusual, the castle ruins are not. It is clear that 'the main draw for visitors at the site of Tintagel is the alleged connection with King Arthur'. (Morris *et al* 1999a:206). To approach the site, visitors must run the gauntlet of shops named after and specialising in souvenirs related to the Arthurian legend. Until 1900, the village was known as Trevenna (Thomas 1993:22). Tintagel was the name for the headland and the parish dependent on the isolated church opposite. In the wake of Tennyson's *Idylls of the King*, in which Merlin discovers the miraculous baby Arthur on the shore at Tintagel, the village was reinvented to deal with the influx of Arthurian tourists (Radford and Swanton 2002: 39).

The legends of King Arthur indisputably cast a long shadow over Tintagel. English Heritage works with the concept of Arthurian mystery as a visitor hook. While this seems modest and understated in the context of the New Age excesses of the village ('a distasteful straggle of knick-knack shops and spurious Arthurian peepshows', Radford and Swanton 2002: 39, quoting Professor Charles Thomas), there is a clear effort to place Tintagel as a prime Arthurian site. Although we are told in an introductory audio-visual presentation that King Arthur 'is unlikely to have come to Tintagel', the commentary continues 'It is as a castle of the imagination that [Tintagel] holds us spellbound ... you can believe what you want to believe' (English Heritage text, quoted by Gallen).

The positioning of Tintagel as 'King Arthur's Castle' and the premier Arthurian site is quite odd. It plays only the most peripheral part in the medieval legends, as the place where Arthur was conceived. Perhaps its appearance, on the opening page of Malory's *Morte d'Arthur*, fixed it in the minds of casual readers who did not manage to read any further. Perhaps it is the fact that, unlike Camelot or Avalon, or Arthur's battle sites, its location is certain and not vulnerable to rival claims. Yet now, in 1998 it, alone of all the sites, was yielding up proof that Arthur had his headquarters there.

English Heritage called the inscribed stone 'the find of a lifetime' which added 'a new dimension to the possibility of there having been a real Arthur on whom the mythical figure was based.' Its spokesman confirmed that 'as a historical figure Arthur almost certainly did exist as a successful soldier fighting battles across the country in the sixth century.' The BBC noted that 'Tintagel relies heavily on its connection with King Arthur, and the new stone will enhance that link' (BBC News).

A Citadel of the Rulers of Cornwall

Tintagel had been introduced to the world by Geoffrey of Monmouth in the 1130s. He described it as an *oppidum*, a fortified settlement, on a readily defensible peninsula. It was one of the residences of Duke Gorlois of Cornwall, in which his wife Igerna was besieged during a war with their overlord, King Uther Pendragon in about the year 500. Thwarted of his desire to sleep with her, Uther called on the assistance of the prophet Merlin. Merlin used his arts to transform Uther into the likeness of Gorlois, in which guise he was able to enter the fortress and sleep with the duchess. 'That very night she conceived the renowned Arthur' (HRB:VIII.19).

This episode occurs in the numerous retellings of the birth of King Arthur, but compared with Camelot or Avalon, Tintagel was always a rather minor Arthurian location. It became more prominent in Victorian times, with Tennyson's more oblique version of Merlin 'discovering' the baby Arthur there.

The archaeologist Ralegh Radford wrote in 1942 'Arthur ... reigns supreme at Tintagel and few would wish to displace him' (Radford 1942: 41). His own excavations, however, led him to the conclusion that Geoffrey had been wrong and that Tintagel had been a fifth/sixth-century monastery (Radford 1968: 64). This interpretation held sway through the heyday of 'Arthurian' archaeology at Cadbury/Camelot and still appears in reprinted books from that period. A counter suggestion (Burrow: 1973) led to a re-evaluation of the finds (Padel 1981, Thomas 1982) and the conclusion that this was wrong. Spindle whorls, for instance, suggested the presence of women at the site, as spinning was a specialist craft 'carried out by women' (Thomas 1993: 71). Padel suggested that what he called 'Cornish folklore traditions' attributing a court of the ruler of Cornwall at Tintagel might have 'an element of truth' in them (Padel 1981: 29).

A potentially disastrous fire in 1983 cleared the ground and opened the way for a complete survey. This decisively demonstrated that the monastery hypothesis was wrong. It identified 'one vast and continuous site with a hundred or more components... No Celtic monastery so far identified looked anything like this' (Barrowman et al. 306, ref 15).

Further work (Batey, Sharpe and Thorpe 1993) and the arrival of Chris Morris in 1990 led to 'a reassertion of Tintagel's status as a secular site, most probably a 'citadel' of the rulers' (Morris 1999b: 19) between the mid-fifth and mid-sixth century. Morris was leading a team from the University of Glasgow. For local historical knowledge they relied on Professor Charles Thomas. Morris and Thomas had both decided, before any archaeology was done, that the Arthurian legends had no relevance to the site. Thomas argued that the idea of 'kings' of Cornwall at Tintagel would exclude 'the hypothetical Arthur' as he was not a king (Thomas 1993: 88). The team's view was that although 'one cannot recover twelfth century folklore', it 'would have been completely non-Arthurian' (Morris et al 1990: 846).

Morris's 1990 work included an element of pure research, sponsored by Mobil (Morris et al 1990: 848). This resulted in 'a promotional programme of TV, radio, press and on-site coverage (including a helicopter visit from Dr C.A. Ralegh Radford) [and a] simultaneous "community archaeology" programme laid on for the people of Tintagel' (Morris et al 1990: 848). Christopher K. Pacey, Mobil's Public Affairs Manager, explained in his introduction to the glossy interim report that the company was launching an unmanned natural-gas platform which they had decided to call Camelot. 'Camelot! It was legendary, available, evocative and British. Further Arthurian fields would follow – Lancelot, Gawain, Guinevere, Avalon' (in Nowakowski and Thomas 1990: v). 'Our quest [to celebrate the founding of 'this gaseous dynasty'] led us ... to the sponsorship of an excavation at Tintagel, the legendary birthplace of King Arthur ... the quest goes on' (in Nowakowski and Thomas 1990: v). Morris et al responded to this largesse by reiterating (1990: 843) 'commercial sponsorship ... depended, curiously, on the Arthurian reputation of the place – a reputation the work is likely yet further to undermine.'

Continued research strengthened the model of Tintagel as a fifth/sixth-century royal citadel. In contrast to some of the other Arthurian sites, it does not have a complex early history. There is no evidence it served as an Iron Age promontory fort (Barrowman *et al.* 309). The Romans made no use of it, though a couple of displaced Roman route markers have turned up in the area– an early fourth century one was found in Tintagel churchyard. If a late Roman route did lie in the area, it is likely that it was associated with an increased exploitation of Cornish tin (Barrowman *et al.* 310). Tin was a vital component to bronze making, as well as being used decoratively, for example to give armour a 'silver' appearance.

Arthurian Tintagel

The naturally narrow entrance to the Tintagel promontory is guarded by the Great Ditch 'a massive feature of imposing grandeur and proportion' (Barrowman *et al.* 314). In the ditch, washed down from its contemporary ground surface, were fragments of imported pottery and wood which could be carbon dated. The very latest dates were AD 530–670 (95 per cent confidence). All the rest were earlier. The excavators concluded 'There can now be no doubt that the Great Ditch necessarily fits firmly as the enhanced landward boundary of the fifth to seventh century site at Tintagel' (Barrowman *et al.* 314). The Great Ditch is 'unequivocally' dated to the immediately post-Roman period (Barrowman *et al.* 320).

Not only does the work in building the Great Ditch itself testify to the power and resources of whatever authority ordered it, the resulting enclosed site was in a league of its own. At 30 acres (12 hectares) (Barrowman *et al.* 320) it is larger than any other site of the period. This includes South Cadbury Castle, 'where the refortification in the post-Roman period encloses some 18 acres (7.3 ha)' (Barrowman *et al.* 335).

All the dates derived from the promontory beyond the ditch were similarly clear. A building of AD 340–530 (95 per cent confidence) and an area of intensive food preparation including animal bones of AD 450–500 (68 per cent confidence) (Barrowman *et al.* 314), for instance. This was no stockade occupied in a brief period of emergency. One structure showed 'occupation and activity extending from the very end of the Roman period through to the seventh century' (Barrowman *et al.* 320). It originally contained (perhaps stored?) ceramics from AD 415–535, then was rebuilt or replaced by a structure dated to 560–670. (Barrowman *et al.* 320).

There was obviously quite a lot of pressure from domestic activity, showing the large site had been well populated. Terraces on the sides were created or enlarged to provide flat areas for buildings. Some buildings were fully stone built, others had stone foundations on which less substantial walls of timber and turf were placed (Barrowman *et al.* 320). Local trees, such as oak, hazel and birch were used for construction and also for fuel (Barrowman *et al.* 319), indicating a more wooded landscape than its current bleak appearance. Other finds included perforated slates, which had formerly been roof tiles, stones with large notches which had once been structural supports and 'spindle whorls, gaming counters and whetstones from everyday domestic' activities (Barrowman *et al.* 318).

There is insufficient evidence to determine whether the site was seasonally or permanently occupied (opinions differ on how habitable the windswept promontory was in winter!), or what structures existed at the same time. As yet there is no sign of a single big high status building, a hall (Barrowman *et al.* 335).

We can tell a lot about the eating habits of the Dark Age inhabitants. Cereals, mainly oats, along with meat and fruit featured in their diet (Barrowman *et al.* 319). More intriguingly, they dined off fine ceramic tableware, fragments of which were concentrated in the vicinity of the medieval great hall (Barrowman *et al.* 317). We might imagine that this particular prominent flat area was attractive to builders in both eras and it may be that the medieval hall obliterated traces of an earlier Dark Age one. More important than the tableware, though, were the massive numbers of imported storage containers.

It had long been recognised that this was a distinguishing feature of Dark Age Tintagel. Similar ceramics from other sites were referred to as 'Tintagel ware'. 'In terms of overall quantities … Tintagel far outnumbers all other sites of the period in Britain' (Barrowman *et al.* 317). The containers had once held wine, olive oil and other Mediterranean luxuries. Some had come from Spain and North Africa, and there was some glass from south-west France (Barrowman *et al.* 318). The vast majority, however, was from much further afield, 'the Argolid region of Greece, the Eastern Mediterranean, probably south east Turkey, Asia Minor and probably North Africa' (Barrowman *et al.* 317). This distribution shows we are not simply dealing with rulers with Mediterranean tastes. In that case we would expect the nearer and cheaper versions to predominate. What characterises the areas represented is that they were provinces of the surviving Roman Empire. While the logic of trade would suggest that the ruler of Tintagel was sending the Romans cargoes they valued in return – tin being an obvious one – we cannot overlook the possibility that these were diplomatic gifts, and that the Roman emperor required nothing more for them than professions of loyalty.

Archaeologists disagree on whether these fragments represent ongoing trade or small scale gifts, perhaps only sufficient for the ruler and his high table. Carl Thorpe interpreted the fragments as adding up to 150 amphorae, the larger containers, and 80 red slipware vessels, for dining. Alcock on the other hand estimated the finds as the fragmentary remains of 1500 vessels (both quoted in Barrowman *et al.* 329), which would point to substantial economic activity. Similar arguments involve the length of time over which these fragments accumulated. Some have argued for a very brief period of intense activity, 450–530 or 475–550, but the excavations have tended against this narrow focus (Barrowman *et al.* 332).

Along with the fragments of imported pottery, the excavators found stoppers made from local slate, used to re-seal the containers after their original pottery stoppers were removed (Barrowman *et al.* 318). 'Most specialists dealing with the imported "exotic" material of this period will now assert the existence of a significant, even if not extensive, trade network into south western Britain in the fifth and sixth centuries originating in the Mediterranean' (Barrowman *et al.* 330). Finds of tin ingots from elsewhere in Cornwall, as well as written evidence from the Byzantine 'Life of John the Almsgiver' (Barrowman *et al.* 331) and Procopius indicate that tin was the main exchange commodity.

It might be thought that Tintagel would be quite an obscure place for a trade centre. The best landing place would be, as it was in the Middle Ages, the 'Iron Gate', which has been described as a 'natural quay' (Barrowman *et al.* 329). However this is on the far side of the peninsula to a ship coming from the continent. The alternative is that the finds indicate the supply of an individual ruler powerful enough to attract merchants to his fastness, perhaps as Dark suggests a Dumnonian 'over king', with his retinue.

The Arthur Stone

This was the state of evidence when, in 1998, Morris's team discovered 'a securely stratified inscription on a piece of slate acting as a cover for a drain' (Morris 1999b: 21). The context was the 'post-Roman (fifth/sixth century) horizon' (Morris 1999b: 21). The slate was discovered in its second period of reuse. It was in the floor of a structure from the fifth/sixth century interpreted as 'occupied by a retinue at specific periods of the year or a caretaking group' (Barrowman *et al.* 56).

The major element of the inscription, at the top, is very fragmentary. Deep cut lines seem to read 'AXG'. There is very little this could mean. [P]AX is ruled out by the fact the unreadable letter before A ended in two parallel vertical strokes, like an H or II. Thomas makes the case for this being an 'idiosyncratic' cutting of AVG (Barrowman *et al.* 197). This is exceedingly common in Roman inscriptions, being the abbreviation for 'Augustus', the official title of the emperor. If this is accepted, the inscription becomes much more straightforward – either II AVG (the Second Legion 'Augusta') or H. AVG – The emperor Honorius.

Below this and partially across it, thus more recently inscribed, is the more interesting inscription. It is much shallower and far from impressive, suggesting 'that these are essentially graffiti on a pre-existing inscribed stone no longer in use' (Barrowman *et al.* 318). The inscription reads:

PATERNI
COLIAVIFICIT

ARTOGNOV

COL

FICIT

The inscription runs into the broken edge of the slate and we have no idea how far it continued beyond the break. On a conservative estimate, extending it sufficiently by the minimum to make it parallel to the unbroken left side of the slate, Charles Thomas suggests (Barrowman *et al.* 193) that there would have been enough room to complete the second COL with –IAVI. This would make a two part inscription '*Paterni Coliavi Ficit. Artognou Col[iavi] Ficit*'.

Charles Thomas compares the letters with those from other fifth- and sixth-century inscriptions and convincingly demonstrates that it is closest to sixth century Welsh inscriptions (Barrowman *et al.* 198), concluding that the inscription is 'perhaps after rather than before 550' (Barrowman *et al.* 200).

Morris originally published the slate as reading 'PATER/COLI AVI FICIT/ ARTOGNOV' (Morris 1999b: 21). Thomas translated this as 'Artognou, father of a descendant of Coll, has had (this) constructed' (Morris 1999b: 21). He took the first word as '*Pater*' ('father') and understood '*Avi*' as a separate word ('of a descendant'), although it actually meant 'of a grandfather'. I argued in *The Reign of Arthur*, following Andrew Smith in *Ceridwen's Cauldron*, that this was wrong. Thomas was clearly unaware that the inscription ended at a break and was most unlikely to form a complete sentence. It was apparent to me, too, that the first word was '*Patern*', as Thomas has now agreed. He reads a further upright stroke to the right of the N, making the word '*Paterni*' ('of Paternus') It could be part of a V, hence 'PATERN[VS]' 'Paternus' or could continue for several letters more, such as PATERN[INUS] or variations on that, all of which are far less common names than Paternus (Thomas in Barrowman *et al.* 199). An 'I' would rule out PATERN[OSTER] 'Our Father', a common Christian graffito.

COLIAVI could mean 'of Grandfather Col' written as a single word. Thomas has now rejected this in favour of the idea that the name Col 'has been extended with a known British hypocoristic or "pet-name" ending, -iau' (Barrowman *et al.* 199). Col is 'conceivably the same as Coll-, meaning uncertain, found in Celtic name formation' (Barrowman *et al.* 199).

It was the third name, Artognou, that everyone was interested in. It starts with 'artos' 'bear' (the European brown bear *Ursus europaeus*, thought be some to have been still extant in parts of Britain in Roman times), and a second element -gnous, the sense of which is 'know' – perhaps 'known-as, known-to-be'. The name crops up in Brittany in 882, in the more modern form of 'Arthnou'. Thomas suggests that this was the spoken form even as early as 550 and that the slate preserves an archaic spelling. In this case writer knew that 'Arthnou' was spelled 'Artognou' much as we know that the word 'nite' is spelled 'knight', quite a high degree of literary awareness.

Thomas notes that 'the element art- appears in other early Welsh male names like Arthfael, older Artmail' (Barrowman *et al.* 199). Although its derivation is, as we shall see, disputed, the name Arthur is a much more familiar one to modern readers, and is frequently interpreted as having the same 'Art-' element. The first recorded instance of the name is in Adomnan's *Life of St Columba*, written in 700 (Barber 1986: 11), far nearer in time to the slate than the first instances of 'Arthmail'. Even Arthur (our 'King Arthur') is recorded earlier.

Various writers have argued that 'Artos/Bear' was a *nom de guerre* for some differently named war leader, yielding a legendary 'King Arthur' (Philips and Keatman 1993, for example). An inscription of a sixth-century Briton signing himself 'known as the Bear' would actually tend to reinforce that argument. Gildas addresses an exact contemporary of the slate, Cuneglassus, as '*Urse*' (Bear), showing the practice existed at the time, whatever we are to infer from it (DEB 32).

Thomas's reconstruction yields a possible translation of

[the mark, or name] of–Paternus/Paterninus
[the mark] of–Coliauus – made [it]
[the mark] of Artognou
[the mark] of Coliauus
He made [it]
(Barrowman *et al.* 200)

To explain this, he has to come up with a rather strange scenario in which Colliau, cramped by the extravagant descenders carved by Paternus, decides to carve out his inscription again, this time dividing his name and Ficit' between two lines to give it more space. This is inspired by the speculation that a different person carved '*Coliau ficit*', albeit with the same implement and at the same time (Barrowman *et al.* 195). This seems unnecessarily complicated. More likely '*Coliau Ficit*' was a repetitious formula, easily copied, while slightly more care was needed over 'Artognou' and 'Paternus'. It is hard to imagine Colliau bothering to carve all his inscription again when the first was perfectly legible and fitted on a single line.

It is just as possible that 'of Colliau' is a (partial) description of Patern and Artognou.

Paternus [] of Coliavus made [it]
Artognovus [] of Col[iavus?] made [it].

An obvious assumption would be that the missing word was '*Filius*' – the men were sons of Coliavus. If '*Avus*' is a description of Col, it would mean 'Grandfather Col', and it may be that Paternus and Artognovus are not brothers but cousins, sharing a common grandfather or more distant lineage founder.

✄

Thomas notes that (Barrowman *et al.* 200) 'nothing of this can inform us who these people were' but the mix of Latin and British names is 'entirely in accord with names already known', apparently from inscriptions. This is equally true in Gildas, where two tyrants have Latin names and three have British ones.

Was 'Artognou' Arthur?

It was not the substance of the inscription but the single name 'ARTOGNOV' which caused all the fuss. Morris's assessment was 'There has been much media speculation about the inscription, but suffice it to say that it does NOT read as 'Arthur'. We must dismiss any idea that the name on the stone is in any way directly associated with that legendary and literary figure' (Morris 1999b: 21).

English Heritage, on the other hand, tended to use the form 'Arthnou', possibly because it had more letters in common with 'Arthur' and was, like it, a disyllable, making it much easier for readers to make the connection which Morris denied. Unsurprisingly, many people did make that connection, as shown by the early press releases. Conscious that the web would now be awash with articles on 'The Arthur Stone' and that 'the letters pages of several national papers have hosted a lively debate on the historical and literary merits (and demerits) of the myth of King Arthur' (Glasgow), Morris and his team posted their own initial views on the University of Glasgow website. They provided photographs of the uncovered fifth and sixth-century buildings, the slate and its inscriptions, and their assessment that 'Tintagel is a major settlement site, and its claim to high status – if not royal status – is clear' (Glasgow).

They came out strongly against an Arthurian connection:

> Although Tintagel is often associated with the mysterious and mythical past, we must dismiss any idea that the name on this stone is in any way to be associated with the legendary and literary figure Arthur. Arthur was only associated with Tintagel through the work of Geoffrey of Monmouth in the twelfth century, six hundred years later.

The team was anxious to distance itself from an Arthurian connection, what Hutton calls the remarkable spectacle of all involved 'bending over backwards to avoid appearing to give credence to the medieval tradition' (Hutton 2003: 56). True to form, in the final publication, Thomas adds the obligatory swipe that the slate 'has aroused great public interest including misleading and ill-informed speculation, which can now be set aside' (Barrowman *et al.* 200). Far be it that archaeology should arouse public interest! Thomas provides no references to or arguments against this 'ill-informed speculation'. All the published 'misleading speculation' revolves round his 'father of a descendant of Col' translation, which I demonstrated in 2004 was not correct.

✂

I agree with Hutton that the reaction of the archaeologists against the slate was wildly intemperate. They took every opportunity to deny a connection with Arthur, and the snide side-swiping was then taken up by other academics (e.g. Green, *Concepts of Arthur*) without a moment's consideration. Remember, even before they started digging, the team had already made up their minds (Morris *et al* 1990: 843) that their 'work is likely yet further to undermine the Arthurian connection'. They assumed from the start that Arthur was a 'literary and legendary figure' and that it was impossible a sixth-century slate with his name on could turn up anywhere in Tintagel. Without any argument, the Arthurian connection to Tintagel was dismissed as 'tenuous at best' (Barrowman *et al*. xiv).

Although this is not explained directly in the excavation reports, the archaeologists started from a certainty that the Arthurian connections with Tintagel were spurious and that Padel had 'proved' the only dark connections were with the Mark/Tristan cycle. It was into this hostile atmosphere that the 'Arthnou' stone made its embarrassing appearance.

The hostile argument, as far as we can deduce it, since it is not made explicit in the report, seems to be that the name is not Arthur and that, furthermore, the connection between Arthur and Tintagel is late and comes from Geoffrey of Monmouth. Setting aside the fact that Tintagel's connection with the Tristan cycle is even later and stems from writers who were more clearly romancers, this argument is very weak. We do not need to make any judgement on whether Arthur was real or whether he and Artognou were the same person. It is surely not wildly speculative to suggest that the merest sniff of a sixth-century character called Arthnou at Tintagel was probably all Geoffrey would have needed to incorporate it in his story of Arthur. It is arguable that this is what he did with Atrwys of Gwent to link Arthur to Caerleon, for instance. We don't even need to fall back on the idea of oral tradition, as we know the name was physically preserved at the site (on the slate) and could have been on other inscriptions visible in the twelfth century.

Many authors have suggested (e.g. Phillips and Keatman 1993) that Arthur or Arth was a by-name for a character with a different given name. Green, though denying any historical Arthur, suggests there was a taboo against the use of the specific name Arthur, only broken later in the sixth century (Green 2007: 196). The inscription by someone 'known as the Bear' only strengthens these arguments. Gildas confirms that one of his contemporary tyrants was known, to Gildas at least, as 'Bear' and obliges us, in this case, by giving his real name as well.

The focus on Arthnou/Arthur has meant no attention being given to the other names. It was obvious when the first high resolution photography of the slate became available that there was an 'N' at the end of Patern. This was ignored by the official team, who allowed the mistranslation 'father' to stand uncorrected in Morris 1999a and 1999b. Until the stone went on display in the Royal Cornwall Museum at Truro every discussion of it used this erroneous reading. There was consequently no official engagement with the connection between Patern and the Arthurian cycle. This is bound to raise suspicions in the minds of pro-Arthurians. Whatever the status of 'Artognov', any Arthurian scholar would be aware that there was a pre-existing connection between Patern and Arthur. They feature as adversaries, later reconciled, in the early twelfth-century *Life of St Paternus* (Wade-Evans 1944), one of several Saints Lives in the same manuscript which connect fifth/sixth-century saints with Arthur. These are legends earlier than, and entirely independent of Geoffrey of Monmouth.

If Arthurians had been asked to come up with a list of pre-Geoffrey names that might conceivably turn up in archaeological investigations of the sixth century, we would almost certainly have included Paternus in it. His credentials are impeccable. He is the eponym for Llanbardarn Vawr in South Wales. The early twelfth-century *Life of St Paternus* shows him confronting Arthur. Arthur is a rapacious tyrant who covets the saint's fine tunic. Paternus causes Arthur to sink into the ground until he repents. It is so far from the mainstream of Arthurian literature that it is commonly seen as representing a genuinely variant tradition, perhaps offering a glimpse of the nature of the real Arthur. The *Life* is a product of the South Welsh and obviously concentrates on Llanbadarn, but even a cursory glance at the Saints' Lives shows the connections between the cults in Cornwall. Most of the famous Cornish eponymous saints are said to be scions of South Welsh dynasties and Lives such as that of St Carantoc show their protagonists operating in both areas. As we have seen, the inscription itself is of a style suggesting a South Welsh origin.

Paternus is of interest beyond this because of the glimpses we have of variant legends. A Patern Red Coat appears in the first of the Harleian Genealogies, and, under the later Welsh version of his name, Padarn, he is given as the owner of a coat which is one of the 13 treasures of Britain. The list includes many other Arthurian or related items. This suggests that a character called Patern and his fine coat are features of the Arthurian tradition, of which the idea that he was a saint and his tunic of ecclesiastical origin just one variant.

The importance of Patern makes it almost inexplicable that no mention was made of him in any of the discussions from the archaeological team. Perhaps an argument about Arthur and Patern, side by side on a sixth-century slate as in the sixth-century Saint's Life was seen as too difficult. Too difficult, certainly, to refute on the grounds of the Arthurian connection to Tintagel being the product of a single late source.

What if the other person on the slate, Col/Coliau, were connected with Arthur too? Like several Arthurian enthusiasts, I immediately connected Col Avus (Grandfather Col) with Coil Hen (Old Coil, 'Old King Cole') from the Welsh genealogies. Andrew Smith (1998) suggested a nearer connection with Coll son of Collfrewy, which I now find more convincing.

Coll, (Charles Thomas's version of the name on the slate) appears only in the Triads, brief mentions which give a glimpse of the legends which once featured him (Bromwich 1978: 56). He first appears in the Triad of the Three Powerful Swineherds. Rather than being extraordinary farmhands, they are powerful and famous men who at one time in their careers had to act as swineherds. The most celebrated in an Arthurian connection was Drustan son of Tallwch (Sir Tristan), who defended the herd of King March against Arthur, Kai and Bedwyr, even against March himself. Here, Arthur is put into the same milieu as characters from the March/Tristan Cycle, in a Cornish context. Once again, it is in the rapacious predatory mode seen in the *Life of St Paternus*.

The next powerful swineherd is Coll son of Collfrewy. He is also in Cornwall, looking after the monster sow Henwen. The sow escapes and is followed by Coll across western Britain, as she gives birth to monstrous offspring. The last, which Coll throws into the sea at the Menai straits, grows up to become the fearsome Palug's Cat, one of the three oppressions of the Isle of Anglesey.

Although only a later version of the Triad specifically connects Coll with Arthur, any contemporary hearing the story would make the connections themselves (Bromwich in Bromwich *et al* 215). The chase is an ironic reversal of Arthur's boar hunt from *Culhwch and Olwen*. The writer is familiar with this corpus, as the third powerful swineherd is Pryderi son of Pwyll, whose legend is always found in the same manuscripts as *Culhwch and Olwen*. Arthur had been seen as a famous boar hunter since the ninth-century *Historia Brittonum*.

More directly, we know from the earliest surviving Arthurian poem, *Pa Gur*, that Arthur's companion, Kai was famed for going to Anglesey 'to fight lions', taking on the monstrous Palug's Cat and killing it. Variant continental sources made Palug's Cat responsible for Arthur's own death. We thus have a picture of Coll sharing a milieu with Arthur, operating in the same location (Cornwall) and at the same time.

The next two Triads amplify the material in the first and were presumably traditionally grouped together. Coll, we learn, is actually an enchanter. What his enchantment was we are not told, perhaps it was obvious to listeners who knew his story. Here he stands alongside Uther Pendragon, who passed his enchantment to Menw son of Teirgwaedd. Menw is a shape-shifting enchanter at Arthur's court featured in *Culhwch and Olwen*. Menw is part of the team searching for Mabon son of Modron. Mabon is an equally early part of the Arthurian legend, appearing in *Pa Gur* as a 'servant of Uthyr Pendragon'. And the enchantment of Uther Pendragon is, of course, the shape-shifting magic he used to get in to Tintagel and beget Arthur.

My suspicion is that the revised transcriptions of the Artognou inscription were not rushed out with the same bravado as the first precisely because they broadened the Arthurian debate. It was relatively easy for Morris to dismiss Arthur and Tintagel as a connection made by a twelfth-century 'romancer', although Geoffrey had in fact been spot on in his identification of the time period and function of the remains on Tintagel, as far as Morris's team now interpret them.

However, once Patern and Col came into the equation, the problem was much more complex. It could not be solved by recourse to the Penguin Classics translation of Geoffrey of Monmouth, the only Arthurian 'primary source' in the archaeologists' bibliography.

So is there a connection between 'Arthnou' and 'Arthur'? Although Green denies any historicity to the Arthur of *Historia Brittonum*, his idea that there was a taboo against the use of the name 'divine name' Arthur, until it was broken in Irish circles in the late sixth century fuels the concept of by-names, as does the translation of 'Artognou' as 'Man known as the Bear'. We know for certain that (whatever we are to make of it) an instance of calling men with other names such as 'bear' did exist in sixth-century Britain, as is shown in Gildas's denunciation of Cuneglassus as '*Urse*'. If there was an actual taboo on the use of the name Arthur among the insular Britons, Arthnou might be as close as anyone was prepared to go.

Of course, Arthnou and Arthur are not the same name but there are ample analogies from the Arthurian legends of names drifting just as far from their historical originals; Magnus Maximus appears in Welsh legend as Macsen (Maxentius) and in Geoffrey of Monmouth as Maximianus, three different names with only their first letters in common. Variant legends provide the names Cato, Cador and Cadwy, as a sixth-century ruler of Cornwall, quite possibly all intended to refer to the same character. Gorlois, Duke of Cornwall and Gormund, chief elder of Cornwall may be the same character. Once again we see the first three letters or the first syllable remaining the same while the ending varies from source to source.

This is not to say that any of these legends are true or connected with the slate. It is exceedingly unlikely they literally describe events in sixth-century Britain. What they do suggest is that there are more substantial grounds for speculation than three shared letters and some post medieval 'traditions' about Arthur's birth, on which the initial interest in it was based. It is surely improbable that the fact these names were all found together in a sixth-century context in a prime Arthurian location has no bearing at all on their later appearance in the Arthurian legend. Whatever connection the Artognou stone may have to the historical Arthur, it is undeniable that it strengthens the hands of those of us who believe the later legends were attached to real characters and incidents properly located in the fifth/sixth century. It cannot be used to support the current academic orthodoxy, accepted implicitly by the excavators, that the Arthurian legends concern figures of folklore and mythology, arbitrarily pegged to the sixth century on the whim of the writer of *Historia Brittonum*.

The archaeologists' refusal to engage with any of this struck Hutton as 'unbalanced'. He quotes Padel, in the face of accumulating evidence from Tintagel supporting the traditional narratives 'one hardly dares to make such a suggestion for fear of what may be made of it in some circles' (in Hutton 2003: 56).

4

THE RULER OF DUMNONIA

Morris's web article on Tintagel, and the publications which followed (Morris 1999a and 1999b), showed the tendency of archaeologists to treat the sub-Roman period as 'prehistoric' (Snyder 1998: xvi), making no reference to historical material which might illuminate their discoveries. A case in point is the claim that the inscribed slate 'demonstrates that Latin literacy survived the collapse of Roman Britain among the entourage of the rulers of Dumnonia' (Glasgow 1998). This sense of wonderment and discovery continues in the excavation report. The excavators view the fifth/sixth century as a prehistoric period, sporadically enlightened from the outside by written flashes such as the seventh-century Byzantine *The Life of John the Almsgiver* (of which more later) and Bede. To them, the inscribed slate appears as 'a remarkable recovery of evidence for post Roman literacy' (Barrowman *et al.* 125), 'attesting to the continuance of Latinate literacy in the immediately post-Roman centuries'(Barrowman *et al.* 318).

Yet this is one of the few aspects of sixth-century Cornish history which has never been in any doubt. Gildas's *De Excidio Britanniae* is a work in sophisti-cated Latin (Dark 1994: 181), which includes a section specifically addressed to a ruler with the Latin name of Constantine, 'tyrant whelp of the filthy Lioness of Damnonia'(DEB: 28). This tyrant is one of five named rulers castigated by Gildas and it is all but certain that Dumnonia (Devon and Cornwall) is the land he rules.

Two recent analyses of Gildas' work (Higham, Dark) have separately come to the conclusion that he was writing in the land of the Durotriges (Dorset and Somerset), the neighbouring polity to Dumnonia. This is not a new conclusion. It also appears in the twelfth-century *Life of Gildas*. Even if he is not entirely specific about Constantine's location (and almost all commentators believe he is), he also attacks Vortiporius of Demetia, whose lands faced Tintagel across the Severn Sea. Yet somehow the excavation report nowhere cites Gildas. He is not in the index or the bibliography. It could be argued that no finds specifically referred to Constantine of Dumnonia, hence his absence from the index too. Yet reference is made to Richard of Cornwall as the originator of the thirteenth-century castle. This equally derives from external written history, rather than the finds themselves.

Gildas gives a name to the 'royal', 'princely' or 'magnate' ruler of sixth-century Cornwall, a man so steeped in (Eastern) Roman culture he even bore the same name as some of its emperors. This man was either very literate in Latin himself or employed courtiers with this skill, since Gildas expected him to understand the complex scholarly Latin of *De Excidio Britanniae*. He was no distant figure, since Gildas knew he was still alive, and that he had committed some of his heinous crimes that very year.

Constantine is the missing man in the interpretation at Tintagel (Hutton 2003: 55). He indisputably existed, a tyrant or king of Dumnonia around the turn of the sixth century. He was clearly 'a powerful ruler and Tintagel is the most important site yet found in his dominions' (Hutton 2003: 56). He is very much the person who could be connected to works of that time of 'royal status' at Tintagel. Geoffrey of Monmouth made him King Arthur's cousin and successor, a position he retained in the romances. It seems quite likely his guilt by association with the Arthurian legends has counted against him in archaeological interpretation.

Luxuries from Overseas

By ignoring Gildas, the archaeologists have robbed themselves of any supporting material on subjects with which they wish to engage. Gildas lived in sixth-century Britain. He knew about trade and about different types of settlement, yet the excavators prefer to turn to sources distanced by time, geography and culture, like the *Life of John the Almsgiver*, Bede and Eddius Stephanus.

At the beginning of his work, Gildas explains that Britain was blessed with the Thames and Severn estuaries, by which luxuries from overseas had once been brought by ship '*olim transmarinae deliciae ratibus vehebantur*' (DEB 3:2). This is generally read as meaning that by Gildas's time the supply of luxuries had dried up entirely. What are we then to make of the extensive finds of overseas luxuries at Tintagel? Do they happen to date from periods before or after Gildas wrote? This seems unlikely. There is no obvious clear start or cut off point for these imports. Much more likely is that the wars with the Saxons had exactly the effect Gildas said – the luxury goods could not be brought into the estuaries and thence to the rivers. The Thames was clearly in Saxon hands, while the Wansdyke, a contemporary defensive feature, approached the Severn estuary. The upper reaches of the Severn were evidently a war zone. Faced with this, traders would drop their luxuries at the nearest available site en route for the Severn, Tintagel. This explains, too, why they chose Tintagel over possibly more accessible sites on the south coast – the trade routes were aiming for the Severn estuary, and stopped off short.

Gildas does not directly explain the kind of luxuries arriving in Britain. but in a perhaps humorous passage (DEB 7.1) he says the Romans went back to Italy because of Britain's lack of wine and oil. This shows that he associated those goods specifically indicated in the archaeological record with an overseas and luxurious Roman way of life.

It is clear that, as an archaeological site, Tintagel is in a league of its own. It is superlative both in the number of fragments of imported ceramic discovered and in the huge area covered. Next behind it come Cadbury Castle, Cadbury-Congresbury and possibly Alt Clut (Barrowman *et al.* 334). 'These are the largest of the whole group, which are 'stone-walled, embanked or palisaded – set frequently on hill-tops, promontories or cliff-edges' and arguably to be seen as 'the seats of potentates of varied rank, power and wealth' (Barrowman *et al* note 231) with these very large sites (and their residential potentates) at the top of their social ranking' (Barrowman *et al.* 335).

Faced with such an outstanding site, excavators speculate about the nature of it and the hierarchy of settlement at the apex of which it stands. This 'hierarchy of settlement' concept is very much *de rigueur* in modern archaeology, occupying a hefty part of the analysis of Iron Age Cadbury, for example. It is useful when applied to prehistoric sites, where we have no other information with which to judge relative importance. But Tintagel is not prehistoric. It was occupied at a time when abundant evidence for settlement hierarchy was written down.

Possibly the University of Glasgow team was used to dealing with proto-historical sites, first emerging in the historical record in the works of Eddius Stephanus and Bede. Thus, although these writers had nothing to say about Cornwall and precious little about the sixth century, it is to them that the team turned. Tintagel, they conclude, was a '*civitas*', a word used by those writers for Bamburgh and Alt Clut.

> In the social context of post-Roman Britain … it would … seem perverse not
> to accord sites such as Tintagel and Cadbury Castle 'Royal' status (or 'princely'
> or 'magnate' depending upon the relationship of the relevant potentate with
> any other in the region), with a descending hierarchy of other high status sites,
> individually sometimes identified as an *urbs* or *villa regis*, and therefore meriting
> the term 'royal'. (Barrowman *et al.* 335)

Bede and Eddius Stephanus were writers working 200 years after the period using terms from Roman vocabulary to describe institutions of the Germanic kingdom of Northumbria. To appeal to them to illuminate finds in sixth-century British Cornwall obviously has the potential for distortion. The archaeologists continue:

> Archaeologically, the site is at the top of the social hierarchy in this period,
> and so it is difficult to envisage Tintagel as anything other than a site of the

Dumnonian rulers. It was an enclosed settlement on a hilltop promontory, from which control could be maintained of passing shipping, and indeed of maritime trading activities. (Barrowman *et al.* 336)

If Tintagel was occupied seasonally, then rather than being 'the capital' it would be considered as one of a number of such centres 'comparable with the *villae regales* mentioned by Bede in relation to early Northumbria' (Barrowman *et al.* 335). This is a very important point, which we will return to in more detail when searching for 'the real Camelot'. Dark Age and early medieval monarchs moved constantly between royal locations. This was necessary from the practicalities of feeding their retinue and from the administrative need for the ruler to intervene and be seen throughout his domains.

Tintagel has been recognised for many years by archaeologists and others as a special, if not unique, site, and there is no doubt that it is this quality that has led to the association in the popular imagination with that quintessential representation of the heroic and mythical British past, 'King Arthur'. (Barrowman *et al.* 336)

The Cities of Britain

Unlike Bede, Gildas did, presumably, live in a sixth-century British settlement. We do not need to comb his book for vague hints or clues about the number and size of settlements in his country. At the start of his book, in the same passage in which he wrote about overseas trade, Gildas tells us that Britain had 28 *civitates* (cities? towns?) and some *castella* (castles? villages?) '*bis denis bisque quarternis civitatibus ac nonnullis castellis*' (DEB 3.2). Bede is hardly an independent witness at this point, as he reproduced the same passage, virtually word for word, at the start of his ecclesiastical history and it presumably informed his use of the terms (Bede HE I.1).

The *civitates* seem more important than the *castella*. It is as *cives* 'citizens' that the inhabitants of Britain are distinguished. In Gildas's day the 'cities' themselves are not populated as they used to be (DEB 26.2). They were deserted (DEB 19.3) first during the Pictish raids and later during the Saxon revolt. Instead, the Britons fled to 'steep fortified hills, dense forests and cliffs on the sea coast' (DEB 25.1), indicating that Gildas sees these refuges as different from the *civitates* they abandoned. If anything characterises Tintagel, Cadbury, Cadbury-Congresbury and Alt Clut it is this passage. They are exactly the types of refuge Gildas suggests and thus, to his mind, different from the *civitates* in which the Britons should have been living.

Gildas is not bound by the technical Roman meaning of *civitates*, county-sized administrative units. His '*civitates*' are clearly towns or cities. He distinguishes between cities and fields '*civitates agrosque*' (DEB 24.1) devastated by the Saxons and his descriptions of *civitates* always include urban features. *Civitas* is a word used in his version of the Bible (e.g. 51.1) for the 'cities' of the Holy Land. The fact that he thinks Britain has 28 of them shows he is thinking of something more common and thus including smaller settlements than the cities which were technically *civitates*.

Gildas knew various words for structures which were purely military. He refers to '*munitionibus*' 'fortresses'. You can see '*deserta moenia*' – deserted city walls which are old Roman structures, decorated as they are with carvings of pagan deities (DEB 4.1).

A stone wall (Hadrian's Wall) has '*arcis*' 'citadels' for its garrison (DEB 19.2). On the south coast are '*Turres per intervalla*' – towers at intervals protecting it. These particular structures still stand, massive fortresses of the Saxon shore. Gildas thus clearly means something more than the translation 'towers' implies.

So, although Gildas's word for smaller settlements, *castella* evokes images of castles to us, he carefully distinguishes them from the '*munitionibus*' – fortifications. *Castellum* is also a word used in the Latin version of the Bible, for villages such as Bethany compared with neighbouring cities such as Jerusalem. Unfortunately it does not occur in any of the quotations used in *De Excidio Britanniae*, leaving the exact meaning Gildas gave to it uncertain.

Two other words for settlements are also used by Gildas. Did he, though, intend his readers to attach any particular significance to them or was he simply casting around for synonyms for 'town' to vary and enrich his prose? One is *urbes*; Hadrian's Wall runs from sea to sea between towns '*a mari usque ad mare inter urbes*'. One of these, we know, is Carlisle, *civitas* capital of the Carvetii, so clearly a settlement of size. *Urbs* means a large city, the seat of a bishopric, to Gildas, or at least extends to include cities of this size, as he refers to St Ignatius, Bishop of Antioch '*antiochiae urbis episcopus*' (DEB 74.1). Other than the ones on either end of Hadrian's Wall, the only *urbs* Gildas refers to in Britain is the City of the Legions '*Legionum urbis*' (DEB 10.2). This has a martyrs' shrine so may well have a bishopric. Verulamium, named in the same sentence, has St Alban as one of its citizens *cives* and so is presumably at least a *civitas*. The three towns of Roman Britain with legions attached to them were York, Chester and Caerleon, whose claims we will examine later.

The other word is *coloniae*. Technically these were specific large towns where army veterans were settled. There is no reason to think that when Gildas says all the *coloniae* were laid low by battering rams during the Saxon revolt he did not mean precisely what he wrote. Even if he uses the word loosely, though, his *coloniae* are clearly significant settlements (DEB 24.3). They have walls and towers as well as houses, requiring siege-craft to breach them. They were seen by the Saxons as potential providers of the monthly allowances they wanted and the leaders who would supply them. Crucial to Gildas's understanding is that the *coloni*, the people who live in the *coloniae*, include the leaders of the Church –'*praepositis ecclessiae*'. These leaders are distinct from the ordinary priests '*sacerdotibus*'(DEB 24.3). They are therefore bishops and the *Coloniae* are their sees. The organisation of the Christian Church into bishoprics based in major cities mirrored the Roman civil administration. It was quite a conservative pattern and ensured that a concept of 'settlement hierarchy' persisted even when urban dwelling was in decline.

Urbs and *coloniae* are used historically by Gildas, describing the situation of Britain in the past. Unfortunately, in his own time he does not connect his tyrants to settlements. Cuneglassus (DEB 32.1) is called 'charioteer of the bear's stronghold' '*receptaculi ursi*'. If this is somewhere he lives or a site of one of his victories, rather than, say, a geographical feature in his land, then it seems rather smaller than a town or city. A frequently cited possible location, Bryneuryn Dinarth (Bear Fort) in Gwynedd opposite Deganwy, is a small site enclosed in this period (Alcock 1988: 24).

Briefly, then, we can conclude that Gildas did have a concept of a hierarchy of settlement. At the top are *coloniae*, seats of provincial and church government. They are destroyed and perhaps deserted in Gildas's time. Next are the *civitates*, including some *urbes*, which are of significant size, include Carlisle and either York, Chester or Caerleon, and probably support bishoprics. *Civitates* also include towns which are smaller than regular *civitas* capitals, since there are twice as many of them. They are deserted or at least not inhabited as they used to be. Below them are *castella*, villages or small towns of some kind. At the bottom of the scale are the towers, walls and fortifications.

Isca Dumnoniorum (Exeter), the *civitas* capital of the Dumnonii, must count as a *civitas*. On average we would expect each Roman '*civitas*' administrative region to support two or three of the settlements Gildas would call a *civitas*. That makes it just possible that Tintagel was of a size and importance in Dumnonia to rank alongside Isca. However large and impressive Tintagel would have been, its identity as a recently fortified cliff-top must count against it. What is clear is that the *civitates* from which the citizens fled must, to Gildas, be different from the fortified hills and sea cliffs to which they fled. It is impossible that he would not have classed Cadbury, Congresbury and Tintagel among these defensive sites. If they are not fortified cliffs and hills, then nothing is. Besides which, they were, of course, not abandoned in this period. Logically, therefore, they must be ranked in his lesser classes of *castella* or fortifications.

We can see that Gildas, a contemporary and probably local writer, could have provided the archaeologists with many more words and concepts for settlements than the vague '*civitas*' and '*villa regis*' they were able to glean from Bede. With so much to offer, why was Gildas ignored in favour of ideas from a different age, culture and region? I suspect he was ignored for being one of the 'usual suspects' in the historical Arthur debate, a debate the archaeologists were desperate to avoid.

Double Standards in the Dark Ages – The *Life of St John the Almsgiver*

The general scepticism by archaeologists about the sources previously used to provide narrative to the period, has led to other more obscure sources being sought out. These are preferred for being untainted with Arthurian connections but are rarely if ever subjected to the same sort of hypercriticism which even Gildas must answer. A case in point is the *Life of St John the Almsgiver*. This is often dropped into recent accounts of Dark Age Cornwall as if it was an unassailable witness to conditions and society there (e.g. Snyder 1998: 152, who goes so far as to locate the captain's arrival at Topsham outside Exeter). It even beat Gildas to inclusion in the Tintagel excavation report so must surely, I at first supposed, be better founded than the latter's fanciful account of contemporary Britain. Then I decided to read it. It is about a century later than Gildas, from the mid-seventh century, by two writers who knew the early seventh-century Alexandrian Patriarch John the Almsgiver. There is one incident concerning Britain. A sea captain, down on his luck, applies to John for alms. He uses the donation to buy a ship. The ship is wrecked. This is because the captain mixed unholy goods with holy ones in its cargo. John gives the captain some more alms. The result is the same, except this time the ship is wrecked because he put holy cargo in unholy ships. Third time lucky. Generous John gives him cargo and ships, and with a fully holy inventory, the captain sets off. For the whole voyage the ship is in darkness. No-one can see where they are going, but every night John the Almsgiver appears miraculously at the tiller, steering them through. After many days, the darkness lifts and they find they are in Britain. A leader from a town comes and tells them there is a famine. He begs them to sell him their cargo of (holy) grain, offering either tin or an inflated amount of money. They agree to take half money, half tin and sail back again. When they arrive in north Africa and have the tin assayed, they find it has miraculously turned into silver. (Dawes 1948)

From this, academics who think the list of Arthur's battles in *Historia Brittonum* is implausible because it shows Arthur fighting unrealistically distant campaigns, and that even Gildas is unreliable, are happy to accept the testimony of the hagiographer that Britain had a town with a leading man and that this was probably in Cornwall (because of the tin). It is difficult to see how any aspect of this tale that could be true (except perhaps the absurd generosity of John the Almsgiver in such a hopeless case) but not a fraction of the hostility the Arthurian sources attract has been directed to it.

Geoffrey of Monmouth

It is normal practice in archaeological reports to consider the excavation results alongside the earliest documentary information. Frequently sites emerge for the first time in the written record centuries after they were built or inhabited. Very often in England it is in the Domesday Book from the 1080s that they first enter the pages of history. Tintagel was too obscure to figure even in that exhaustive record of settlements prepared for the new Norman overlords. It was to be another 50 years before a churchman took up his pen to name it, describe it and attribute a history to it. He describes the site before it was altered by the construction of Richard of Cornwall's fortress. He gives it a status and function in AD 500 which could be measured against the finds for accuracy. This should have been a godsend.

Of course, the writer is Geoffrey of Monmouth, and the archaeologists' comments show he was not the sort of company they wanted to keep. There is no indication that anyone on the project read Geoffrey of Monmouth in anything other than Lewis Thorpe's popularist (and inadequate) Penguin Classics translation. That is the only text given in the bibliography, a shocking oversight. They thus have no idea what words Geoffrey actually used to describe the site. Even that is generous, since there is no evidence that they even read the Penguin translation, so convinced were they that Geoffrey could be ignored with impunity.

In a large, and in most other ways comprehensive report, it is astonishing how little space is devoted to the earliest written source. Near the start, the archaeologists write (Barrowman *et al.*: 3):

> Traditionally Tintagel is connected with the legendary king Arthur: the source of this tradition, Geoffrey of Monmouth's *History of the Kings of Britain* (*c.*1135–8) places Arthur's conception by the union of Uther Pendragon and Igerna, the wife of Gorlois, Duke of Cornwall at Tintagel, Gorlois's safest maritime fortress.

That is it. The quote is referenced to Thorpe's translation and Padel's 1984 article, which dismissed the Arthurian connection. This is followed up with a pithy direct quote from Professor Charles Thomas.

No-one would deny Thomas's expertise and experience in the area, but he has always been committed to an anti-Geoffrey and anti-Arthurian position. His hold over the archaeologists and their interpretation of the site is clear from the acknowledgements, where he is thanked twice before contributing himself by thanking the people who have thanked him. Twenty-seven of his works are included in the bibliography, a bibliography which, remember, includes no primary works by Geoffrey of Monmouth or Gildas, no reference to the Triads, to the *Life of St Padarn*, no general work on the Arthurian connection, even, which might have drawn attention to the names of Paternus and Coll.

The contemptuous attitude of the team to anyone with anything other than a wholly negative view of the Arthurian connections of Tintagel is clearly revealed. Thomas is thanked for sharing

> with the director [Morris] the frustrations of both genuine and 'fringe' interest from the press and public over the finding of the 'Arthnou Stone and the other 'A' word.

Most archaeologists working on publicly owned sites would, I imagine, be only too happy to deal with the frustrations of … genuine … interest! Kevin Brady, a member of the team who has never published anything indicating a level of knowledge of the Arthurian material, is thanked for demonstrating 'unsuspected talents for dealing with innumerable requests for information about [the inscribed slate], "King Arthur" and the so-called "Arthurian period"'.

The excavations were not an environment where the possibility of a connection between the finds and the Arthurian legends could be discussed dispassionately. True, nothing in the excavation decisively confirmed the Arthurian connection, but equally nothing confirmed Padel's view that Tintagel was connected to the (non-Arthurian) Mark/Tristan cycle or academic orthodoxy that Arthur was a legendary superman only linked with Dark Age history by *Historia Brittonum*. Indeed, those two contentions fared rather worse than Geoffrey's version as a result of the excavations. Arthnou may or may not be Arthur, but he certainly wasn't Mark or Tristan nor can any connection between the other names and that cycle be argued. All three names belonged to men capable of 'making' something in the sixth century, not mythological figures. The lack of any desire of the team to progress beyond the Penguin Classic paperback, an academic already committed to an anti-Arthurian position before the slate was found and an archaeologist with an amateur interest in Arthuriana is shocking and should not go unchallenged.

So what did Geoffrey say? At the turn of the sixth century, Tintagel was one of two fortified centres for Gorlois, the *Dux* of Cornwall. *Dux* is a perfectly plausible term for a ruler of that period. Gorlois's successor is known as *Dux*, occasionally as *Rex*. Gildas calls his contemporary rulers variously *Duces* (DEB 33) and *Reges*. In Geoffrey's own time there were no 'dukes' in Britain – he is not grasping at some anachronistic peerage title, as 'Duke of Cornwall' now sounds in English translations.

Tintagel is not the capital of the *Dux*. It is one of his chief '*oppida*', a word Geoffrey would have known from Caesar, used for the hill forts of the Gallic Wars. Another is nearby Dimilioc. Gorlois uses it as a refuge for his wife because he believes it the safest place under his command, when he is attacked by his rapacious overlord.

Geoffrey knew from Gildas that sixth-century Britain was riven by civil wars, that the rulers and their wives were guilty of adultery, and that it had fortified hills and sea cliffs, places where the Britons of the generation before the Battle of Mount Badon had held out. He may, of course, simply have mined Gildas's work for these details, but the origins of the specific Tintagel and Arthur material must lie elsewhere. Geoffrey's description of 'The fort of Tintagel, a safe place of refuge on the coast … it stands completely surrounded by the sea and can be reached only by a narrow cliff' (HRB VIII.19), is spot on.

Geoffrey tells us no more about Tintagel or the internal workings of Cornwall, so there is no place for elucidating the imports and pot sherds which loom large in archaeological considerations. However, the general sophisticated ambience of the Cornish court is indicated by the fact that Geoffrey thought it was a suitable place for Guinevere, 'a woman of noble Roman ancestry' (HRB IX.9), to be brought up. The use of the site as a residence for ladies like Igerna and Guinevere is demonstrated by the spindle whorls, those feminine objects which did so much to dispel the all-male monastery model.

All this is as accurate as it could possibly be. It is exactly the time period, function and status which the excavation report describes, just with a few proper names added, including that of the site. This is particularly impressive considering all Geoffrey could have seen there was a small recently modified chapel barely 100 years old (Barrowman *et al.* 322). Tintagel parish Church, the most substantial standing building in Geoffrey's time, was on the mainland, not the promontory. The archaeologists agree that the first medieval castle building on the site should be attributed to Earl Richard in the thirteenth century (Barrowman *et al.* 322), possibly influenced by Geoffrey, rather than influencing him.

The crowing that the excavations would further disprove the Arthurian tales was completely wrong. To the embarrassment of all concerned, the excavations agreed with Geoffrey's version in every particular. His view of Tintagel being one of several fortified residences of an independent ruler of Cornwall *c.*AD 500 is entirely in accord with the archaeologists'. The date range established by the Phocaean red slipware found there dating from AD 475–550 (Campbell 1996: 85) was just what he implied (HRB: XI.2). Morris is fully in accord with Geoffrey:

> fifth to sixth centuries AD … most probably a 'citadel' of the Dumnonian rulers … it would seem perverse not to accord Tintagel … 'Royal' status.' 'a major post-Roman 'citadel' of the Dumnonian rulers of the time. (Morris 1999b: 19-21)

As for the personalities connected with Tintagel by Geoffrey, Morris and his team have neither proved nor disproved any of them. The story of Arthur's conception lies well outside the realms of archaeology. What on earth could any archaeologist find which would disprove that Arthur was conceived there? A monastic site or one uninhabited in the period would have argued against it, but what was discovered seems as near as we will ever get to 'proving' the case.

'There was conceived Arthur, the most famous of men'

Modern historians tend to approach Geoffrey from the perspective that his tale of Merlin magically disguising Uther Pendragon so he can beget Arthur must be fiction, so the rest of the story is suspect. The paradigm in which Geoffrey worked would not have made him or his readers predisposed to doubt the story for this reason. Geoffrey was well acquainted with the miraculous conception stories in the Bible and hagiography, as well as classical parallels. The most obvious is in the *History of the Battles of Alexander the Great*, a Latin translation of the Greek romance from the eleventh century (Stoneman 1991: 30). In this, Egyptian king Nectanebo uses his magic arts to take on the form of Ammon to seduce Queen Olympias, who gives birth to their son, Alexander the Great. It in no way would have raised any doubts about the historicity of Alexander, Olympias and Nectanebo, or Alexander's conception at Pella. Closer to home, *Historia Brittonum* makes the absolutely historical fifth-century British leader Ambrosius a fatherless prophet conceived by a Welsh virgin (HB 41).

If Geoffrey of Monmouth were nothing more than a 'romancer', unfettered by anything other than his imagination, why did he write what he did about Tintagel and Arthur's conception there? He was not supporting a Tintagel tourist industry and we can see no ulterior motive for aggrandising this site. If he had a truly blank canvas to work with, we would have expected Arthur to be conceived at Caerleon, Geoffrey of Monmouth's favourite Arthurian location. The Alexander romance provides us with an answer. Its writer needs to balance conflicting traditions, one that Alexander was the son of Philip and Olympias, thus legitimate heir to Macedon. It is a claim from the start of Alexander's career and incidentally true. The other is that Alexander was the son of the god Ammon, a claim which became politically expedient after his conquest of Egypt and was promoted by his successors in Egypt to whom the Macedonian claim was less relevant. As a Christian, the writer follows the euhemerising line that the god Ammon was not actually involved, only a human impersonating him.

Geoffrey seems to be stuck with a similar dilemma. He needs to reconcile the idea that Arthur is the son of Uther Pendragon and part of the dynastic succession to Constantine and the Breton/British 'royal family' with the idea that Arthur is a scion of the Cornish royal house. He takes the same route of impersonation and deception to provide Arthur with two possible fathers.

Presumably, he does this because he needs to deal with pre-existing Cornish traditions. In the *Prophecies of Merlin* Arthur is referred to as the 'Boar of Cornwall', but in the *History* proper only the story of his conception is offered to provide this link. It might be that Geoffrey needs to reconcile Arthur with his successor, the Cornish ruler Constantine (from Gildas). If this was of particular importance to him, however, it is surprising that he does not detail exactly how Arthur and Constantine are related. According to Geoffrey, Constantine is Arthur's '*cognatus*', meaning they are kinsmen, but not exclusively in the male line. Arthur is the son of Uther Pendragon and Igerna. Cador, Constantine's father, could be a son of Gorlois and Igerna. We know nothing about Igerna's family, but she is only a member of the Cornish dynasty by marriage, so there is no blood connection between Arthur and the Cornish dynasty. Constantine of Cornwall is not descended from the earlier Constantine nor is there any particular reason for him to inherit the throne of Britain, if this is taken to be hereditary. It is obviously the need to juggle these conflicting ideas which makes Geoffrey reticent to spell out the exact link between Arthur and Cador and Constantine.

There are other indications that the Cornish material is not just a product of Geoffrey's imagination and the recurrence of similar names but different stories connected with Dark Age Cornwall is one such. Gorlois in Geoffrey is matched by Gormant and Goreu, both from *Culhwch and Olwen*. Cador obviously has some connection with Cato, from the *Life of St Carantoc*, and Cadwy son of Gereint from the genealogies. Constantine (from Gildas) also appears as Custenhin, father of Goreu in *Culhwch and Olwen*.

Geoffrey uses skill and imagination which convert a possible genealogical wrangle into a memorable story, but this is hardly grounds to dismiss everything he had to say on Tintagel. It is true that Geoffrey is distanced by some 600 years from the time of the episodes he relates. But remember that the written history of Tintagel starts with Geoffrey. The gap is not filled with references to the site denying it an Arthurian connection, which can falsify Geoffrey's claims. That it did have a sub-Roman history is confirmed by the archaeology and Geoffrey's success in pointing this out ought by rights to be celebrated rather than vilified. It is hardly Geoffrey's fault that, as Thomas points out (1993: 24) 'almost every subsequent writer was able to expand the conception of Arthur at Tintagel to his birth there and by implication, ownership and even residency'.

Seeing the Stone

A replica of the Artognou stone is displayed in the visitors' centre at Tintagel Castle, with an account of its discovery. The visitor experience opens with an introductory video 'Searching for King Arthur', 'a magical mystery audio-visual tour through the ages, introduc[ing] visitors to the castle, its legends and history.' (English Heritage Property 316). The video aims to show 'how myths are made and how they lead us back to history'. The reality of the Dark Age residence at Tintagel is stressed, and the role of legend, folklore and later writers in creating the figure of Arthur is made clear. The positioning of the concepts of Arthur and the mystery attached to the stone at the start of the visit is significant.

On the site, care has been taken to work with an Arthurian interpretation without committing the curators to supporting it. A general board covering '2000 years of history' says the history of the site is 'shrouded in mystery. What is known provides little basis for the Arthurian legend. However, when the mists come swirling through Merlin's cave, it is easy to see how the myth has survived to this day.' Signs relating to the sixth-century occupation refer to an unnamed 'Dark Age Cornish King'. In an evocative reconstruction drawing above the Haven, he is shown as a monarch viewing the arrival of luxury imports. Perhaps he is intended to be Constantine of Dumnonia, but as he is never named; the identification with Arthur is left open. The caption reads in large red letters 'The Legendary birthplace of King Arthur'. In the small print underneath Arthur is written twice, in inverted commas, and he is described as 'real or fictitious', before being dated 500 years earlier than the castle but contemporary with the Dark Age 'stronghold' and its imports. Structures of the medieval castle are labelled with sufficient latitude for visitors imagining Arthur as a medieval king to place him in that context.

The real stone is on display in the Royal Cornwall Museum in Truro. Truro has no Arthurian tourist industry to satisfy and indeed does not even mention Arthur, one of the county's most famous 'sons' on its website. The stone is displayed as 'inscribed slate 2', accompanied by a detailed analysis of the writing on it.

For visitors attracted to the stone by all the media hullabaloo about Arthur, the curators have no comfort to offer: 'It has absolutely no connection with the medieval name Arthur', the sixth-century form of which might be 'Artorius'. Geoffrey of Monmouth is dismissed as a twelfth-century 'romancer'.

The most positive 'Arthurian' spin on the Artognou stone originates with English Heritage. This is meshed, somewhat indiscriminately, with the concepts of mystery, legend and romance. The archaeologists, on the other hand, are over-keen to distance themselves from the legends. Even though their interpretation is all but identical to that presented by Geoffrey of Monmouth, this is not commented on, nor is the significant contemporary evidence given by Gildas compared with the site. The true value of the stone and the excavations which recovered it surely lies between these two extremities. As a result, an exceptional opportunity to fully interpret the realities of sixth-century Britain has been lost.

5

CAMELOT!

King Arthur: Camelot!
Galahad: Camelot…
Lancelot: Camelot…
Patsy (shrugs): It's only a model.

Monty Python and the Holy Grail (1974)

Of all the mythical places associated with King Arthur, none has the resonance of Camelot. If ever there was a prime Arthurian site for English archaeologists to discover and the heritage industry to capitalise on, this is it. For some, Camelot is 'a medieval dream-city which it would be misguided to locate on a map' (Ashe 2002: 211) but this has not stopped others from trying. 'Let these young critics, bless them, in this sort of context recall the epic battles and victories of Troy long ago, and of a certain Heinrich Schliemann…' (Wheeler in Alcock 1972: 2).

Schliemann, famously, was inspired by the Iliad to go in quest of Troy (Renfrew and Bahn 2004: 32). His excavations at Hisarlik made him 'archaeology's original mythic hero' (Romer 2000: 106) and were presented as proof of the Trojan War. Even though nothing he discovered even confirmed the name of the city, his success held out the hope to others that their cherished stories might equally be built on historical reality (Gazin-Schwatrz and Holtorf 1999: 12).

Leonard Woolley (Renfrew and Bahn 2004: 36) was able to present the Mesopotamian site of Tell el Mukkayer as 'Ur of the Chaldees' (Romer 2000: 128) while Arthur Evans named a whole civilisation after the mythical King Minos, having discovered the Labyrinth of 'Knossos' at Kephala on Crete (Romer 2000: 204). In 1960s Britain it was to be the turn of Camelot.

The name 'Camelot' first appears in the form 'Camaalot' in *Lancelot*, a romance by the late twelfth-century writer, Chrétien de Troyes. His Arthur was an itinerant

iii. THE ARTHURIAN SOUTH WEST

monarch, as was normal at the time, holding court at various locations from Carlisle to Nantes. In *Lancelot*, he is once shown holding court at Camelot (*Lancelot* 34, trans Owen 1987: 185).

Chrétien knew from the French translation of Geoffrey of Monmouth that Arthur would be killed at Camlan, which could be the source of the name. However, he was a classicist (*Cliges* I, trans Owen 1987: 93) and probably aware, from Pliny's *Natural History*, 'a work which was certainly much read in Western Europe in the twelfth century' (Alcock 1972: 14), that there had been a British city of Camalodunum (sic) (Rivet and Smith 1979: 294). This is the city now called Colchester which has, on these grounds, been suggested as the original Camelot (for example in Morris 1977: 138). Colchester was occupied at the beginning of the Arthurian period (Snyder 1998: 145). No archaeologist, however, seems to have dug there looking for Camelot. (Pryor 2004: 173 quotes the excavator Philip Crummy as saying the occupation of Colchester 440–450 was like a squatters' camp!)

There are no 'Camelot' tourist attractions and no mention of Arthur or the sub-Roman period in the otherwise comprehensive Castle Museum. The museum's website gives this curt reply to what seems to be an irritatingly frequently asked question: Is there any connection between Colchester and King Arthur?

> No. King Arthur is a semi-legendary character who led the resistance against the invading Anglo-Saxons. Any historical Arthur can only have lived in the west or north of Britain. At the time Arthur is believed to have existed Colchester lay in the heart of enemy territory. (Colchester Museum)

A website supporting the identification of Camulodunum/Camelot prints the text of what it claims to be a standard letter from the curators on the subject. The letter begins by raising the possibility that Arthur may not have existed at all, and that even if he did, the early sources when stripped of all later accretions are very meagre. Next, the Colchester area is within that settled earliest by the Saxons, and an Arthur as military leader against the Saxons would have operated in the areas which had not been settled, the north and west where many of the legends relating to him are based. Furthermore, 'we also know from archaeological evidence that during this time Colchester itself was largely deserted' (Camulos.com). There is, in fact, evidence that the Essex area was one where sub-Roman kingship evolved (Dark 1994: 86), and there are plenty of scenarios which could see its rulers joining with other kings in resistance to the Saxons. The idea that Arthur was a defensive general, who would not have operated in occupied territory, is at variance to the view of the period given by Gildas. For him what marked the Britons from the time of the siege of Mount Badon (subsequently attributed to Arthur) was that they took the fight to the enemy (DEB: 25).

The curators' letter rightly ascribes the introduction of Camelot into the Arthurian legends to Chrétien de Troyes and therefore late and fictitious. The curators take the question of Camulodunum and Colchester head on. They concede that it was just about possible for Chrétien to have come across the classical Roman texts relating to Camulodunum. However, the identification with Colchester was not established until the late eighteenth century. This is illustrated by reference to Geoffrey of Monmouth. The letter concludes with material on the connection between the city and Arthurian writer Thomas Malory.

Colchester Museum clearly has a lot of knowledge about the supposed Arthurian connection. If the website is to be believed, this is a frequently asked question. However, the establishment view that the connection is wrong means that the issue is not addressed at all on the main pages of the website. This is a missed opportunity. Arthur is a well known figure and this could be used as a hook to draw the visitor into discussion of issues the museum thinks are more relevant. The main display, for instance, simply leaves a 200-year gap between the end of the Romans in 410 and finds from the East Saxons in 600. The transition between the two is a subject for continued speculation with new arguments and discoveries constantly being put forward. The story of the re-emergence of the Roman literary texts and the identification of Camulodunum with Colchester might be another approach.

Other Camelots

Chrétien took the background for his Arthurian material from, ultimately, Geoffrey of Monmouth. Geoffrey's ancient kings were itinerant too, but Geoffrey chose Caerleon-on-Usk as the capital of Britain. Caerleon is only a few miles down the road from Monmouth, and its standing Roman remains impressed twelfth-century sightseers like Gerald of Wales (Snyder 1998: 164). For Geoffrey it was the see of the Archbishop of Caerleon, the leading Christian priest, who crowned King Arthur and accompanied him on his campaigns. Geoffrey spins the reference in Gildas to the martyrdom of Saints Julius and Aaron in the City of the Legions to a glowing description of the wonderful ecclesiastical shrines dedicated to them in Caerleon in Arthur's day. A fantastic *tour de force* of Arthur's plenary court at Caerleon fixed the image of an Arthurian court *par excellence* (HRB: IX. 12).

Caxton, in his introduction to the *Morte d'Arthur*, tells his readers that in Camelot, in Wales, great works of stone and iron can still be seen lying on the ground (In Vinaver 1977: xiv). This part of Wales, Gwent, became a Dark Age kingdom (Dark 1994: 84), one of whose rulers, Atrwys ap Meurig, is sometimes advanced as 'the real king Arthur' (e.g. Gilbert, Blackett and Wilson 1998).

Cadw, the Welsh equivalent of English Heritage, makes nothing of King Arthur at Caerleon, or in any of the sites under its care. The former Chief Inspector of Cadw (the late Richard Avent) told me

The only site with legendary associations is the Roman amphitheatre at Caerleon. In a fictional epic, written in the thirteenth century, Geoffrey of Monmouth identified Caerleon as the court of King Arthur. His *History of the Kings of Britain* proved so popular in the Middle Ages that Caerleon soon appeared as Arthur's court in medieval Welsh and French romances. (pers. comm.)

Now, the Arthurian connection goes back at least as far as the Vatican recension of *Historia Brittonum*, 200 years before Geoffrey, and a reliance on twelfth-century material has not stopped Tintagel and Glastonbury cashing in on the associations. To not interpret any of this at all seems peculiar.

Caxton was very familiar with Malory's text. However, his description of Camelot being in Wales is at odds with Malory's identification. Sir Thomas tells his readers that Camelot is now called Winchester (Vinaver 1977: 58). Perhaps he knew no more than Winchester had been the 'capital' of England. Most likely, though, he was influenced by the fact that King Arthur's famous Round Table was hanging on the wall of the Great Hall in the castle there, something Caxton points out as proof of the existence of Arthur (Vinaver 1977: xiv).

Unsurprisingly, the prime Arthurian focus in Winchester is on the Round Table. Every kind of Round Table souvenir, from mouse mats to chopping boards, can be bought in the gift shop. It is interpreted as an incredible survival of high medieval royal furniture. Older works connected it to Edward III, but the more recently published material (Biddle 2000) takes it back to Edward I, broadly contemporary with the hall in which it hangs.

Beyond that, the Winchester Camelot connection is not really interpreted. The Winchester museum does not mention Camelot, nor the Round Table (the Great Hall is the responsibility of the County Council). The principal curator, Geoff Denford, describes the displays as based on 50 years of scientific archaeology of the city. I take that to mean that because the Arthurian connection is not founded on those principles but rather literary speculation, it is necessarily omitted. However, the sub-Roman history of Winchester (Snyder 1998: 153) has been recovered by precisely those scientific methods. In the museum, the Roman Winchester display finishes in the 'Arthurian' period, with the end of Roman Britain, the decay of the town and the first appearance of artefacts of Germanic style. It is a perfect opportunity to at least mention the King Arthur connection. Pagan Saxon Winchester, starting with an introduction covering their arrival in the region, is on the floor below.

Winchester's website (www.visitwinchester.co.uk) hardly mentions Camelot. It is not included in an eclectic list of '20 things you might not know about Winchester', Arthur is not in the list of historical figures, neither are Malory or the *Morte d'Arthur*, of which the 'Winchester Manuscript' is one of its two surviving versions (Lacy 1988: 353), mentioned on the Literary Connections page. To add insult to injury, there is an extensive section on *The Da Vinci Code*. This has absolutely nothing to do with Winchester, except that some scenes from the film were filmed in the cathedral. The History of Winchester section says only: 'Dark Ages 400–600. The era of the legendary warrior King Arthur. Was Winchester 'Caer Gwent', Camelot?' (www.visitwinchester.co.uk:brief-history).

There are other candidates for Camelot, from Westminster to Cornwall, but Colchester, Caerleon and Winchester are the front runners. The fact that none of these promising sites is interpreted as 'Camelot' is strange in itself. If nowhere was described as Camelot, this at least would be explicable – the whole edifice rejected as the anachronistic creation of a late twelfth-century fiction writer. The fact that somewhere else is identified as Camelot is entirely due to archaeologists.

A British Troy

In June 1965, Dr Ralegh Radford took on the role of Chairman of the Camelot Research Committee. Later the even more illustrious Sir Mortimer Wheeler took the helm as President. The founding committee included representatives of the Society of Antiquaries and the Society of Medieval Archaeology. (Alcock and Ashe 1968: 123). As interest in its self-proclaimed 'Quest for Camelot' snowballed, they were joined by esteemed archaeologists Philip Rahtz and Leslie Alcock (who would lead the investigation), representing University College, Cardiff, the Board of Celtic Studies of the University of Wales, the University of Bristol and two special interest groups, the Prehistoric Society and the Society for the Promotion of Roman Studies.

Ideas held by the committee members ranged from 'an uncritical belief in the most romantic and unhistorical of tales, through a vague but uninformed scepticism … to a degree of scholarship unrivalled in the Arthurian field' (Alcock 1972: 23). Founders included the Honourable Society of Knights Of The Round Table and the Pendragon Society. The Secretary was Geoffrey Ashe, author of 'distinguished middle-brow books on the problems of the historical Arthur' (Alcock 1972: 22). Also among the founders was the Somerset Archaeological Society, soon to be joined by Somerset County Council (Alcock and Ashe 1968: 127).

One might wonder what the Somerset contingent was doing there. Where were the archaeologists from Essex, from Monmouthshire, from Hampshire, even from Cornwall or Greater London? Surely they could have provided invaluable aid in the 'Quest for Camelot'? They were not represented because the committee had already worked out where Camelot was. All they needed to do was dig it up – the declared aim of the committee was 'the adequate excavation of one site, Cadbury Castle, South Cadbury, Somerset' (Alcock and Ashe 1968: 127).

In 1542, the Tudor antiquary John Leland wrote 'At ... South Cadbyri standith Camallatte ... sometime a famose toun or castelle ... The people can tell nothing than but that they have hard say that Arture much resortid to Camalat.' (Leland Book 1, part 2: 151). The idea was resurrected by James A. Bennett, the rector of South Cadbury in a paper entitled simply 'Camelot' in 1890 (Alcock and Ashe 1968: 125). He supported this by some amateur digging on the site. 20 years later the site was dug by H. St George Grey, who wished 'to learn more about Camelot' (Alcock and Ashe 1968: 126). It was this line that Radford and Alcock wished to follow.

We might wonder why a brief passage in a source 400 years distant from Geoffrey of Monmouth, should be preferred above all the possible locations with a medieval pedigree. Was it that Cadbury's wild and windswept aspect, with views to the distant Glastonbury Tor, just seemed a more romantic location than Colchester town centre? Was it that the uncluttered site simply offered more possibilities to archaeologists?

The committee decided 'There could be no objection to seeking further funds for a "Quest for Camelot"' (Alcock and Ashe 1968: 128) and money came rolling in from the British Academy, the BBC, Bristol United Press, Hodder and Stoughton, the Society of Antiquaries, the University College of South Wales and Monmouth and private donors. Preliminary investigations used aerial photography, analysis of crop marks and sample trenches and trialled a new device, the soil conductivity meter (Alcock and Ashe 1968: 129). It was in this respect a very modern archaeological investigation. As the first turfs were removed 'in the presence of cameras' it became quite clear that not finding Camelot was not an option (Alcock and Ashe 1968: 131).

Alcock and Ashe (1968: 132) wrote revealingly that 'Cadbury Castle, appropriately for Camelot, was plainly a kind of British Troy'. They wrote candidly of 'optimistically' classing finds from the first season as 'Arthurian'. What turned up, among evidence of 4000 years of occupation, was that an essentially Iron Age hill fort, as Cadbury appeared to be, had been extensively refortified in an era contemporary with post Roman 'Tintagel Ware' by 'an Arthur-type figure, so to speak' (Alcock and Ashe 1968 134).

It was time to raise £5,000 for the 1967 campaign. It certainly cannot have harmed the appeal, to which private donors, the Pilgrim Trust, the *Observer* and Bristol University, eagerly contributed, that cinemagoers that year could watch Richard Harris serenading Vanessa Redgrave about the wonders of Camelot in Lerner and Loewe's eponymous musical. Who could fail to be excited by the idea that this 'congenial spot for happ'ly-ever-after-ing' (Lerner and Loewe 1960) was currently being revealed by the white heat of sixties' technology?

The campaign began with a geophysical survey using four instruments including a 'proto-magnetometer' to take 100,000 readings (Alcock and Ashe 1968: 135). Sub-Roman and Saxon remains were uncovered and interpreted in the light of prevailing assumptions of the 'Quest' (Alcock 1995: 6). 'The Lord of Cadbury was a person as much like Arthur as makes no matter: a person living on a site traditionally picked out as his home, in the traditional period' (Alcock and Ashe 1968: 147).

Alcock published an interim report entitled '*By South Cadbury is that Camelot …*': *Excavations at Cadbury Castle 1966–70* (Alcock 1972). His publishers, Thames and Hudson, helped the public along. They printed in stark bold letters on the spine the words: 'Cadbury/Camelot' and by this name the site became known (e.g. Radford and Swanton 2002: 24).

6

THE FALL OF CAMELOT

The story of Cadbury/Camelot did not end there. In 1982, in the Mortimer Wheeler archaeological lecture 'Cadbury-Camelot: a fifteen year perspective', Alcock stood before his peers like a repentant heretic. He confessed 'my position on the historicity of Arthur is one of agnosticism, and for the present I will discuss Cadbury/Camelot without Arthur', although he appreciated that this might be like discussing Troy without Priam or Homer (Alcock 1982: 356).

Archaeology had played some part in this Damascene conversion – Alcock's own work in northern Britain, and the realisation of the regal and residential rather than purely military nature of Cadbury itself (Alcock 1982: 356). Primarily, though, it was the product of intensive criticism of the written sources. Alcock wrote in 1989 (2001: Xvii) that the new generation of scholars 'have largely undermined the case which I had advanced for the historic Arthur: Indeed, some scholars would claim they have destroyed that case completely.'

It was the work of Dumville, Miller and Hughes (Alcock 1982: 356) which had dealt the death blow. These were not archaeologists but historians specialising in the early texts. The most significant, David Dumville, is described by Hutton (2003: 52) as 'Arthur's executioner'.

Dumville has never once engaged with any of the discoveries of the 1960s and 1970s at Cadbury or elsewhere. His view of Arthur as a legendary, even mythological figure relied on theories from the 1950s, or as far back as 1891 (Dumville 1977: 187). The basis of his attack was that sources like *Historia Brittonum* and *Annales Cambriae* were firmly products of their own time, not pristine survivals from the fifth and sixth centuries. This view is also argued at greater length by Higham (2002). Alcock had previously considered that the *Annales* at least were 'unimpeachable in terms of the normal rules of historical criticism, and to reject them is to display prejudice, not scholarship' (Alcock 1972: 15). Dumville countered (1977:188) 'The fact of the matter is that there is no historical evidence about Arthur, we must reject him from our histories and, above all, from the titles of our books.' Rahtz agreed. He described the term 'Arthurian' relating to the fifth and sixth centuries as 'historically misleading and an example of the trivial personification which bedevils history and historical archaeology' (Rahtz 1991: 3).

The attack was specifically directed (Dumville 1977: 173) at Alcock and John Morris, author of the monumental and (over) imaginative work *The Age of Arthur*. 'By a cruel trick of fate' (Hutton 2003: 53) Morris died suddenly on the very day Dumville's attack was published. He was one of the few historians competent to tackle Dumville on his own ground and his death left Dumville a clear field.

'The effect of this short piece upon academics was immediate and tremendous' writes Hutton (2003: 52). He frequently heard it said that 'Dumville had proved that Arthur never existed... The consensus among historians shifted at once. From then until the end of the century most works dealing with post-Roman Britain have either ignored the subject of Arthur [or] derided it'. Dumville had provided the excuse the archaeologists needed to ditch the inconvenient baggage of Dark Age historiography (Hutton 2003: 55).

Archaeologists of the Cadbury/Camelot generation had spent their formative years in a world at war (Wheeler 1972: 7). For them the picture of a beleaguered Britain, heroically resisting invading Germans (Higham 2002: 14), had been accepted instinctively. Now archaeologists were reacting against the traditional picture of heroes and savage fighting, preferring 'slow and peaceful infiltration' (Hutton 2003: 55). A wider discussion of this trend can be found in Ward-Perkins (2005).

The written sources universally portrayed the fifth and sixth centuries as an uncomfortable world of violence, bigotry and inter-ethnic strife. Jettisoning these as mythical freed modern archaeologists, as we saw in the case of Tintagel, to rewrite the Arthurian Age as 'prehistoric' (Alcock 1988: 22), a blank canvas to paint more satisfying mythic compositions.

Welcome to Camelot

Cadbury Castle is privately owned and there is hardly any interpretation on site. Instead, the local authority (South Somerset District Council) provides guidance for potential visitors, describing the Iron Age origin of the site and its role in the Roman Conquest. Although it mentions a 30ft section of the wall 'uncovered during the 1967 archaeological season', it describes this as 'almost certainly Saxon' and dates 'probably' to AD 1010 (South Somerset Museums and heritage site).

The website www.somerset.gov.uk says only that Arthur's name is linked to Glastonbury and Cadbury, speculating on his role as a Roman-style cavalry general. It concludes that in the absence of conclusive proof of his existence 'Arthur remains a mythical figure and a subject for further study and debate.'

Without on-site or internet support, all the interested visitor can do is pick up the official English Heritage excavation report (Barrett *et al.* 2000). This is in many ways an admirable piece of work, presented in a quasi-narrative form 'developing an argument about the way the hill was physically transformed and occupied' (Barrett *et al* 2000). It is horrifying to discover that there are but two references to Camelot and Arthur in the whole report: in the introduction. It explains the research programme of the Camelot Research Committee in 1965 as the converging of interests in 'the mythical association of Cadbury Castle with Camelot; the potentially historical association with Arthur and the recognition of imported Mediterranean pottery dating from the fifth and sixth centuries AD among the existing collections of material' (Barrett *et al* 2000: 1). Although the committee was obviously interested in the fifth and sixth centuries, it was committed to a holistic approach covering all periods (Barrett *et al* 2000: 4). And that is it. Its definition of 'early historic archaeology' does not even reach the fifth century.

I am not the only one to cry 'foul' over this. Alcock was dismayed to discover that English Heritage had abandoned the chronologically inclusive element of the research programme, and was compelled to publish separately on what he called 'the early medieval archaeology' (Alcock 1995: ix).

There are still only two references to Arthur and Camelot in this volume. Alcock repeats his recantation of the Camelot attribution 'the present excavation report is not the place to discuss the Arthurian problem; and the military and political significance of Cadbury Castle in the later fifth and sixth centuries will be considered ... without reference to Arthur' (Alcock 1995: 6). If Leslie Alcock's official excavation report on Cadbury/Camelot was not the place to discuss the Arthur problem, one might legitimately wonder 'where is?'

Alcock concluded that the castle was the home of a powerful late fifth-century king, an 'immediate fore-runner of those kings of western Britain whom Gildas castigated around the middle of the sixth century' (Alcock 1995: 172). Gildas did not name this immediate forerunner, but the very first time he was named (HB 56) and subsequently (e.g. HRB XI.2) he was called Arthur.

Readers of the excavation reports survey the same, bleak uninterrupted vista as offered by the windswept summit of Cadbury Castle. Encouraged to follow a mythical quest by reputable and distinguished archaeologists, they are abandoned at the culmination of their journey, with only myth and pseudo-archaeology to guide them.

Peasants and Kings

This is not to say that archaeological work in the Cadbury area has ended. Far from it. The South Cadbury Environs Project continues to research and publish. In keeping with modern archaeological trends, the focus is firmly on 'ordinary people', providing the context of South Cadbury, rather than on the elite who presumably commissioned and used it.

Davey (2004: 52) rejects the Anglo-Saxon account of the conquest of Dorset/ Somerset by the West Saxons as pseudo-historical, and predictably interprets the work of the environs project as demonstrating the 'peaceful emergence of a new cultural identity in the seventh century'. The stable nature of field and estate boundaries in the area, coupled with the evidence from Hicknoll Slait of a 'sixth to seventh century cemetery exhibiting a mixture of Romano-British and Saxon burial customs' (Davey 2004: 52) indicates there was a 'slow process of acculturation' in the area. This suggests that 'if any truth can be gleaned from the Anglo-Saxon Chronicle, the emphasis on military conquest is certainly misleading. Nevertheless, the approximate date for the west Saxon absorption of Somerset is broadly correct' (Davey 2004:52). This immediately raises the question of why the locals' response to the peaceful process of absorption by the West Saxons through a process of acculturation was to reoccupy a giant hill fort and to construct a vast earthwork, the Wansdyke, between them.

Davey, representing the project, argues that:

> perhaps, then, on the collapse of central authority in Britain, sometime in the fifth century, the Durotrigian *civitas*, having retained a strong identity, was able to assume regional autonomy without the need for social upheaval. In this scenario the reoccupation of Cadbury Castle in the middle of the fifth century might be seen as a symbolic separation from Roman authority and a link to the Durotrigian past, rather than a response to external stress. In reality it was probably a response to both of these factors.

This idea is something we will return to later.

The basic idea is that the Romans divided the *civitas* of the Durotriges, creating a separate *civitas* of the 'Lendinienses', based on Ilchester (Lindinis) in the third century (Davey 2004: 49). The third-century economic strength and restructuring of the South Cadbury environs gave way to the reversion of marginal land to unenclosed wood, marsh or downland some time between the fifth and seventh centuries. It is not clear whether the principal cause was the collapse of central Roman authority at the beginning of the fifth century, or climatic disaster in the middle of the sixth century. A shift of central place from Ilchester to Cadbury Castle in the middle of the fifth century is coupled with the continuous conspicuous consumption of imported goods into the middle of the sixth century.

This suggests that the true situation cannot be simply ascribed to a monocausal explanation (Davey 2004: 52).

This has important implications for the interpretation of South Cadbury. Far from a collapse of civilisation back to scattered fortified bunkers, or the militarisation of a wasted buffer zone, the evidence seems to show that the Cadbury environs must have continued to produce an agricultural surplus in the fifth and sixth centuries. This in turn enabled the construction and manning of the earthworks and the accumulation of luxury items such as wine and oil. Far from being a windswept military base, South Cadbury is taking on the aspect of a prosperous royal centre once again.

7

KINGS OF THE BRITONS

I noted briefly in the introduction how the popular image of Arthur as a medieval king came about. Although the sources were clear that Arthur was envisaged as living some time around the year AD 500, it was a commonplace for medieval fiction writers to portray their heroes, whether the Bronze Age denizens of Troy, the Iron Age soldiers of Macedon or the Dark Age Paladins of Charlemagne, as though they were contemporaries. There was an extraordinary flourishing of Arthurian romances between the 1130s and the 1230s. It was in this period that such well-known Arthurian motifs as the sword in the stone, Excalibur emerging from and returning to the lake, the Round Table, the forbidden love of Lancelot and Guinevere, the quest for the Holy Grail and its achievement by Sir Galahad were first devised. These created a template on which writers of the later middle ages based their versions.

As often as not, we can see how these motifs took shape and were developed. We can follow the steps, for instance, by which a grail, a sort of dish for serving fish, evolved into 'The Holy Grail', Christ's own cup and the repository for his blood (Barber 2004). The Round Table went from being a supernaturally large structure 'where sixteen hundred and more can easily be seated' (Lawman 11434) to a relatively smaller disk or ring shaped piece of furniture at which the king and a select group of his elite knights dined. Attempts to find 'the Holy Grail' or 'the Round Table' by archaeology are thus by their nature doomed to failure.

The sword Excalibur has often been the source of 'archaeological' speculation. It is a superlative weapon (called 'Caliburnus') in Geoffrey of Monmouth's *History of the Kings of Britain*, forged in the Isle of Avalon. It appears (called 'Caledfwlch') in early Welsh sources and may well be an element of the Arthurian legend of some antiquity. The idea that it was pulled out of a stone as proof of Arthur's right to rule appears later. Geoffrey presents Arthur as universally acknowledged as his father's son and heir. The other story, that Excalibur is a replacement sword presented by the Lady of the Lake and reclaimed by a mysterious hand from the water, also appears later. It is wildly unlikely that either of these versions dates back to Arthur's time or beyond into prehistory, without leaving any trace in even the most comprehensive earlier accounts of the legend. Attempts to link the sword in the stone back to by Bronze Age storytellers describing the process of casting bronze blades in stone moulds (e.g. Pryor 2004: 18) would have to explain this very patchy record of transmission. Likewise, tracing the throwing of Excalibur into the water as a memory of Iron Age Celtic votive deposits would need to explain why this story was not preserved by Welsh bards, arguably direct inheritors of the Celtic tradition, but by courtly French writers.

In truth, even if we concede ancient antecedents to these stories, we do not need to buy the whole package of 'oral survival'. The romance writers had a relatively direct hotline back to the early Iron Age world and the imagined Bronze Age world beyond it, not through bards but from the classical texts with which they were certainly familiar. The legend of Theseus told how the hero proved his right to rule by lifting his father's sword from under a stone. Practices not dissimilar to those of the ancient Britons persisted with more recent barbarians: fifth-century ruler Attila had been presented with a sword found stuck in the ground which proved his right to rule. Scarcely more than 200 years before the romances, Vikings were casting real weapons into the Thames, presumably for votive purposes, and the medieval inhabitants continued to throw miniature weapons and knives, along with coins and pilgrim badges in during the heyday of the romances. The front cover of the paperback version of Francis Pryor's *Britain AD* has a well-chosen image of a thirteenth-century sword recovered, along with many others back to prehistoric examples, from the River Witham. Pryor argues convincingly that this shows a continuity of ritual practice associated with this liminal or boundary location (Pryor 2004: 218). This also shows, though, that the practice was a contemporary ritual to the writer who first imagined Arthur's squire casting Excalibur back into the water at the liminal point in Arthur's life. The writer need know nothing about the Arthurian past to invent this potent symbolic act.

Thus, unfortunately, although the newspapers eagerly seize on reports of the Grail, the Round Table and Excalibur as the sorts of finds likely to be recovered by Arthurian archaeology, even the most enthusiastic archaeologists of the Cadbury/Camelot era were unlikely to make such claims.

Life after Rome

If Arthur and his contemporaries did not inhabit a feudal 'medieval' society, it is still difficult to pin down the exact nature of society in the fifth and sixth centuries. The Cadbury excavations certainly had a lasting impact on the archaeology of the 'Sub-Roman' period. This had often been dug through en route to more durable Roman remains beneath. Now it came to be studied as an interesting period in itself. All kinds of archaeological theories of the peaceful transition kind found support in the period. Currently the two most interesting theories are the 'Late Antiquity paradigm' and the 'failed state'. Both take more notice of the written record than their anti-migrationist predecessors, but still not to the point of including Arthur in their indexes, let alone their titles.

The arguments for and against the Late Antiquity paradigm arose from the archaeology of western Europe and have only relatively recently been brought to bear on the British experience. It acknowledges that at one end of the period there was a society characterised by the official use of the Latin language, stone monuments of stereotypically Roman kind, complex urban life, institutions of the Roman state such as its governors and army, and so on. These were present in Britain certainly in 381, when Magnus Maximus was proclaimed emperor. 300 years after, all these had gone. But was there a sharp break, a 'fall of the Roman empire – departure of the Romans' which someone living at the time could have noticed, or was the process more or less imperceptible, with continuity more likely to be the norm? The fictional King Arthur, as he has appeared in historical novels in the late twentieth century, is sometimes cast as a 'Last of the Romans' type of general or as a Celtic warrior chieftain, a physical embodiment of the two contrasting societies on either side of this transitional period.

Neil Faulkner (2004: 6) sees the crucial defining feature as the towns: 'Towns were essential features of Roman imperial civilisation … they were local centres of political authority where tax collection and law enforcement were organised'. Just as important was their role as 'centres of 'Romanisation', uniting the many local elites who governed the Empire into a single ruling class which 'shared cultural identity and uniform social inspirations … the decline of towns … represent the passing of an entire political order that depended on them'. Without them, sub-Roman Britain looks very different:

> there were no towns in Britain after *c.*AD 375, because on no site can a level of activity be demonstrated – whether measured by buildings under construction or buildings still occupied – sufficient to justify the description 'urban'. It is not sufficient simply to demonstrate continuity of activity at a site. (Faulkner 2004: 7)

This is by no means a unique view. C.J. Arnold (1984: 158) argued that towns were not directly relevant to the study of fifth-century Britain as 'these once grand Roman institutions had already failed'. Instead, Faulkner offers a list of features indicative of the early Dark Age British society which succeed it:

1 Fortified secular sites e.g. hilltop enclosures, including reused hill forts, coastal promontory forts and reused Roman walled settlements.

2 Ecclesiastical sites – cemeteries, churches, monasteries, mostly new foundations but some continuing or reusing Roman sites.

3 Small coastal trading sites – promontory forts with harbours or beaches.

4 Small farms, often enclosed, sometimes reusing high status Roman sites, sometimes continuing low-status Roman sites, sometimes new foundations.

5 Small stone round-houses, small rectangular halls in stone or timber and some larger rectangular halls with aisles and partitions in timber.

6 Small and impoverished local assemblages including domestic pottery. High status artefacts include penannular brooches with decorated terminals and hanging bowls with decorated escutcheons.

7 Imports of luxury goods from the Byzantine east and Frankish Gaul.

8 High status inscribed memorial stones.

We have already encountered nearly all these features in the cases of Glastonbury, Tintagel and Cadbury/Camelot and they are, as Faulkner argues, diagnostic of sites associated with 'the Age of Arthur'.

Faulkner's 'overtly political' (Davey 2005: 122) explanation of how this came about is open to challenge. In his view in the earlier part of the transition, say 375–450, the urban Roman institutions were actually overthrown in a period of anarchy. Withdrawal of some troops and the inability to pay the rest opened the way for revolting peasants, equivalents of the '*Bagaudae*' in Gaul, egged on by radical egalitarian Christian preachers, analogous to the Circumcellions in North Africa. They seized the land from the elite and ended the surplus production on which it parasitically depended. I suggested the involvement of *Bacaudae*-like elements in the 'Saxon revolt' in Gildas but we should be careful of seeing them as solely working class. Wood (1984) shows that the Gallic *Bacaudae* included not only the poor but the victims of political oppression. Salvian, the one fifth-century writer to actually use the word *Bacaudae*, says they were victims of evil judges under whom they had lost their liberty and their rights to call themselves Romans. This is closer to the way Zosimus describes the establishment of an independent Britain, with the Britons driving out the officials appointed by usurper Constantine III.

There is some support for the concept of the fifth-century Britons as social liberators. The Roman play *Querolus* has a fictitious deposed heir contemplating going off to join the British freemen on the Loire (Wood 1984: 4). That these Britons were not operating as a proletarian anarcho-syndicalist commune is shown by the letters of Sidonius Apollinaris. He wrote directly to the king of the Britons operating in Gaul, Riothamus (3.9) complaining that certain Britons had been enticing slaves away from their masters. It is these Britons operating on the continent who formed 'Brittany' in what had been Armorica. Riothamus is presented as 'the real king Arthur' by Geoffrey Ashe (eg. Ashe 1982: 128). While this character would certainly repay investigation, he cannot in my view 'be' Arthur.

The identification involves jettisoning key features of Arthur's identity, such as his victory at Badon Hill and his death at Camlan, in favour of later ideas such as conquests in Gaul.

Liebeschuetz (1993: 288) studying the rise of private warbands as a feature of the late Roman military scene also doubts that the *Bagaudae* are simply participants in a peasants' revolt on jacquerie. He notes that the legal strictures used against them are those intended against long-term deserters from the Roman Army and the private armies to which they were attracted (*latrones, duces, coloni*). He concludes that 'these upheavals were perhaps no more than extreme forms of local armies and dependents' jostling for supremacy.

Faulkner's surplus-free, primary producer-led society before the mid-fifth century is at variance to that reported by Gildas. For him it was a time when (DEB 21. 2) 'the island was so flooded with abundance of goods that no previous age had known the like of it'. Cruel kings were 'anointed' by bloodshed, overthrowing each other in the general atmosphere of luxury the unparalleled prosperity engendered. Faulkner's characterisation of Gildas as a (fellow?) 'red' (2004: 10) hating the kings and their clerical toadies is wide of the mark. Gildas castigated errant rulers but shows no sign of opposing the whole system of elite rule which they represent. He bewails the fact that in the pre-Saxon period 'any king who seemed gentler and rather more inclined to truth was regarded as the downfall of Britain' and writes only with approval of the kings and public officials, as well as private individuals, who 'kept to their stations' in the era of the Battle of Badon (DEB 26.3).

Faulkner is mistaken when he characterises the succeeding period (450–550) as seeing the new elites of warlords and chieftains using 'increasingly sophisticated legitimation strategies includ[ing] "the invention of tradition" [and] fake genealogies'. There is no indication of this in any contemporary source. Patronymics are not used of any of Gildas's tyrants, or of Coroticus, a tyrant written to by St Patrick or many of the Gododdin heroes, still less any more complex genealogies. Gildas only refers back to the generation of their fathers in most cases – they seem to be new men. His longest genealogical link, from his contemporaries back to their great-grandparents is in the line of Ambrosius and is used to castigate rather than legitimise them. Faulkner has back-dated the process we can see beginning in *Bede* and *Historia Brittonum* and brought to its fruition in the Harleian Genealogies, contemporary with the tenth-century *Annales Cambriae* they accompany. These are products of a succeeding age anxious to link back to the 'chieftains' of the fifth and sixth centuries, not products of that age itself.

Many of Faulkner's characteristic Dark Age features were also singled out by Leslie Alcock (1988), from his own very different standpoint. He notes the existence of halls, like that at Cadbury where imported wine was drunk, built by the potentates of the time, as well as the enclosed sites and the carved and inscribed monuments asserting to the potentates' use of 'craftsmen who were literate in arcane symbolism, whether that of the Roman script in various forms or the ogam stroke alphabet or the Pictish symbols' (Alcock 1988: 28).

Esmonde Cleary (1993: 59) takes a not dissimilar starting point:

> late Romano-British society was integrated to a greater or lesser extent over a wide area ... had a deep and elaborate hierarchy ... specialisation by occupation ... by location, such as town dwellers [or] countrymen.

The scale, hierarchy and specialisation of society was to be drastically reduced in the sub-Roman period. Surplus extraction was the key to this and when Roman social structures necessary for this collapsed it 'led to the disappearance of Roman rule and culture in Britain and of their archaeological manifestations' (Esmonde Cleary 1993: 61). He checks the evidence against what Gildas has to say to conclude that the 'four horsemen' of war, famine, plague and death often seen as bringing about the fall of Roman culture were actually symptoms of the collapse. Gildas's 'memorable plague' even if it was as destructive as the later Black Death, came long after the collapse. Besides which, in his view plagues do not of themselves cause cultural change. Without visible manifestations of Roman rule, the countryside remained by and large open and cultivated from the Romano-British to the Anglo-Saxon period. The inhabitants however reverted to a 'localised, agrarian, kin-based society' (Esmonde Cleary 1993:61).

Although this picture will need to be refined, we have here essentially the archaeological consensus of what the 'Arthurian' period looks like; how sites like Cadbury and Tintagel are interpreted currently. Making a sharp distinction between Roman and post-Roman cultural on these lines, however, misses two important considerations.

Kingdoms of the West

Equating Roman culture with urban culture ignores the fact that in Roman times the vast majority of the population did not live in towns. They, like their predecessors and their successors until the late nineteenth century, lived in small rural communities and worked in agriculture. There was no real reason why the imposition of a minority urban population need have impinged greatly on their daily life. Faulkner's extreme position demands he ignore the rural evidence of continuity (Davey 2005: 122).

Secondly, what part of Britain do we mean? The successor states of the north and west arose in places which had never been urbanised anyway. Exeter was the only city, the only Roman town, in Dumnonia. There were no towns in the interior of what became Wales. Roman settlements around the perimeter were military bases more than urban settlements. The Gododdin, coming to the aid of their compatriots in Catraeth, using Roman loan-words and concepts like the days of the week, came from lands which not only had no Roman towns but also had no other instruments of Roman rule which Faulkner says characterised Roman-ness. And it is precisely in these areas that the archaeological signifiers of 'post-Roman' Britain seemed to originate and in which they concentrate. They are, coincidently or not, also the areas most likely to be connected with Arthur.

> We know that structures of life in most of Devon and Cornwall were affected relatively little by 'Romanized' styles between the 1st and 4th centuries ... only small amounts of characteristically 'Roman' imported objects are found on many sites in Cornwall ... 95% of all pottery from Roman-period sites in the county was locally produced on the Lizard peninsula. This echoes the situation during the preceding Iron Age. (Turner 2004: 26)

Here, in short, the presence of the infrastructure of the Roman state further to the east made no more difference to most of Dumnonia than its absence did.

The division is incredibly sharp on the ground:

> nowhere is this regional variation more pronounced than in the south west, where a line approximately along the watersheds of the Quantock and Blackdown Hills divides the highly Romanised landscape of eastern Somerset and Dorset from the rest of the south west where very little Romanised material culture has been recovered from a rural settlement pattern that retained a largely prehistoric character in all but the immediate hinterland of [Exeter]. (Fyfe and Rippon 2004: 161)

Fyfe and Rippon theorise that this 'presumably represents the boundary between the Iron Age tribal groupings of the Durotriges to the east and the Dumnonii in the south west.'

Archaeological sites with strong Arthurian connections are found on either side of this divide, with the *civitas* of the Durotriges and the *civitas* of the Dumnonii equally good candidates for providing 'kings of Britons' to resist the Saxons.

Some archaeologists have seen this as merely the resurfacing of Iron Age tribal identities barely submerged by the occupying Romans. Evidence that it is something more than this, assertions of new, post-Roman identities can be found in the characteristic burials associated with the western communities. Rahtz (2004: v) points to 'cemeteries that appear to be of indigenous British in the west, but not conventionally Roman or Anglo-Saxon. They are characterised by being sparse in grave-goods. The graves are orientated west-east, mainly in rows.' He cites his own recently published excavations at Cannington in Somerset as the type site. Rahtz actually excavated this in the Cadbury/Camelot period (1962–63) but it did not contribute to the debate then as, for some reason, it took nearly 40 years for the results to be published.

The burials were seemingly associated with Cannington hill fort. As the cemetery 'provides ample material of the fourth century' (Rahtz *et al* 2000:424) it is quite possible the hill fort was reoccupied even before the end of the Roman Empire. 'Radiocarbon determinations are apparently continuous into the fifth century; any finds associated with thus phase are likely to be indistinguishable from the Roman ones.' As other nearby settlements did not continue beyond the Roman period, Rahtz and his team speculate that it is possible that 'it was only in a more remote, backward, rural area that settlement continued to be economically and politically viable, with its hill fort nucleus becoming increasingly important in difficult times' (Rahtz *et al* 2000: 423). In fact radiocarbon dates showed there was no break in the use of the cemetery for three or four centuries. Settlement intensity must have had no break either.

Cannington is typical of the pattern: 'burial practices established in Britain by the late fourth century remained unchanged throughout subsequent centuries in those areas not affected by the Anglo-Saxon incursions of the fifth, sixth and early seventh centuries' (O'Brien 1999: 185).

There is something 'Christian' about this type of burial 'unfortunately, for the archaeologist, the Christian dead were almost invariably buried in shrouds without associated grave-goods' (Henig 2004: 18). To be buried this way was a public assertion of identity, be it Christian, Roman or British. Exactly which is not clear. Evidence for Christianity (other than the burials) is sparse in late Roman Somerset. Rahtz (2000: 418) gives Wells and the Glastonbury Tor complex as rare examples, saying that his Cadbury/Camelot-era interpretation of the Tor as a chieftain's residence is 'not now so convincing' and 'based … on the dubious evidence of animal bone'. West-east graves with few grave goods occur at Henly Wood (also in Somerset), Caerwent in Gwent and Llandough in Glamorgan. Although they are difficult to date precisely within the date range established by Cannington, they come to dominate in the fifth century (Petts 2004: 81).

At first the burials are limited to those parts of the western Roman province of Britannia Prima which had been most Romanised in the fourth century, but the tradition is then introduced into the more westerly areas. When they occur in the un-Romanised west they are clustered rather than in the 'managed' rows of the Roman cemeteries. Crucially, though, it is in the west they first become connected with the epigraphic tradition seen by Faulkner as characteristic. 'Most carved stones are bilingual or purely in Latin. The range of formula used, particularly "*Hic iacet*" show clear parallels with the wider epigraphic tradition of the western Roman Empire' (Petts 2004: 81). Apart from the occasional outlying in Silchester and Wroxeter 'this type of fifth century epigraphy was not used in the more distinctly sub-Roman areas of England'. Not Dorset, Somerset east of the Parrett, little in south-east Wales (Petts 2004: 81). If the burial of Arthur had been associated with a carved stone, rather than a lead cross, it would have fitted well into this pattern.

Of course the inhabitants of western Britain did more than die. In life they consumed and produced. Exotic pottery, metal working particularly of iron, pins and combs, leather working and pinning are attested, although there was no minting of coins. The diet of the inhabitants was weighted in favour of stock rearing, though porridge and bread were also important (Alcock 1988: 25). Although Cannington shows burial continuity, Rahtz notes (Rahtz *et al* 2000: 424) 'it is the later fifth and sixth centuries which appear to mark an important phase in the Somerset hill forts, principally dated by the fortunate occurrence of pottery imported from the Mediterranean'. This in itself demonstrates a (continuance of? revival of?) surplus production, not only for trade, if that was how the luxuries were acquired, but also because the works on the hill forts imply the removal of able-bodied persons from agricultural food production (Alcock 1988: 26).

Unlike the Cadbury/Camelot approach, and presumably because of it, there is a deep reluctance to attach any narrative to the finds.

> No clear name can be given to the community burying in the cemetery. Adjectives such as sub-Roman, early Christian, Dark Age and Anglo-Saxon have their uses in specific contexts, but do not describe a community living, dying and being buried in the area over several centuries. Cannington was a burial place for people who lived in the area, whoever they may have been. (Rahtz *et al* 2000: 425)

This strikes me, from the perspective of a historian, as a timorous avoidance of the totality of the evidence. Gildas was convinced, writing apparently from a nearby location, that any Saxons there may have been in the area earlier were invaders who had since returned 'home' to eastern Britain, and are therefore hardly likely to be part of a burying continuity in Cannington. The West Saxon rulers of the area, according to the laws of the late seventh-century king Ine, thought Welsh and Saxon communities were sufficiently clearly demarked that different legal values could be placed on them. Saying that the people of Cannington were no more than the people of Cannington is symptomatic of the 'nameless dead' who rob this period of any historical connection. Providing a narrative involves synthesising more than one form of evidence.

8

BRITAIN HAS GOVERNORS

The search for King Arthur in an archaeological context must always be one of fitting names to sites and artefacts. Driscoll and Nieke (1988: 1) write of:

> an ambivalent relationship between the archaeologist and the artefact. On the one hand we expect richer deeper interpretations from historical archaeologists than we do from prehistorians, yet such interpretative efforts are not likely to satisfy the criteria historians establish for historical knowledge: archaeological events are imprecisely dated and the identification of an individual's actions nearly impossible.

Whereas the Cadbury/Camelot excavations were all interpreted in the context of a historical narrative, Davey's current work on the South Cadbury environs explicitly avoids this:

> to focus on individual events such as the point at which Roman culture could be said to end, or Saxon culture begins is to abuse the archaeological evidence and to give too much credence to dubious historical sources ... archaeological evidence is not suited to answering these essentially historical questions. As archaeologists we can identify and interpret the socio-economic systems which underpin historical events but not the events themselves. (Davey 2005: 126)

This ought to be an eloquent argument for synthesising history and archaeology to produce a single narrative, but is all too often taken as licence for archaeology to operate in a vacuum, refusing to draw inferences. I might also add that this should cut both ways. The unsuitability of archaeology to answer historical questions did not prevent Morris and his team using the archaeology of Tintagel to attack the Arthurian interpretation of the site.

It is possible to put some kind of narrative on these remains without turning to legendary materials. Gildas is absolutely clear that the Britain of his time had

iv. LATE ROMAN BRITAIN

Carvetii

BRITANNIA

Brigantes

SECUNDA

Decangli

Ordovices

FLAVIA

CAESARIENSIS

Cornovii

BRITANNIA

Dobunni

Trinovantes

Demetae

Catuvellauni

MAXIMA

Silures

London

PRIMA

CAESARIENSIS

Durotriges

Dumnonii

kings (*reges*). He goes on to refer to them as tyrants (*tyranni*), judges (*iudices*), leaders (*duces*) and princes (*principes*) which it is easiest to see as synonyms. He gives us the names of five 'tyrants' whom he denounces with lavish details of their sins and lifestyles. Unfortunately it is very rare, as we saw with Constantine, that archaeologists take the trouble to cross reference these written accounts with the physical remains. An additional distorting factor is that these tyrants are all too frequently interpreted not on the basis of what Gildas wrote but what later Welsh sources made of them. Three of the tyrants, for example, appear in a collection of ninth-century genealogies. The fact that these genealogies make free with practically any characters from history their compilers could remember or invent, from Antony and Cleopatra to the Virgin Mary, has not stopped even the most cautious of historians drawing inferences from them. I prefer to consider these tyrants primarily from Gildas's work.

A breakthrough in the understanding of the origins of the sub-Roman British kingdoms came from Ken Dark. In *From Civitas to Kingdom* he proposed that, with the collapse of the Roman central government, power devolved to the *civitates*, county-sized units. Some of these survived to become the Dark Age kingdoms. Although Dark made unnecessary distinctions between the *civitates* of the west, whose rulers he thought were actually 'kings', and those of the east who were not, in general I support his theory and agree with many of his conclusions.

The only tyrant specifically located to a *civitas* by Gildas is Vortiporius, tyrant of the Demetae. He is an old man and his father was a good king, so we can deduce that kingship was established there sometime before Gildas. Constantine is a 'tyrant whelp of the filthy lioness of Damnonia', which is taken by most historians as saying he was of Dumnonian origin and probably tyrant of the *civitas*/kingdom of Dumnonia. In Dark's analysis there were two *civitas* kingdoms between Dumnonia and Dyfed, those of the Durotriges and the Dobunni. Gildas has one tyrant (Aurelius Caninus) between Constantine and Vortiporius. If there is a geographical logic to Gildas's list, then Aurelius may rule one of these two. Dark deduced that Gildas was writing in the land of the Durotriges (which is actually what the twelfth-century *Life of St Gildas* said too) so maybe his own ruler was not one that he thought deserved criticism. The next tyrant, Cuneglassus, could be from central Wales and the last, Maglocunus, from North Wales, which is where *Historia Brittonum* placed him, followed by all subsequent sources.

As luck would have it, a memorial stone almost certainly to one of the tyrants survives. It calls him Voteporix, with the title 'protector', and was found in Dyfed. There may well be other monuments with names of the other tyrants out there waiting to be discovered. Unfortunately, apart from this memorial, the actual kings of the Britons are hard to detect archaeologically. Kingly jewellery, for example, is not really to be found before the late sixth century with the Anglo-Saxon kingdoms. (Henig 2004: 16)

From my point of view, Dark scores in being able to give some sort of logic to the areas which resisted Anglo-Saxon settlement in the fifth and sixth centuries but which did not end up as Dark Age kingdoms. Without it we would have no way of referring to the political units which are visible archaeologically, such as those of the Durotriges, Dobunni and Catuvellauni/Trinovantes. Those areas were doing something – in Durotriges building some very impressive fortifications – but without the *civitas* model we would have no way of describing or explaining the sort of organisations responsible. On the other hand, the big successor kingdoms of the Britons, Gwynedd, Rheged, Gododdin, Deor, Berneich and Elmet have nothing to connect them to *civitates*.

One thing I would correct is Dark's view that the 'Honorian Rescript' specifically referred to *civitates*. In fact our source for this, and Zosimus's account of the British resistance which followed, never uses that word, being in Greek, and we have to decide what specific term they were translating by the word '*poleis*'. They might mean *coloniae* – towns in general or local political units (tribes? Provinces?) – just as easily as they could the *civitates*.

The *civitas* kingdom theory forms the basis of Stuart Laycock's 'failed state' theory. The *civitates* took their names and their approximate boundaries from the pre-Roman Iron Age tribes. In Laycock's view these submerged tribal identities resurfaced once the Roman veneer was lifted. Furthermore, the regionalised military traditions, earthworks and refortifications suggest that these were from the outset antagonistic against each other.

There is no doubt that there was civil war amongst the tyrants of Gildas's time. It was one of the principal crimes of which Gildas accuses them 'they wage wars but only civil and unjust ones' (DEB 27). These are not exclusively between their kingdoms however, as many are usurpations or fought against close family members. There were also civil wars in Gildas's past, but these are harder to pin down. In his narrative they follow the death of Magnus Maximus, therefore before the establishment of British rule. From what little we know of these from Roman history, these were primarily military coups aimed at setting up rival western emperors, culminating in the regime of Constantine III. His fall was followed by what seems to have been a united British response to drive out his supporters. Certainly by the start of the Saxon invasions, Gildas seems to have the Britons united under a single government of a council and the Proud Tyrant, who have responsibility for defending against Picts and Scots, can decree settlement in the eastern part of the island and dispense payment to them from cities in the west.

For the most part, the sub-Roman defensive works cannot be dated precisely enough to answer the question of whether they pre or post date the Saxon settlements. Strong regional differences are not to be wondered at. The agricultural world of the modern British counties in the eighteenth and nineteenth centuries are probably just as detectable archaeologically.

Back to Cadbury

Davey's South Cadbury environs work provides an intriguing insight into these controversies. Davey, I think unfairly, characterises Dark as coming from an entrenched position with 'a personal agenda to interpret *all* evidence as representing political continuity in Britain from the fourth to seventh centuries' (Davey 2005: 122). Equally, though, he also sees no evidence for a failed state or revolutionary transition. There was no chaotic disruption of the rural economy or the system of land tenure, nor a collapse of the population around South Cadbury. What seems to be the case is that the 'hyper-coherent imperially driven economy' of Britain as part of the Western Empire did collapse at the end of the fourth century, indicated by the severe collapse of Romano-British material culture. The resilience of the underlying structures, however, meant there was significant continuity in land tenure and rural infrastructure (Davey 2005: 133). 'A best guess is that the society that emerged in the fifth century was based partly on a reinvention of Iron Age tribal organisation and an impoverished sense of what it meant to be Romano British' (Davey 2005: 122).

Davey thinks it is possible that the post-Roman owners of the estates centred on South Cadbury, Ilchester, Sherbourne, Silchester and Wroxeter may actually have been tribal leaders. He suggests that if this is the case the rise to supremacy of the ruler of South Cadbury over the surrounding countryside need not have come about as a result of internal conflicts leading to one victorious individual. Instead it may have been a rather more consensual, 'considering the continuity of and pride in Durotrigian identity retained throughout the Romano-British interlude' (Davey 2005: 132).

There is ample archaeological evidence from the South Cadbury environs to support the contention that the countryside was already divided into estates in the fourth century and that the heirs of these estate owners retained control of them in the fifth century, possibly through the use of armed retainers. By this time each of the sub-Roman estates had acquired central places in highly defendable locations such as hill forts or old walled towns. Davey sees a large number of these estates co-existing. Ilchester, in his theory, continued to function as an estate focus even after the occupation of South Cadbury. This suggests a thriving economy and incidentally puts to question the idea that the resources of a whole kingdom would be necessary to perform re-fortification works.

The evidence is synthesised by Davey into a picture where South Cadbury plays the role of an estate centre in the context of an itinerant kingship of the Durotriges, rather than an anachronistic one of 'capital city' or 'forward military base'. Although there is no definite evidence that this system of itinerant kingship existed prior to the seventh century, this is only because there is so little evidence at all. Davey quotes Charles-Edwards (1989: 28), who argues that it must have existed, both on the analogy of the later 'King's circuit' in Ireland and Wales, and also on the grounds of necessity;

> In the whole of the British Isles all but very minor kings kept on the move in order to survive. Itineration was an essential economic basis of kingship. No large household could stay in one place for more than a few weeks without a long distance trade in all essential foodstuffs.

The king might have his own halls distributed round his kingdom, or enjoy the hospitality of magnates or monasteries. Roman emperors, Davey notes, were itinerant too, and the presence of Mediterranean pottery – and presumably the less durable Roman luxuries which accompanied them – enhanced the ruler's stature by association.

The Mediterranean imports presumably arrived at South Cadbury via Cadbury-Congresbury. As Davey finds it hard to imagine what the Durotriges had to give Byzantium in return, he imagines the trade is actually with the Dumnonians, who receive the goods for tin. The Durotriges are thus in a subordinate position to Dumnonia.

In whatever way one particular member of the sub-Roman elite managed to attain his position of supremacy over the Durotriges, it is likely that he used his control of exotic goods and their dissemination through gift exchange to maintain it. In such an itinerant system, the estate owner of South Cadbury would maintain suitable lodgings in the hill fort for the lord whenever he arrived. His own status would be reinforced through association with the acknowledged lord, a system of reciprocation and consensus which remained stable for over 250 years.

> It is possible that the aisled hall at Cadbury was one of many in the region serving a similar function as a temporary residence for a petty 'king' or 'tyrant' in the fifth and sixth centuries. It may have been at the time of such visits that imported wine was consumed with the head of the estate bathing in the reflected glory of a ruler who retained some of the trappings of the ancient civilisation of Rome… Whether this hypothetical proto-king initially gained position through inherited tribal status or economic advantage, the ability to disseminate the elite trappings of Rome would have maintained and enhanced his stature. Mobility would have been necessary to such a system and possibly reflective of late Roman imperial authority. This person would command respect and be looked to for the dissemination of justice. (Davey 2005: 131-2)

Arthur Resorted Much to Camelot?

Although Davey never mentions the name Arthur in his published work, his shadow must always be present behind this luxury dispensing 'proto-king' feasting and distributing justice throughout Dorset and Somerset, with strong reciprocal ties to the Cornish dynasty of Tintagel. In many respects it is closer to the Lerner and Loewe *Camelot* King Arthur and his romance antecedents than the head of homeland defence envisaged by Alcock. Is it fair, as Alcock did, simply to use 'Arthur' as a convenient name for the unknown ruler who fortified South Cadbury? The same man could be the one who ordered the Wansdyke too, since that great earthwork seems contemporary and to be protecting the same *civitas*.

The problem with using Arthur as a convenient name is that we might equally use it for other unnamed rulers of the fifth and sixth centuries responsible for archaeologically significant sites, with equal or better support from the legendary material. He could, for instance, be the man who dug the great ditch at Tintagel, creating the largest refortified sub-Roman site. A potential 'Arthur' refortified Silchester, blocking all the roads, and defending the enclave around it ensuring no Saxons settled there in the period (Snyder 1998:156). Silchester has a better pedigree as an Arthurian location (he is crowned there in Geoffrey's book) than South Cadbury or indeed Camelot.

Actually, Arthur is never connected with building mighty defensive works in any source at all. In Geoffrey he takes them, and foreign rulers build them for fear of him. All the literary Arthurian sieges put Arthur on the offensive. The only major defensive siege is in the early thirteenth-century *Morte Artu*, part of the *Lancelot-Grail* or *Vulgate Cycle*, where Guinevere is besieged by Mordred in the Tower of London. Even here the Tower seems an ancient fortress (it was commonly ascribed to Julius Caesar), not one built or refortified by Arthur. The vision of Camelot as a superlative fortification is a modern one. In Geoffrey of Monmouth, Caerleon is an incomparably sumptuous city, but it is the walls and gates of London which are covered at most length. In Chrétien's work, Windsor Castle is described much more lavishly than Camelot. It is not clear in the *Lancelot-Grail* cycle that its Camelot is superlative. Castles, like Lancelot's Dolorous/Joyous Garde are more impregnable.

Gildas says that the Britons fled to fortified hills '*collibus ... vallatis*' (DEB 25.1). We would therefore expect that when, two paragraphs later, he refers to the siege of the Badonic mountain '*obssesionis Badonici montis*' he expects us to understand that the Britons are besieged. Saxon fortifications have never been mentioned in his text, or even hinted at. Gildas's victors, whether Romans or God-guided Britons are never shown besieging enemy fortresses and if this were uniquely the case at Badon we would expect him to clarify his meaning. Saxons, on the other hand, are shown assaulting settlements with their battering rams. The victorious Britons whom Gildas applauds, are precisely the ones who did not cower in the fortifications so the only explanation which fits is that the victorious Britons relieved a siege of the cowering ones by beating the Saxons. This concept of victors coming swiftly to the rescue is the view Gildas has of the previous wars too, assumptions doubtless projected back from his own time. This is the logic which directs me away from the fortified sites as associated with 'Arthur'.

If size of fortification is not a viable test of an Arthurian connection, there are other diagnostics which might connect archaeology to Arthur. The legendary Arthur is always associated with wealth and generosity, which might mean we should look at the imported luxuries which dominate the archaeology of Tintagel or, to a lesser extent, Cadbury-Congresbury and South Cadbury, as signifiers.

Although Arthur is connected with various regions, in no sense in the legendary material is he the local king of them. He is generally their overlord. In *Historia Brittonum* his defining feature is that he is the leader of battles of the kings of the Britons, with whom he fights against the Saxons.

There are many models for how the kings of the Britons could form a common purpose in this way. They might make an alliance, spurred by fellow-feeling and cemented by religious oaths (Gildas castigates Constantine for swearing such an oath and breaking it (DEB 28.1)) or dynastic marriages. One king might come to dominate the others, as Gildas suggests Maglocunus does and as the Anglo-Saxon Bretwaldas did.

Since we have come to this position by examining the late Roman system of local government, it seems sensible to start with the higher regional structures under which they were supposed to operate. The *Notitia Dignitatum* is a list of the officials of the late Roman Empire. It explains how the officials should be addressed and who they report to. Although its actual date is not clear, and duplicate entries for military units show it was 'live document', responding to changes, in Britain it must deal with the last years of the fourth century, since the full Roman administrative framework is described. The Diocese of Britain is ruled by the vicar or viceroy of the Britains or British provinces. Terms like vicar and diocese were appropriated by the church from the civil government but as Francis Pryor notes wryly (2005:106n) serve to give a whimsically ecclesiastical feel to the late Roman government.

Under the vicar were five British provinces (the Britains). Maxima Caeasariensis and Valentia had higher-ranking governors than the other three, Britannia Prima, Britannia Secunda and Flavia Caesariensis. We don't know where Valentia was. It was a subset, it seems, of one of the other four (possibly, given the rank equivalent it was part of Maxima Caesariensis).

It is clear that Gildas's 'Proud Tyrant' and 'Council' must collectively have an authority which crosses provinces, hence in some way diocesan level. These are the people he sees as responsible for letting in the Saxons to settle in the island. At first Gildas concentrates on the council, only later adding the tyrant to the picture. It is not clear whether (as later sources would have it) the tyrant is the decision-maker, advised poorly by 'his' council, or whether on the contrary the council is the decision-making body (representing, say, the provinces or the *civitates*) and the tyrant is a regional ruler persuaded to accept Saxon settlers for the greater good. He might be a man with military authority for fighting back the Picts and Scots. Whatever their status, it is clear that this form of authority does not survive the shock of the Saxon revolt. The council is never heard of again and when the Britons organise a resistance it is under Ambrosius Aurelianus, a '*vir modestus*' or ordinary man.

Bede says that Ambrosius's parents were of 'royal rank and title' (HE I:16), based on Gildas's claim that they had 'worn the purple'. I argue in *The Reign of Arthur* (Gidlow 2004: 80) that this is a mistaken inference. In Gildas, wearing purple robes is never given as a sign of royal or imperial rank. It is only used, and used frequently, of the blood of the martyrs. Gildas says that Ambrosius's parents had been killed in the Saxon revolt and had surely 'worn the purple' meaning they had died martyrs.

Archaeologically there is nothing particularly to support the case for a continued diocesan authority, except perhaps on the level that Saxons were allowed to settle within the diocese rather than opposed. The provinces, though, do seem to have had some measure of continuity which can be seen in the archaeological record. White, in his in-depth study of the westernmost province, Britannia Prima, shows that someone in the west was producing military metalwork, home-produced versions of the standard military brooch and belt sets. This suggests that some kind of army continued there and prompts him to wonder (White 2007: 154) 'did Britannia Prima continue to exist as an entity even though the diocese and the hold of imperial government on Britain had ceased?'

There is no doubt that Britannia Prima saw extensive and characteristic military activity in this period. The vast majority of the refortified hill forts like South Cadbury are within the boundaries of the province. This was accompanied by bank and ditch linear systems, the dykes, which were thrown up apparently by the *civitates*. Wat's Dyke runs from Oswestry to Flintshire between the *civitates* of the Deceangli and the Cornovii, seemingly to protect the hinterland of Chester. The great Wansdyke runs to the north of the lands of the Durotriges. Stantonbury hill fort is at the centre of the two halves of the Wansdyke, and other forts like South Cadbury are to the south of it. It is of course possible that the dykes and forts are signifiers of endemic strife between these British kingdoms, on the failed state model. They do indicate at the very least a common military doctrine, as the pattern is not repeated in the other provinces. More importantly, though, they suggest a common response to the most pressing military issue, the Saxons. Bokerly Dyke defines the boundary of Britannia Prima on the eastern boundary of the Durotriges 'Both Bokerly Dyke and Wansdyke can thus both be interpreted as a response to the occupation by the Anglo-Saxons of the *civitas* of the Belgae from the mid fifth century' (White 2007: 175).

It could be that the internal dykes like Wat's Dyke are characteristic of the age of warfare between the Britons in which Gildas lived. The feuding kings may have misapplied military techniques intended for common defence. Clearly fortified hills did exist at the time of the Saxon revolt, but as noted Gildas does not make a connection between them or indeed any fortifications and the fight back initiated by Ambrosius Aurelianus. On the contrary he regards the flight to defensive locations misguided and ungodly, and not a tactic adopted by victorious Britons.

It is in the treatment of the Saxons that differing provincial responses are most evident. Maxima Caesariensis and Flavia Caesariensis show clear signs of the encroachment of Saxon culture, evidenced in archaeology we will consider in the next chapter. Britannia Prima shows none in the fifth and early sixth centuries. There are some foreign settlers but the evidence of Irish Ogham-inscribed artefacts shows the source of these settlers is Ireland (White 2007:194). It is possible that the policy of settling pagan barbarian mercenaries to deal with a manpower shortage was common across Britain, but that Britons on the east coast used Saxons and on the west Irish, based on availability. It is also possible that the Irish settled where they could with no regard for the Britons. The evidence is against this, however. Ogham inscriptions are always found in conjunction with standard British remains. Voteporix's memorial stone, in Latin and with a Christian cross on it, also proclaims his identity in Irish Ogham. The legendary Irish source 'The Expulsion of the Deisi' tries to appropriate Vortiporius and his dynasty as Irish. It is certain that this was not true of the historical figure, since Gildas, who has nothing good to say of the Scots (as he calls them) is adamant that Vortiporius's father was a good king. Clearer evidence that Irish settlement was indicative of a different British policy is found at Silchester. Archaeologically this city was at the centre of a 'Saxon free zone, highly distinctive from the Saxon remains around it. Not only was the city refortified, its hinterland was protected by dykes cutting Roman roads. This policy was obviously successful, as the town never became Saxon. At Silchester the most easterly Ogham-inscribed memorial was also found (Snyder 1998: 156), to an Irishman called Tebicatos (babelstone).

White concludes (2007:201) on balance that at least initially there was a provincial government in Britannia Prima capable of making decisions for the province as a whole. It must have had some means of enforcing these decisions. The extensive production and use of military belt fittings, including the kit identifying a 'Roman officer' at Kingsholm, and the discovery of weapons in some of the towns of the province suggests a concerted and coherent plan executed at high level. Instead of handing military control over to the allies, they used their own resources. The proof of this is the evidence for the successful resistance to the Germanic incursions in Britain.

The northern province, Britannia Secunda, also shows clear signs of a policy of resistance to the Anglo-Saxons but by different means, as we shall see later.

That is not to discount the possibility of co-operation between the two provinces. *Notitia Dignitatum* records a cohort of the Cornovii (the inhabitants of what would be Powys) in Newcastle, and work parties from Britannia Prima left their names there.

An interesting point is that Gildas does begin by saying that Britannia still has *rectores*. This ought to mean that it still has provincial governors, which is the technical meaning of the word. We cannot unfortunately be sure this is exactly what he does mean, but it is certainly arguable. Although *Notitia Dignitatum* has a different technical name for the Governor of Britannia Prima, one of them, Lucius Septimius, set up a column in Cirencester, the provincial capital, on which he described himself as 'Rector of the First Province' (White 2007: 85). On the other end of the spectrum, one of the warriors of *The Gododdin*, Tudfwlch, has 'rector' as one of his epithets along with 'helmsman', 'rampart' and 'citadel' (B2 36). He is a chieftain from Edinburgh and certainly not the holder of an official Roman title. The question of where on the spectrum between the two Gildas lies is not easy to answer.

The two tyrants Gildas connects to regions, Constantine of Dumnonia and Vortiporius of Demetia, are connected to Britannia Prima, and all the theories about the others also place them within this province. If Gildas is seen to be writing from the *civitas* of the Durotriges, as Higham and Dark suggest, this could mean that his picture of resistance to the Saxons followed by complacent civil wars is specifically focused on this province.

The Saxons may have retained a memory of the western province as a place of co-operating British kings. In the Anglo-Saxon Chronicle the decisive thrust into the province comes with the Battle of Dyrham in 577. Here the deaths of three British kings, Coinmail, Condidan and Farinmail are recorded, along with the capture of three 'Chesters' Bath, Gloucester and the provincial capital of Cirencester. Very frequently the kings are described as the kings of the named Chesters, though as Sims-Williams points out (1983b:33) they are not specifically linked to them. They would be pretty minor figures if they had been clustered in such nearby locations only one of which, Cirencester, was identified as the nucleus of a *civitas* kingdom by Dark. I think it is equally possible that the Chronicle is conveying an impression of neighbouring British kings rallying unsuccessfully to the defence of a key area, the provincial capital and the link between 'Wales' and the West Country. Sims-Williams dismisses any idea the entry suggests an early written source but points out that two of the names are actually linked to the borders of central Wales. Condidan may be a mistake for Condilan (the hero of Powys Cynddylan) and Farinmail is Fernmail, the name of an early ninth-century ruler of Builth in *Historia Brittonum*.

White (2007: 206) accepts, probably unthinkingly, Bede's characterisation of the alliance between Cadwallon (of Gwynedd) and Penda (of Mercia) as 'unholy'. In fact it seems eminently reasonable that they should join forces against an aggressive common enemy. If there was a tradition of Britannia Prima kingdoms working together in defence, then Cadwallon and Penda did rule over a lot of the province, despite their different origins.

Rather than trying to identify the historical Arthur with the *civitas* kings and connect him with their hill forts and estates, a more fruitful line might be to consider evidence for a higher unifying authority, leading the kings of the Britons in a united front against the Saxons. The provincial governor of Britannia Prima or his military commander would be a better fit for the Arthur of *Historia Brittonum* than the king of the Durotriges or his estate manager at South Cadbury.

9

THE SAXON INVASIONS

Bede and the Anglo-Saxon Chronicle established the historiography of the fifth and sixth centuries. They told of a violent Saxon conquest leading to the destruction or expulsion of the Britons of eastern Britain. This is the crux of the controversy. It was relatively easy for the archaeologists of the 1960s to find a place for Arthur in the Dark Age history of Britain since they accepted the general picture presented by the written sources. All the historians writing about the Dark Ages believed that the Saxon conquest of England was essentially a military one. It had been accomplished by violent means leading to the subjugation, expulsion and even extermination of the Britons formerly living in the area. It was to be expected that the Britons had tried to resist this, and on this again all sources agreed. All that was left was to assign a name, the name of Arthur, to the leader of this resistance movement.

The crucial question is was this true? Surely, in theory, a process of widespread invasion, settlement, swift replacement of one people by another ought to be obvious in the archaeological record. To the early archaeologists indeed it was. Settlements of the Romans and Romano-Britons ceased to be used. New settlements using building techniques from lowland Germany sprang up in their place. Regimented cemeteries of graves empty of anything but bodies, aligned west to east, outside Roman towns gave way to burial grounds with cremations or where the deceased were accompanied by dress accessories and other items familiar from the German and Scandinavian shores. Not to mention the obvious change in language and place names which still marks England as a distinctly Germanic country.

As late as 1986, when I was just starting my research into the historical Arthur, veteran historian J.N.L. Myres published *The English Settlements*, volume 1b in the *Oxford History of England*. It starts with the obligatory sideswipe at the historical Arthur 'no figure on the borderline of history and mythology has wasted more of the historian's time' (Myres 1986: 16), then goes on to fill 200 pages of the exploits of Aelle of the South Saxons, 'the extent of Cerdic's power', and archaeological

v. SAXONS IN BRITAIN

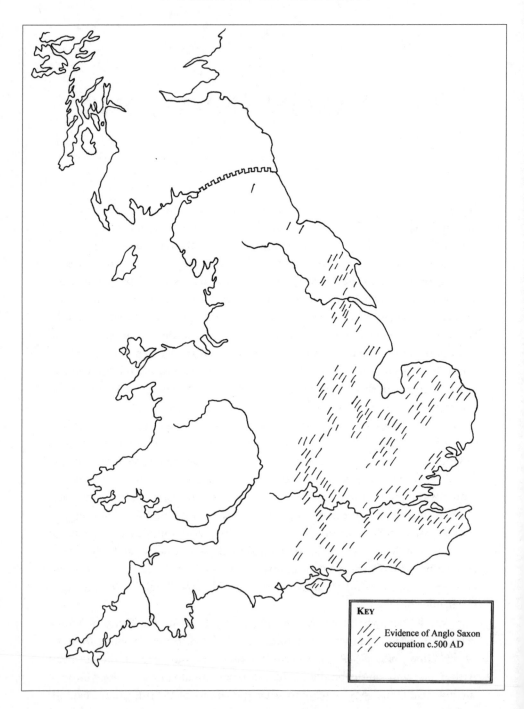

KEY

/// Evidence of Anglo Saxon
/// occupation c.500 AD

proofs, primarily via pottery styles, of the Anglo-Saxon Chronicle's story of the establishment of the Anglo-Saxon kingdoms. This was something of a swan-song and none of it would survive unscathed the assault on the written sources and the assumptions which underlie them.

The idea of the initial settlement of Saxons as federate troops has plenty of parallels on the continent. Federates were of two kinds, tribal groups who settled or garrisoned regions and received *annona* in return for military assistance, and units recruited for the duration of campaigns. The first three shiploads recorded by Gildas were arguably of the second type, recruited for the imminent attack by the Picts. The second wave clearly intended to settle and Gildas uses the technical terms of *annona* and *epimenia* to described what they considered their dues, and is explicit that they broke their *foedus* when they revolted. Although Gildas considered the decision to use Saxons against the Picts and Scots was blind folly, it was certainly in keeping with the methods of the time. In the first half of the fifth century, regular troops became unimportant compared with the federates in the rest of the western empire. 'The men who increasingly came to decide battles were barbarian federates' (Liebeschuetz, 1993: 267).

Although some archaeologists even doubt the initial settlement of federates, scepticism is usually reserved for the idea that this was followed by waves of Saxon settlers, what Williams (2004: 90) describes as the 'culture-historic paradigm that dominated traditional Anglo-Saxon archaeology'. He characterises this with the example of:

> the large urn-fields of hundreds and sometimes thousands of cremation burials dating to the fifth and sixth centuries AD [which] form a discrete cluster in the 'Anglian' regions of Anglo-Saxon England, namely East Yorkshire, the East Midlands and East Anglia ... the traditional approach to these burials has been to regard them as the clearest possible evidence of intrusive and immigrant Germanic groups settling in Eastern England during the fifth century AD. (Williams 2004:90)

This view was rejected as too simplistic. Burial practices were a symbol of cultural change, not indicative of a wave of urn-buriers. After all, the fourth-century fashion for west/east burials without grave-goods already noted wasn't ascribed to waves of invading Christians.

Dark Age England was by no means unique in having its archaeological record interpreted in this way. The arrival of agriculture, the fashion for including clay 'beakers' in graves, the change from burial in long barrows to round barrows, the working of bronze then iron, the spread of the Celtic languages were all once taken as evidence of conquest by foreign invader groups.

Archaeologists of the late twentieth century more or less unanimously turned aside from this style of interpretation. For them the archaeological record certainly did record the spread of ideas, of lifestyles and societies, but there were many ways of accounting for this of which conquest and extermination were seen as the least likely. Roman columns found at Colchester near a large Iron Age fortification did indeed show that a Roman invasion had changed the political landscape of the area, but did not prove that all those who lived in the buildings they supported were Italians who had replaced the former Trinovantian inhabitants. For every well documented invasion there were counter examples. Britain had not been overrun by Christians who massacred the pagan Romans and replaced their temples and burial grounds with archaeological features of their own. The spread of seventeenth-century baroque architecture associated with the Catholic absolute monarchies of Europe in England, epitomised by St Paul's Cathedral, built above a clear layer of urban destruction and abandonment, does not indicate the conquest of England by Louis XIV. In fact it stems from a period when that expansion was actively resisted.

The invasion theory was roundly condemned for all the prehistoric cultural changes. Megaliths, round barrows, beakers and iron swords are mute witnesses, amenable to a variety of interpretations. The overwhelming tendency was to apply exactly the same reasoning to the upper levels of a site. If beakers did not equal invading beaker people then why should Saxon brooches equal invading Saxon people? And if there were no invading Saxon people, then the whole edifice of Arthur and his resisting Britons collapsed as well.

In this cultural shift, I think it is fair to say the archaeologists won and the historians lost. The history of early Dark Age Britain has become more or less unwritable. Dates, reigns, political manoeuvrings and military strategies, the stuff of history since it was first written, have been banished from academic works on the subject. As with the Iron Age, historical texts are mined for names to attach to the broad cultures or political entities, but the names and personalities of individuals are generally removed from the picture.

My view is that the shift has been too extreme. We know that the Roman remains in Britain were indeed symptomatic of military invasion and conquest. We know that the Norman remains at the other end of the Dark Ages equally represent the effects of conquest. Contemporary sources are quite clear that the Scandinavian settlements were accompanied by violent military Viking activities. Why should the most momentous of these cultural changes, that from Roman and British Britain to Anglo-Saxon England be resolutely framed in non-military and non-historical interpretations?

Francis Pryor is a leading opponent of the invasion theories but this surely leads him to overreact when, considering Gildas's Anglo-Saxon revolt, he writes 'if it happened' (Pryor 2004: 176). Gildas is inspired by his fear of an imminent return of warfare with the Saxons to write his book. He isn't making up a Saxon revolt for his own ulterior motives. He furthermore needs to convince people whose grandfathers and presumably fathers fought against the Saxons as recently as 40 years before. How he expected to get away with this if there had never been a Saxon revolt is a mystery!

Anglo-Saxon archaeology was traditionally tied to demonstrating the version given in the Anglo-Saxon Chronicle. Sims-Williams (1983b: 29) cautions 'any attempt to reconcile the chronicle with the archaeological evidence is premature until it has been shown that the quality of the traditions the Chronicle preserves justifies the exercise.'

The credibility of the Chronicle is not easily tested archaeologically through distribution maps of pots or spearheads, especially as much was deposited in non-military contexts. As is frequently overlooked or denied in the archaeological interpretation of both Gildas and the Arthurian battle list, 'Britons and Anglo-Saxons might both wage battles far outside their own areas of settlement, which is what archaeology usually tells us about' ('the Entebbe factor') (Sims-Williams 1983b: 31).

Demonstrating to his own satisfaction that the Anglo-Saxon Chronicle entries for the period are unreliable, Sims William (1983: 41) regrets that newer disciplines such as archaeology:

> are hardly likely to give us a detailed *story* of the settlement of England such as our ancestors enjoyed in the chronicle and its successors. On this note of regret I conclude with Kemble's words [Saxons in England 1.22] of 1849 'from what has proceeded it will be inferred that I look upon the genuine details of the German conquests in England as irrevocably lost to us'.

Britons vs Saxons?

Whether it is even possible to separate Britons from Anglo-Saxons archaeologically has been hotly contested. Rahtz (Rahtz *et al* 2000: 416) uses the Cannington example to illustrate the difficulties. The few artefacts are associated with the cemetery include items from all the areas in contact with the region. They also include items from the Mediterranean, Anglo-Saxon areas or Germanic homelands, Cornwall, north-west Britain or Wales 'the majority of the finds are, however, indigenous'. Though the people might have examples of local inbreeding, there is no evidence they were distinct from other Roman or Saxon groups.

The concentration on burial practices as evidence of cultural identification forces us to ask the question why might you be buried with Saxon-style accoutrements, alongside other people buried with Saxon-style accoutrements and away from and unaligned with Christian sites?

The old answer, the simplest answer, is that you did this because you were a Saxon. That raises other questions, of course. It is possible the Saxons believed in an afterlife, in which particular possessions might be useful either 'practically' by the dead or as some form of distinguishing insignia. We do not in fact know if the Saxons did believe in life after death. In a memorable passage, Bede has one of King Edwin's men say 'of what went before this life or of what follows, we know nothing' (HE II: 13). The medieval Icelandic writer Snorri Sturluson gives his account of Viking mythology which is often taken as indicative of Anglo-Saxon beliefs (as a writer of the early thirteenth century he is actually even more removed from the fifth century than the romance writers). He does have various forms of afterlife, but no indication that real items might be of any use to the dead. Snorri and the Anglo-Saxon poem *Beowulf* describe, on the contrary, the deposition of precious objects as being a way for the living to honour the dead. The key element in such a system would be the importance to the burying community of identifying the dead as its own.

We should be careful of suggesting that people have a completely open choice in how they are buried. This is rarely the case. You will live as part of a community which has its own views as to what constitutes appropriate and dignified treatment of corpses and provides the specialist personnel, from priest to gravedigger, responsible. Thus a trip to a modern cemetery will find atheists and agnostics buried in west/east orientation, without grave goods and with grave-markers inscribed with vaguely Christian sentiments. Whatever the dead individuals' personal views you will not find them exposed on platforms in trees, in Towers of Silence picked clean by birds, mummified in pyramids surrounded by golden treasures, disarticulated and displayed in megalithic chamber tombs or, for that matter, consumed in a ritual feast by their loved ones. Similarly, a person dying in an area without Christian priests and with only pagan Saxons to carry out the funerary rites would be found in the archaeological record cremated or buried as a Saxon.

It is a truism, often overlooked, that the dead person is not responsible for their own burial. They may express wishes while alive but once dead the responsibility passes to others, usually relatives. These people also enter into the equation. They have social appearances to keep up. What will the neighbours say or think of them? Will they be happy opting out of a consensus, to possible ostracism, or do they need to prove their loyalty and commitment to the status quo. How will they keep the memory of the departed alive? Deciding to bury their loved ones with nothing, when surrounded by neighbours to whom due reverence for the departed meant leaving them with clothes at the very least, may have been a social gesture few felt strong enough to make.

If we suppose that burials north-south, or in a variety of positions, and with grave goods, are a signifier of Anglo-Saxon identity in life, we can see that even this pattern is not homogenous. Burials of the Anglo-Saxon kind are not always exclusive where they are found. O'Brien (1999: 60) notes that those buried extended without grave goods form a tiny minority in those cemeteries where grave goods are the norm. Of course, Britons could have assimilated with

Anglo-Saxons, but 'the continuation of … earlier British practices within cemeteries characterised by Anglo-Saxon grave goods constitutes an archaeological argument for an historical thesis, namely that Britons survived to an extent under Anglo-Saxon rule and that they adopted Anglo-Saxon practices such as clothed burial.'

On the other hand, the idea that west/east burials without grave goods and burials with grave goods represent the identities of distinct groups is supported by a similar co-incidence of such finds and areas settled by barbarians on the continent (Petts 2004: 85). More recently, the idea that actual Germans were involved, albeit in a generally peaceful way, has regained ground. There is nothing like a consensus on the scale of this or the interpretation of its implications among the archaeologists. The only agreement is that the idea of a British resistance, let alone a King Arthur leading it, is never entertained.

Let's start with C.J. Arnold (1984:161).

> while absolute figures are impossible to reach, there is every indication that there was a marked reduction in the level of population between AD 300 and 500, brought about by such causes as emigration, epidemics exacerbated by low levels of hygiene and changes in the rates of fertility and mortality. The very small numbers of Germanic immigrants will have done little to alter the situation. On the basis of the very limited evidence currently available, most of the migrants were male, whose intermarriage with native women may be responsible for a notable lack of women in the late fourth-century phases of Roman cemeteries.

I'm not sure what to make about the 'low levels of hygiene'. If Arnold is thinking about the introduced practice of public bathing or of piped public water, then their prevalence did not lessen the impact of plagues on the Mediterranean world. Once the germ theory of disease took hold in the nineteenth century it became clear that these public amenities often contributed to the spread rather than the reduction of epidemics. It is unlikely they offset the unhealthy effects of living in a densely populated city rather than a sparsely populated countryside. That oddity aside, this picture is not very different from that presented by Gildas and followed by other Dark Age writers. A memorable plague caused a short-term drop in military manpower. This was offset by the settlement of a small number of Saxon warriors, initially only three boatloads.

Not that Gildas, Bede and the Anglo-Saxon Chronicle get any praise for a historiographical tradition which mirrors this minimalist school of thought. Instead, the study of the written sources tends to pooh-pooh the small numbers. Francis Pryor, for example, without apparently having read the full text, frequently links Gildas with the (in his view) erroneous concept of 'a massive influx of Saxons' (Pryor 2004: 12). Yet when he focuses on the 'three keels' passage he pours scorn on the small numbers, suggesting that the three boatloads of ravening Saxons are somehow derived from the Trinity (a concept of which Gildas, as an ortho-dox Christian writes only with approval) or the three ships which sailed in on Christmas Day bearing 'our Saviour Christ and his Lady' (from a seventeenth-century carol) (Pryor 2004: 126). With this kind of logic it is difficult to see how many ships Pryor would accept as an alternative to 'a massive influx'. It seems Gildas cannot win whatever line he takes.

The reason is, I am sure, that just as with Tintagel, Gildas is lumped in with the secondary 'inadmissible' sources which followed him. Dumville, Sims-Williams and Yorke are all very scathing of the Dark Age written records. For Yorke they are the surfacing of a tradition which mutated constantly to reflect current reali-ties (Yorke 1993: 46).

> The corpus of written sources which purport to describe the Anglo-Saxon history of the fifth and sixth centuries has, unlike the archaeological evidence, remained static. Only the views of historians toward the sources have changed with the result that there is currently some confusion about how the written evidence is to be regarded, particularly by those who seek to synthesise histori-cal and archaeological material. Some archaeologists have argued that we would be better off disregarding written sources altogether and treating the fifth and sixth centuries as a prehistoric period. (Yorke 1999: 45)

Thus, although Arnold has a theory which could very well fit the written record, he decides not to make this attempt. His view of the Saxon migrations on the ground could hardly be more different from the picture presented by Gildas and Bede:

> whether or not there were occupants of rural sites, of any type, to offer a greet-ing to the inflow of migrants, there is a growing number of villa excavations which indicate that the migrants settled on such farmed land close to the *old* farm buildings; major changes between Romano-British and Anglo-Saxon agriculture are not apparent. (Arnold 1984: 160)

What Arnold doesn't do is try to pinpoint an *Adventus Saxonum* with any degree of precision. Sometime in the late fourth century, in a Britain in the process of being depopulated after 300 seems to be his preference.

Scull (1993: 70) presents a different case:

> there can be no reasonable doubt that south-east Britain saw settlement by people from north Germany and south Scandinavia in the fifth century. The historical and linguistic evidence is overwhelming, and is corroborated by archaeology ... however the traditional model of an *Adventus Saxonum*,

implying a short period of migration and settlement, if not a single event, in the mid-fifth century must now be abandoned in favour of a scenario which allows settlement over a longer period, varying in intensity with time and place.

He gives the example of an unrecorded migration from west Scandinavia to eastern England in the late fifth or early sixth century. There is no evidence that settlers were settled under late or post-Roman rule in East Anglia. The evidence from Song Hill in Norfolk 'suggests a high proportion of individuals of the original community … burying here hailed from the same specific locality in Schleswig-Holstein' (Scull 1993: 71).

Scull's characterisation of a 'traditional model' is overly simplistic. Gildas is clear that the initial arrival and settlement of three boats of Saxons was followed by a period of increased migration to the eastern parts of the country, initiated by the Saxons rather than their British employers. This goes some way to offering a record of this 'unrecorded' migration. Bede's account of the settlement of Kent and Bernicia is hardly an exclusive record. He knows that Angles have entered East Anglia, Mercia and Deira, Saxons various parts of the south-east and Jutes, Hampshire and the Isle of Wight. The Angles come from just the area that Scull would have them come. The Anglo-Saxon Chronicle fleshes out the arrivals of some of the Saxons but it too leaves the origins of the East and Middle Angles open. The archaeological date range, though much closer to the written accounts than that offered by Arnold still dodges the historical question. Late fifth or early sixth century could equally mean the era of the Saxon revolt or (like Bernicia) after the end of the period of British resistance. As it occurs in an area under 'Saxon Rule' it might have occurred during the period of Gildas's life without him being aware of it.

Esmonde Cleary (1993: 61) sees the weakness of the Britons without the Roman administrative structures as providing an explanation for Saxon dominance without needing large numbers of aggressive Saxons: 'reversion to a localised, agrarian, kin-based society … such a situation helps to explain the ability of incoming Anglo-Saxon groups to establish themselves in Britain, and why their culture was not swamped by that of the indigenous population.'

The German archaeologist Heinrich Harke is the most active current exponent of a traditional view, the mass migration of Germanic peoples into eastern Britain. He argues this from skeletal analysis and from interpretations based on similar evidence from Europe. In English historiography he is seen as a maverick throwback to the 'culture history paradigm'. Harke addresses the different reactions to his work in the journal *Current Anthropology*, which is very much in keeping with my own view, that interpretations of the 'Arthurian' period are mainly driven by current preoccupations of the archaeologists rather than the evidence itself.

Harke writes (1998: 19) 'analysis of male burials of the fifth to seventh century AD in England had suggested to me that about half the men buried in early Anglo-Saxon cemeteries were of native British rather than immigrant Germanic origin, with further Britons living in separate enclaves'. He argued that this shows that there must have been substantial migration of Germans (as in the traditional model) and at the same time this must have been accompanied by a substantial survival of the native population, as recent revisionist archaeologists would suggest. Instead of pleased acceptance of what could be seen as an archaeologically based compromise, which would fit the written sources and the archaeological ones, 'the British reaction has been characterised by disbelief at the suggested scale of the immigration, a reaction perfectly in line with current anti-migrationist tendencies in British archaeology' (although he accepts some of the reaction was against his skeletal analysis to deduce ethnicity, another technique which has been under suspicion since its abuse to support racial theories in the early twentieth century).

The German reaction, on the contrary, was of disbelief that so many Britons had survived. If that were true, how was it they had not resisted adopting German dress and customs? Harke argues that these reactions show nothing about the evidence and everything about the societies from which the interpreting archaeologists are drawn. He identifies the British reaction with British post-colonialism, an emphasis on political evolution rather than military solutions and autochthonous development rather than invasions. He also sees a stubborn British insularity, perhaps as evidenced by our half-hearted attitude to the European Union, in refusing to acknowledge European solutions to the archaeological response. To be fair, though, he also acknowledges the German experience which predisposes its archaeologists to the folk migration interpretation. The German Empire was created by large scale settlement eastward, the British Empire by 'elite transfer'.

Although detailed examination of Anglo-Saxon archaeology is beyond the scope of this book, research over the past 20 years has not reached a consensus on the scale, date or method of Saxon migration to Britain. However it is safe to say that all the current theories are compatible with Gildas's work and the hypothesis that Britons led by King Arthur fought against them some time after their arrival. Where Anglo-Saxon archaeology differs greatly from that of the Britons is the willingness of the archaeologists to engage with, if only to criticise, the traditional explanations and written sources. Legendary founding figures of the Anglo-Saxon kingdoms at least find a place in the index of these studies. If their existence or quality of the written sources is questioned, this is at least argued in print.

In 1989 Steven Bassett edited a collection of essays on *The Origins of Anglo-Saxon Kingdoms*. It began with an essay (Brooks 1989) which attacked the literary tradition of the Anglo-Saxon invasions as serving later political purposes and including material which was at base mythological. These are very familiar criticisms also levelled at Arthurian material in *Historia Brittonum* and *Annales Cambriae*. This does not prevent almost every other contributor name-checking at the very least the early Anglo-Saxon kings of their chosen regions. One contributor (Welch 1989) on the origins of the South Saxons is happy to accept the basic idea of a military conquest of the area, adding 'we can accept that Aelle was an extraordinary military leader of great renown.'

Aelle is a figure from Bede (though this has not saved Hengist and Horsa from attacks on their historicity) but Aelle the renowned military leader is a figure from the Anglo-Saxon Chronicle. Yet he fits the facts, does not require to be explained away by over elaborate charges of mythologising and trivialising and the author sees no reason why he should not stay as, if nothing else, the sort of character who the archaeological evidences seems to suggest existed. Just one more example of the double standards applied to King Arthur.

Who were the Saxons?

The debate about the Saxons seems rooted in the assumption that the only real 'Saxons' are people from Saxony. It is my view that ethnicity is a much more fluid concept. It combines ideas of how an individual defines themselves as a member of a community, and how they are defined by those outside the community. These seem rather more potent drivers of society than your DNA, skeletal measurements or where your tooth enamel was formed. Someone who dresses as a Saxon, lives in a Saxon-style house, is buried according to Saxon burial practices is effectively a Saxon. In life they chose to live in a kingdom which manifested a Saxon identity and, if being armed or adding to the productive economy of those kingdoms means anything, participated in them.

These people are the 'Saxons' who the states of Britannia Prima and Britannia Secunda resisted, regardless of whether they had been born in Schleswig Holstein or Maxima Caesariensis. It is quite possible too much is made of the overseas origins of the Anglo-Saxon kingdoms. In the developed 'Heptarchy' before the Viking invasions, the kingdoms of the East, South and West Saxons and the East Angles harked back in their identities to Germanic homelands or peoples. Mercia was however simply 'the borders', Northumbria took the large estuary as its defining boundary while Kent simply used the ancient Roman and Iron Age name for its land. The earlier kingdoms subsumed into them were even more varied, Lindsey, Bernicia and Deira, the Men of the Isle of Wight, the Gewissei made no ethnic claims on the composition of their peoples. These kingdoms were often tied to their locality, regardless of where their ruling family let alone their populations came from. It might be that the kings of the Men of Kent (as *Historia Brittonum* calls them) claimed descent from the Saxon Octha or kinship with the inhabitants of Jutland, but there is no reason why someone born in the *civitas* of the Cantii might not see themselves as participants in a continuing state, even if one under new management.

It is unfortunate that Gildas does not describe the Saxons. Even his perfunctory attack on Picts and Scots contains more information. Sidonius Apollinaris in late fifth-century Gaul provides interesting information on the Saxons of the period. He says that the various Germanic tribes were distinguished by things like hair styles and dress: (8.9) 'the blue-eyed Saxon shaves the edges of his hair to make his face seem larger'. There is a general tendency to picture the Germanic barbarians as excessively hairy and bearded, a criticism Gildas in fact reserves for the Picts and Scots. The only clear example of a Saxon's face we have is the seventh-century facemask of the Sutton Hoo helmet. This shows its wearer as clean shaven but with a small moustache, perhaps also intended to make the face seem bigger.

Sidonius tells us too that when they were ready to return home from their raids, the Saxons sacrificed by drowning or crucifixion one in ten of their prisoners. This may be a form of divination such as Gildas says they performed before setting sail for Britain. Dark Age Britain was thus the home of distinctive communities who can be identified as Britons and Saxons. The Arthurian sources are quite clear that they were hostile and belligerent. How far is this supported by the archaeology?

10

KNIGHTS OF
THE ROUND TABLE

Perhaps even more enduring than the image of King Arthur himself is that of his knights. It is their exploits which dominate the romances. It is therefore no surprise that they are just as significant in the search for the historical King Arthur.

The knights themselves are reflections of the heroic ideals of the high middle ages. They come complete with squires, coats of arms and all the paraphernalia necessary for jousting in fashionable tournaments. It is conceivable, though, that behind these medieval trappings there may be glimpses of historical reality. Warriors feasting around their lord, boasting and listening to accounts of their exploits is a common theme of the Celtic world. Gildas described how his tyrants 'love and even reward the thieves who sit with them at table … distribute alms profusely … exalt to the stars … their military companions, bloody proud and murderous men, adulterers and enemies of God!' (DEB 27).

Building up private armies, linked by personal ties of loyalty, was also a common feature of the late Roman military. Central to these were the *bucellarii*, 'those semi-private household retinues that became the major mobile strike forces of the fifth century'(Liebeschuetz 1993: 289). These retainer-soldiers were defined by a Byzantine writer as 'those who eat the bread of someone, on condition of becoming his trusty'. Procopius calls them 'satellites' or 'those who stand behind when the commander is dining' (Liebeschuetz, W. 1993: 269). The fact that armies would be recruited by a commander personally and would include a strong core of his *bucellarii* was probably the key to the very close ties between the troops and their commanders which Liebeschuetz sees as a feature of the military history of the period.

Thus the idea that military commanders would have their own loyal military companions is certainly not unreasonable. We need to be careful before we leap to the conclusion that these are the original 'Knights of the Round Table' though.

vi. THE BRITISH RESISTANCE

KEY

British & Irish
Inscribed Stones

Imported
Mediterranean Pottery

Elmetsaete

ELMET

Pecsaete

GWYNEDD
Wreocensaete

POWYS

Tomsaete

ERCING

Magonsaete   Arosaete

BRECHEINIOG

DYFED   **GWENT**

GLYWYSING   Cilternsaete

SILCHESTER

Sumorsaete

DYFNEINT   Dorsaete

The earliest references to Arthur do not link him to his own personal war-band. This idea seems to first surface in a Welsh poem called *Pa Gur*. It is of uncertain date, but generally considered later than *Historia Brittonum*, though as we will see some scholars place it earlier.

A lot of energy is misspent in the attempt to place King Arthur's medieval knights back in the sixth century. Certainly armoured heavy cavalrymen existed in the late Roman empire, but they were professional soldiers, often from ethnically distinct groups like the Goths. They were not the aristocratic elite of feudal society as they appear in the romances, which is nothing more than the reflection of the elite patrons of the romance writers. Even this card is overplayed by Arthurian military theorists. Certainly the romances show the knights questing more or less alone (although their support teams of squires and pages are usually on hand when they need to take their armour off or get a new lance). When full battles are depicted, the knights take their places alongside other troops. Medieval battles were not fought and won by knights alone, no more than supposed Arthurian battles would have been. In *Historia Brittonum* the kings of the Britons support Arthur in his battles. This is actually the image carried through to the romances, where the Knights of the Round Table are not highly trained super-troops or bonded soldiers but usually kings and princes in their own right.

The misapprehension that the knights were some sort of unique elite unit is behind the theory, frequently advanced by proponents of the historical Arthur, that Arthur's men were super heavy cavalry, fully armoured and possibly with armoured horses. This in turn has led Arthurians to try to make connections with similar troops in the late Roman army. Certainly according to the *Notitia Dignitatum* there were troops of this kind stationed in Britain. There were Sarmatians, descendants of central Asian tribesmen who fought in this manner, as part of the garrison of Hadrian's Wall, under the *Dux Britanniarum*. Similar heavily armoured cavalry, the cataphracts, were part of the Dux's mobile reserve and another unit of cataphracts was part of the mobile army under the *Comes Britanniarum* (Companion or Count of the Britains). There have been various attempts to argue that these sorts of troops were the prototypes of the Arthurian knights of legend. I see no reason to suppose this. In none of the sources before the middle ages is Arthur described as a cavalry leader, still less a leader of exceptional heavy cavalry. He and his knights only appear in this guise when the patrons of Arthurian literature also happened to fight in this manner, and at the same time as all other past heroes, from Theseus to Judas Maccabaeus, were also being depicted in this way. This seems explanation enough, besides which we can well imagine that in reality troops like the Sarmatians and the cataphracts would be the first to be removed by would-be usurpers like Constantine III in their bids for power against other Roman armies, and the last that native Britons would be able to or feel the need to replace.

In its fully blown form, the 'Sarmatian' theory draws parallels between the legends of the Ossetians of the Caucasus, supposed descendants of the ancient Sarmatians (e.g. Littleton and Malcor 1994). The supposed similarities between the legends are much more easily explained. The storytellers in the nineteenth-century Caucasus (when the tales were collected) had been exposed to tales and motifs which had been the stock of Europe's cultural elite for 800 years, and still were when the tales were collected. The Sarmatian theory supposes that the Britons, exposed to obscure legends over (at the outside) 300 years somehow pre-served then for another 800 years without leaving any trace even in literature like *Historia Brittonum* which concerned these heroes, resurfacing in the thirteenth century. It is far more likely that the fact the patrons of romance fiction were themselves heavily armoured cavalrymen influenced the portrayal of their heroes in this role than that this knowledge was preserved over centuries. Motifs like the sword in the stone or the challenge matches for sovereignty such as we read in Chrétien's *Yvain* may well go back to a distant pagan past, perhaps even to the Bronze Age. But once again we know how. Chrétien was a classicist who boasts of his translations from Ovid. He could simply read these legends in classical texts and get a short cut back to those ancient ideas.

Although the British poetry dealing with the Dark Ages normally has its war-riors mounted, there are some infantry as the *pedyt* (Latin *pedites* 'foot soldiers') raise a cry for Urien's return in one Taliesin poem.

The Tristan Stone

It is often assumed that at least one 'knight of the Round Table' is known archae-ologically. Outside Fowey in the south of Cornwall there is an inscribed stone from the sixth century, known as the Tristan Stone. Its inscription is taken as read-ing '*Drustanus hic iacet filius Cunomori*' 'Here lies [Sir] Tristan, son of Cunomorus'. Sir Tristan's adventures take up a large part of the *Morte d'Arthur*. He is second only in prowess to Sir Lancelot and his adulterous courtly love for Iseult, wife of King Mark of Cornwall as celebrated as that of Lancelot and Guinevere. He is actually a latecomer to the Arthurian legends, featuring in his own epic cycle only peripherally connected to the world of King Arthur. The cycles were only integrated in the mid-thirteenth century, leaving odd duplications like a King Mark of Cornwall reigning at the same time as a King Cador. The ninth-century Breton *Life of St Paul Aurelian* said that King Mark was also called 'Quonomorius', adding a further dimension to the legend (Padel 1991: 235).

Although Arthur is routinely attacked by the archaeologists working in Cornwall, Tristan, Iseult and Mark, along with the Tristan Stone are frequently referenced, even preferred as candidates for association with Tintagel. This is all nonsense. The Tristan legends are far more fanciful and folkloric than the

Arthurian material in *Historia Brittonum, Annales Cambriae* and *Y Gododdin*. The fact that none of the Tristan cycle characters appear in any of these sources, not even in Geoffrey of Monmouth, ought to ring alarm bells about their authenticity. The overwhelming atmosphere is courtly love in the high Middle Ages. The stone however remains as tangible proof.

Ronald Hutton, in his excellent essay 'Arthur and the Academics' traces the origin of this modern archaeological legend. It is more or less impossible to read the top of the inscription on the stone which contains the hero's name. In the sixteenth century, when more of it was legible, it was read as Cirusius. More recent efforts traced out Drustagni or Cirusinius. It was Ralegh Radford in 1936 who first read it as 'Drustaus' and made the Tristan connection. He was digging at the nearby fort of Castle Dore, and the romantic association with Tristan formed the basis of his public appeal for funds. When the donations came in, he was obligingly able to locate the hall of King Mark within the fort. We have already seen the influence of Ralegh Radford on the Tintagel and Cadbury/Camelot story. By the time he contributed to Ashe's *The Quest for Arthur's Britain* he was reading the name as 'Drustanus' and the modern myth was complete (Hutton 2003:45-8).

Setting aside the quest for armoured knights and named heroes, what is the archaeological record on the subject? If there are distinct populations identifiable as Britons and Saxons in Britain during the period, it remains to be seen if archaeology can demonstrate warfare between them. This is the essential background to the Arthur hypothesis and without it, the model will have to be abandoned.

Like Ghosts Instead of Men

After the Cadbury/Camelot era, when sites were routinely identified as military, the trail ran cold. Esmonde Cleary (in Wilmot and Wilson 2000: 89) suggests that 'avoidance of the archaeology of the army may chime with modern liberal views on war and imperialism'. There are, I imagine, similar social reasons for the shift in emphasis from the aristocracy of the hill forts to the workers of the environs. These ought to have no bearing on the interpretation of the historical record, but archaeology has always been a barometer of prevailing social trends.

One clear result from the inclusion of a Late Antiquity paradigm into the interpretation of British archaeology is that both proponents and opponents have now been forced to acknowledge the military aspects of the historical record. Faulkner writes (2004:11), 'I hardly need add that our historical sources imply that the entire period was characterised by conflict and change, including two major phases of warfare between "Britons" and "Anglo-Saxons", the first in *c*.AD 450–500, the second in *c*.AD 550–600.'

Actual warfare can be an elusive thing. Sidonius, having described the piratical character of the Saxon sailors, who give the impression that every oarsman is a pirate captain, issuing and obeying orders, goes on to state 'that enemy surpasses all in brutality. He attacks unforeseen and when foreseen he slips away; he despises those who bar his way, and he destroys those whom he catches unawares'(8. 6). Faced with this kind of barbarian guerrilla war, Roman forces on the continent were forced to adopt similar tactics. There is a story given by Zosimus of how Theodosius tried to deal with the barbarian raiders near Salonika who were hiding in the marshes. His remedy was to take a small band of horsemen and ride continuously around the countryside, hunting them out. They were, says Zosimus, 'like ghosts instead of men'(quoted by Whitaker 1993: 278). Specific advice to this effect was given by the military writer Ammianus. The Roman army should deal with this sort of barbarian invasion 'in small divisions and by stealthy and guerrilla warfare' (31.7.2: *particulatim perque furta magis et latrocinia*' (quoted by Whittaker 1993: 278).

It is presumably of this sort of guerrilla warfare that Scull is thinking when he writes (1993: 70) 'there was undoubtedly conflict between native and incomer, but however traumatic it may have been for those concerned neither its scale nor the power of warleaders should be overestimated: these were not nation states, nor feudal kingdoms.' This is possibly a bit too glib, since the actual impact of a shipload of sword-wielding Saxons on a small village operating at subsistence level could be completely devastating. It does indicate though, that without the resources of a nation in arms, warfare might be on such a scale as to be hard to detect archaeologically. A notable misstep (Rahtz *et al* 2000: 411-2) was the identification of the Cannington cemetery as massed war graves (belied by the long time span covered and the heavy presence of women and children) which resulted in the cemetery being labelled as a battle site of 878 on the Ordnance Survey map!

Against this concept of low-level warfare, Leslie Alcock needs to point out (1988: 23)

> the most conspicuous archaeological monuments of our period and area are enclosed places – stone walled, embanked or palisaded – set frequently on hill-tops, promontories or cliff edges … overwhelmingly they are sited on the coast or beside navigable rivers and estuaries. Rarely are they more than 2.5 km distant from water. Many stand immediately beside sheltered havens or natural harbours.

He goes on to argue (1988: 27) that their 'location and enclosing work argue for a defensive function' more than just against wild animals or thieves. These forts would serve as secure refuges, strategic sites which 'may or must be attacked in the pursuit of politico military aims, or serves to control a territory'. He does acknowledge that these secure places would also serve 'peace-time' functions as administrative centres, domestic or residential sites and symbols of dominance.

The construction of such edifices implies a surplus of production and a political will to employ it in this way. As Alcock (1988:26) puts it:

> the builders of enclosed places, or those who commissioned their construction, had access to the labour-services of masons skilled in dry-stone work; and in the case of timber-reinforced walls or palisades, to the labour of skilled carpenters as well. Moreover, the layout of many enclosures and their relation to the terrain implies the skills of architects or military engineers.

This is not to forget the felling and hewing of timber or the quarrying or gathering of stone, carrying of building materials from source to site, smithing and managerial competence to arrange all these disciplines.

Something similar has been detected in the archaeology of the warlords of Gaul. There is 'considerable nucleation of rural sites ... small farms disappeared, many *vici* were abandoned or removed to old Iron Age hilltop sites' (Liebeschuetz, 1993: 292), though in Gaul large villas also tended to be expanded and fortified. We have the testimony of the early fifth-century Gallic writer Salvian that 'those who, when driven by the terror of the enemy, flee to the castella' effectively found themselves having to become '*inquilini*' essentially 'unfree' tenants of their new protectors.

As well as the enclosed places, we also have the evidence of the dykes. These are often undated, or dated too widely for us to know exactly how they relate to the period. Many cut Roman roads. The Wansdyke comes between the Roman and the Anglo-Saxon archaeology. Their military function is clear but the enemies they were intended to resist are not. Just because the Britons built defensive structures does not necessarily imply they built them for defence against the Saxons. Gildas is absolutely clear that the Britons of his period engage in civil and unjust wars instead of fighting the common enemy. The Wansdyke looks very clearly like a defensive boundary of the land of the Durotriges to the south, a land where refortified hill forts like South Cadbury are relatively common, and some are incorporated in the defensive line. To the north, the land of the Dobunni has no hill forts and seems to have been a different state. The Wansdyke makes a clear detour to avoid Bath, leaving it to the north side. It has been seen, in White's proposal (White 2007: 175), as a defensive line behind which Britons could fall back if menaced by Saxons in the upper Thames Valley. It could equally be the defence of a single *civitas* state against another. Draper (2004:63) notes that the parish boundaries ignore the fact a Wansdyke runs through them. If these boundaries are of real antiquity, as they seem to be around South Cadbury, this would indicate that in peace time movement across it was extensive and that this was not a customs barrier or 'Dark Age iron-curtain'. This suggests it was indeed intended for emergency use and makes no attempt at forcing the locals to chose sides between the two *civitates*. We can certainly say that even if there was animosity between the Durotriges and the Dumnonii, they shared a common policy of not letting Saxons (or the public manifestations of Saxon culture) into their lands.

Swords and Spears

Alcock shows the paucity of archaeological support for the wars (2003: 161). He notes only two fragments of swords, from Dunadd, though quite a lot of spears. The battle wounded are hard to detect. Some have been found in the cemetery at Eccles in Kent, but not in a way which can be linked to the historical record (2003: 178).

The only warlord-like character yet found is the warrior buried at Lowbury Hill, described by Harke. He was a man of the sixth or seventh century, buried with a shield and spear enamelled in the British style, and an enamelled British hanging bowl. These finds would all have been taken as indicators of British identity, had they not been found accompanying a burial, a signifier of being Saxon. Are these spoils of war, pay from British employers or a statement made by a Briton to local Saxons or of his own pagan identity?

> Whether Briton or 'Anglo-Saxon' the Lowbury Hill warrior surely looked rather like the Roman general Stilicho ... we can write about his taste ... but hardly decide whether he was a Christian or not, perhaps a member of the congregation of a nearby British church, or whether he considered himself as a Roman or as a Teutonic barbarian. (Henig 2004: 1)

He is yet another of the nameless dead ruling this proto-historic period.

Another is the putative 'Roman officer' from Kingsholm near Gloucester, referred to by White (2007: 201). He was a young man possibly from the early fifth century, kitted out in insignia reminiscent of the eastern Roman empire.

The warriors of the fifth and sixth centuries might have been difficult to place. Their ethnic origin was often no guide to who they fought for. The Roman *Magister Militum* Aetius was distinguished by his core force of Huns. His greatest victory, however, was against the Huns at Chalons. There his force consisted of the King of the Goths on one wing, Romans led by him personally on the other and Alan federates in between. But the 'Romans' were Franks, Sarmatians, Armoricans, Liticians, Burgundians, Saxons, Riparians and Olibrones, not Roman soldiers (Liebeschuetz 1993: 272).

Barbarian troops could convey just as uniform a look as regulars. Sidonius Apollinaris describes the *comitantes*, military companions of Sigismer of the Franks, attending a wedding *c.*469. They are uniformly dressed, presumably by gifts from their lord, in hairskin shoes, bare lower legs and arms, a tight fitting multi-coloured garment from knee to shoulder, each wearing a green mantle with crimson border, a sword hanging from the shoulder by a studded baldric and a shield of silver with a golden boss 'the gleam from which showed their rank and devotion' (Sidonius Apollinaris *epist*.4.20).

The British Resistance

Alcock (2003: 178) attempts to reconstruct Dark Age campaigns from written sources. Like me he does not see anything implausible about the wide-ranging campaigns. He estimates 40 miles as a three-day march, perhaps faster if the Roman roads were used. He thinks it is a 'reasonable conjecture' that Aethelfrith took the Roman road from York to Chester (2003: 139), a route which was equally available for Welsh leaders like Cadwallon operating in Northumbria or (I would say) Arthur. Alcock pointedly does not even include Arthur in the index of this work.

The simple explanation of the archaeological evidence is that no Saxons were able to settle in the areas broadly defined by the provinces of Britannia Prima and Britannia Secunda. A more minimalist interpretation would be that cultural pressure in those areas was sufficiently strong that any Saxons who did settle there were compelled or impelled to conform to the dominant culture, at least as far as its public expressions in burial practice or dress were concerned. Or, turning it the other way, the dominant culture was sufficiently strong that it was able to counter the tendency of the indigenous population to adopt Germanic cultural mores, at least as far as their public expression in funerary practice and dress. The archaeological evidence for Britannia Prima at least is that a considerable amount of manpower was invested in fortifications, something only seen in scattered enclaves like Silchester in the eastern provinces. It seems too perverse not to combine this with the testimony of the British and Anglo-Saxons themselves that 'cultural dominance' was manifested militarily. It is time to turn again to the figure the Britons said was responsible for this military response.

11

Arthur's Twelve Battles

Arthur is not popularly known as a battle leader. The common image is of him as a rather elderly figure sitting at home while his knights perform individual quests. When battles impinge on this they are fought against hostile rivals in the 'Sword in the Stone' period or, conversely, a last dim battle in the west following which the sword is flung back into the lake. There are no battle names, no Hastings or Waterloo, with which the popular Arthur is routinely associated. The historical Arthur material of the twentieth century, on the other hand, is completely obsessed with locating Arthur's battles. Most 'shared postcode' theories have supposed resemblances between Arthur's battles and local place names at their foundation.

Even if the locations of Arthur's battles were established beyond doubt (in fact all are disputed), the difficulties of discovering the battlefield associated with them are obvious. There is no doubt at all about where Hastings is, or Agincourt or Waterloo, but to hope to find the battlefields associated with them by digging randomly in the general vicinity of the town would be doomed to failure. Very few Dark Age or even medieval battles are established beyond doubt in particular locations, and only rarely is archaeology able to clinch the decision.

The battle site of 'Hastings' is well established by narrative sources and the fact a large abbey was built on the site of the English last stand. There is nothing archaeologically, however, to distinguish the rolling fields around the ruins from any others in East Sussex and, were scepticism about William and Harold to become academic orthodoxy, we would be able to prove that the abbey was several centuries later than the claimed battle, doubtless part of a legitimating strategy by the Anjou-derived Plantagenet dynasty and the Earl of Sussex. None of the narratives is by an eye-witness, the date 1066 is suspiciously sacral (the Millennium and the Number of the Beast) and probably was chosen because a monk decided to peg the folklore story of the year of three battles to the appearance of Halley's comet marked in his Easter annals. Archaeology would be powerless to prove or disprove this hypothesis on the battle site. Our detailed knowledge of the arms and armour

vii. THE ARTHURIAN NORTH EAST

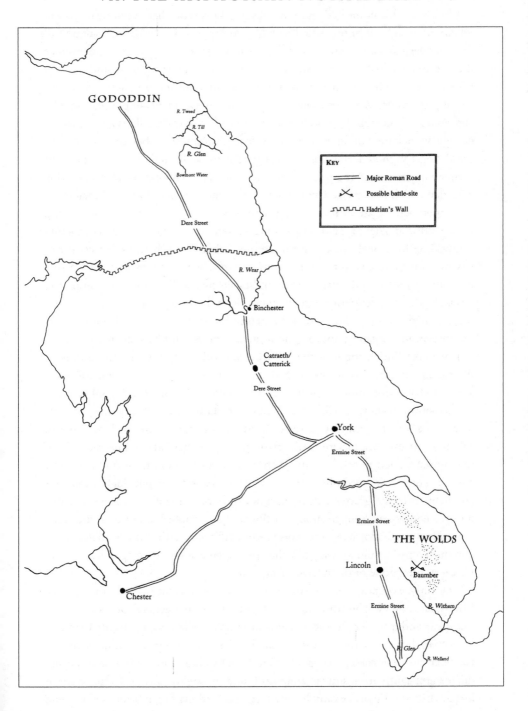

of the participants comes from the chance survival of the Bayeux Tapestry, not from finds in the vicinity of the abbey.

I belabour this point because I am absolutely certain that, without the overwhelming weight of historical information to support the Norman Conquest of 1066, modern archaeologists would dispute its reality on exactly the same grounds they do the Anglo-Saxon invasions. The battle sites and wargear would be irretrievable, the archaeological record would show continuity of settlement and burial patterns between 1000 and 1100, and no displacements of population. The appearance of Romanesque architecture and castles would be shown as a gradual change, with some buildings such as the first Westminster Abbey or some castles, pre-dating a supposed '*Adventus Normanorum*' in 1066. It ought to be clear that an accurate impression of the past can only be gained by synthesising all the available evidence which has survived, not by jettisoning inconvenient historical material.

Remember, we are not struggling with masses of conflicting evidence, using the scientific archaeologists as dispassionate referees to judge between competing claims. The historical sources are unanimous that the fifth and sixth centuries saw migrations of Saxons from the continent to Britain, who extended their rule by military means and were resisted militarily by the Britons. The competing position is a late twentieth-century fantasy. Its wild divergence from the written sources ought to have shown that the methodology which yielded this fantastic interpretation was faulty, not that the written sources must have been wrong.

If we take the example of the hill forts and other earthworks, the problems of proving military activity in the fifth and sixth centuries will be evident. They appear to have some military purpose. They could be defended and would require some sophistication to attack. Some Roman structures were clearly used by military formations for military purposes, and seem in some cases to have been in sub-Roman use. But where is the wargear of their defenders? The relatives of the people buried in the vicinity of these structures did not, for one reason or another, bury their loved ones wearing armour nor did they put shields, weapons and helmets in the graves with them. They did not, generally, just leave valuable military equipment lying around, nor throw it into rubbish pits. Yet all the written sources agree that weaponry was used by fifth and sixth century Britons, and common sense would also suggest this. Yet, barring some fused spearheads from northern sites, none of them have turned up.

The only exception is the iron spearhead and javelin from Four Crosses, Llandysilio, Powys. 'The combination of weapons, a large general-purpose thrusting spear and a projectile spear seem more appropriate to a warrior that to a huntsman, but are without close parallel in Britain, either individually or as a pair' (Barford *et al* 1986 p104). They were found well within the British zone and differ significantly from similar weapons found in English contexts. The javelin is longer than any English examples, for instance. Its short broad blade is at the end of a very long slender shaft which has been previously bent and straightened out again. The spear has a very long tapering head with a central ridge. An obvious inference is that they are British war weapons. As the archaeologists point out, little is known of the weapon types in use in contemporary British territories in western Britain, and although it is possible that they derive from this cultural background, little more can be said until further examples are found (Barford *et al* 1986: 104).

The weapons were found in the vicinity of an ancient barrow, but what they were doing there is anyone's guess. They might have been hidden in the overgrown ditch around the barrow, or buried, either by themselves or in association with the east/west-oriented burials at the site. Whether some Dark Age British warrior defended the barrow, claimed it or wished to be associated with it in death will never be known.

'Then Arthur fought against them in those days'

It is worth repeating what *Historia Brittonum* had to say about Arthur's battles. Hengist's son Octha comes down from the north, leading the Saxons:

> Then Arthur fought against them in those days, with the kings of the Britons, but he himself was the leader in the battles. The first battle was towards the mouth of the river which is called Glein. The second and third and fourth and fifth were on another river, which is called Dubglas and is in the Linnuis region. The sixth battle was on the river which is called Bassas. The seventh battle was in the Wood of Celidon, that is Cat Coit Celidon. The eighth battle was in Castellum Guinnion, in which Arthur carried the image of Saint Mary, ever Virgin upon his shoulders, and the pagans were put to flight on that day and there was great slaughter upon them through the virtue of Our Lord Jesus Christ and through the virtue of Saint Mary the Virgin His Mother. The ninth battle was waged in the City of the Legion. He waged the tenth battle on the shore of the river which is called Tribuit. The eleventh battle was made on the hill which is called Agned. The twelfth battle was on the hill of Badon, in which 960 men fell in one day in one charge by Arthur. And no-one laid them low save he himself. And in all the battles he was the victor. (HB 56)

In *The Reign of Arthur* I looked at various theories about these locations. Instead of retreading this ground, we will see what archaeological support there is for the most plausible of these locations. The easiest to identify are the Wood of Celidon and the City of the Legion, and I will deal with them and the controversies surrounding them separately. Similarly I will cover the Battle of Badon on is its own, as the only battle on the list for which we have independent evidence. Tribuit is a completely unknown location.

Again Arthur's Battles

Detractors who criticise the historicity of the battle list must face the question of why it is so opaque. If the author was trying to make a point about a geographical location for Arthur or in support of a ninth-century patron, why did he not just use names his contemporaries might have heard of? The clearest example of an 'imaginary' list is the catalogue of places Arthur's porter Glewlwyt visited in the early Welsh prose story *Culhwch and Olwen*. These are nonsensical, often rhyming, places spiced up with some 'real' locations like India to let us know these are widely scattered, faraway places. In *Historia Brittonum* the reader generally has to puzzle over the places, and we have been doing that ever since. Many of the Latin names are not derived from obvious Welsh originals. The only one which he glosses is Silva Celidonis.

Thomas Green presents a case for not considering the battle list historical, but goes beyond what is warranted by either his theory or comparative evidence by characterising it as (2007: 32) 'historically highly implausible, especially given that some of the battles were said to be in areas where there were no Anglo-Saxons in the late fifth century and that there were not to be any for some time after' and therefore 'rightly rejected by nearly all … modern researchers'. Quite apart from the obvious lack of correlation between places where people fight and where they settle, and the riposte that they didn't settle there because they had been beaten militarily, this is factually inaccurate. We know for certain, from Gildas, that the Saxons raged from sea to sea in their campaigns against the Britons, in the course of which they laid low all the *coloniae*, one of which was Gloucester. They subsequently withdrew to their homes in the eastern part of the island. That makes an unassailable contemporary case for warfare between Saxons and Britons in areas which were not immediately, or indeed for some time afterwards, settled by them. Green's certainty that the battles are widespread and in non-Saxon areas, prompts the question, 'where are they supposed to be then?'

The supposed immobility of Dark Age Britons can easily be falsified on the ground. The British kingdom of Elmet, in the Leeds region, stood far to the east, hard against the Anglian settlements of the Humber region. But one of its sixth-century denizens, Elmetiacos ('Elmet man') left his memorial stone in Gwynedd (Dark 1994:151), at Llanaelhaiarn, far to the west on the Lleyn Peninsula. We have previously encountered the fifth or sixth-century Irishman Tebicatos commemorated by an inscribed stone at Silchester.

Bede thought that it was reasonable to ascribe Dark Age rulers wide spheres of activity. His King Ethelfrid of Northumbria (603) fights King Aidan of the Scots at Degastan then the Britons at the City of the Legions (Chester). Ethelfrid might, of course, be a mythological superman, but the Northumbrian bodies discovered at Heronbridge south of Chester (see next chapter) argue at least for the plausibility of the campaign. Bede's claim that Edwin ruled all the people of Britain except the men of Kent, including those in the Menevian Isles might be hyperbole. But these claims of wide rule continue as Bede approaches his own time. King Cadwalla of the Britons fights and kills Edwin at Haethfelth in Northumbria (Hatfield?), continuously ravages the English lands and rules the Northumbrian provinces for a full year. If we accept, as *Historia Brittonum* tells us, that Cadwalla was king of Gwynedd then this is a reach easily comparable to that which we can deduce for Arthur. Of course it doesn't mean it is true, and the *Historia's* knowledge of Bede could have led him to deliberate one-upmanship, but it does dismiss the assumption that wide-ranging campaigns were impossible.

Historia Brittonum's use of place names invites comment. At one point Green even accuses the writer of making names up spontaneously (Green 2007: 207). The *Historia* clearly does have a problem. Arthur is preceded by Vortigern's son Guorthemir as the preeminent Saxon fighter. The writer gives Guorthemir and Arthur specific numbers of battles (sacral? traditional? poetic?) but not enough names to fill them. If he were inventing them, his imagination ran out badly for Guorthemir, when he only needed to find one extra name. If he was in the habit of plucking battles from all over time and space, it is astonishing he did not make more of a success of it. If Arthur was the top superman in a prevailing mythology, the *Historia* could have taken Guorthemir's battles to fill out Arthur's list and left Guorthemir, like Outigirn, the next British warlord, with no battles at all. That he did not do this suggests some reverence for external sources rather than a wanton tendency to invent. The fact that hardly any of the names he uses are known, and only the City of the Legion, Caledonian Forest and Badon are in any sense famous, is in contrast to the legendary/mythological material.

Apart from Glewlwyt's amazing catalogue of obviously made up places in *Culhwch and Olwen*, when the action starts most of the places in the narrative are real. In *Pa Gur* the heroes fight in Anglesey and Edinburgh. Most of the imaginary locations in *Preideu Annwfyn* have clear Welsh meanings (fairy, glass, drunkenness, numbness, obstruction, four-cornered). The battle list is unusual in preserving what seem to be real but unknown placenames. *Historia Brittonum's* author could have made a far better job of localising his mythical hero if he had picked known places along the frontier of Wales and the Mercians. He knew there were traditions localising Arthur in this region, in Builth and Ercing, but did not feed this through to his battle list.

The River Glein

There are two rivers named Glen (assumed to be the modern form of the name) in areas which could make them possible candidates. My preference is for the one which appears in Bede as the site of the mass baptism of King Edwin of Northumbria and his court. It is in Northumberland, running below the Anglian royal site of Yeavering. Yeavering is a famous archaeological site, yielding details such as the configuration of the hall which confirm elements of Bede's account. These Anglo-Saxon discoveries have dominated the written accounts of the site, but there is evidence that the site was actually taken over from the Britons. Above it the hill fort of Yeavering Bell was apparently refortified in this period. British burials there point to occupation in the period AD 300–500 (O'Brien 1999: 63).

My feeling is this is the site intended by *Historia Brittonum* because of its author's indebtedness to Bede. The baptism of Edwin is one of the points where he contradicts Bede and would immediately start readers thinking about that river. He would also have specified that Arthur's Glein was in Linnuis too, if he knew the battle was not at Bede's Glen.

The Lincolnshire Arthur

There is another River Glen in Lincolnshire. This identification is given weight by the fact that the next run of battles are, uniquely, actually given their location 'in the Linnuis region'. The most plausible meaning of this is Lindsey, in Lincolnshire. It is easy to demonstrate how Linnuis is an Old Welsh folk/region name derived from British '*Lindes*', in turn from Romano-British '*Lindenses*', the people of the Roman colony Lindum. This is supported by the Old English form '*Lindesige*', from which modern Lindsey itself derives (Green, T. 2007: 3).

Unfortunately there is no Dubglas river in the Lindsey region. Locating the River Glein in Linnuis would involve an implausible set of errors by the writer or the first copyist of *Historia Brittonum*. Alternatively the name of the River Dubglas could have been replaced by an English one. It means 'blue-black', so might refer to the peaty colouration of the Witham (Green 2007. 3 quoting Reavill 2003: 4).

Although Thomas Green, as we shall see, is convinced that Arthur is at root a mythological figure, he argues that some of the historicity attached to this mythical figure derives from a real fighter against the Saxons operating in Lincolnshire, a prototype Ambrosius or Arthur. Green rightly takes to task writers determined to find Arthur in a particular area and by various combinations of 'wilful ignorance' and wishful thinking come up with fallacious arguments of the type 'X sounds like Tribuit, so X is Tribuit' or 'make huge leaps in the translation and interpretation of the names in order to get them to fit places in the locality they are interested in' (Green 2007b: 2). I am also wary of these 'King Arthur shared my postcode' theories and this initially led me to steer clear of Green's theory as he himself comes from Lincolnshire.

The context of an Arthur operating in the Humber area would be the signs of a significant Anglian presence there. There are cremation cemeteries at Sancton in the East Riding of Yorkshire, Cleatham, South Elkington/Louth and Old Bolinbroke, all in Lincolnshire. The sites indicate that this was one of the most

✄

heavily settled sites during the fifth century, with up to 2000 burials, with Sancton being the northerly limit (Green 2007b: 7). The cremation cemeteries steer clear of Lincoln itself, the nearest being 17 miles away. Green plausibly argues that this suggests Britons of Lincoln were able to control and manage Angles settled in their territory (Green 2007b: 8).

> The earliest Germanic immigrants appear to have arrived by *c.*400 and to have lived in Romano-British settlements almost certainly under native control. Before 500 there are signs of new Anglian communities particularly in the Wolds. Thereafter, the Anglo-Saxons expanded into all parts of the area. (Eagles 1989: 212)

This is a key point, which parallels Gildas's account, of different phases of Saxon settlement. The earliest settlement sites date from about 400 and seem to have included Germanic women, from the evidence of their brooches. These are assumed to be *Laeti* settlements specifically to protect Romans in the vicinity. The presence of these German communities mean that other settlers were attracted to them (or directed to them by a controlling authority) during the fifth and sixth centuries. Although fifth-century sites, concentrating on high ground east of or just on Ermine Street, continued into the late sixth century, in the sixth and seventh century settlements spread without check throughout Lindsey (Eagles 1989: 208–10). Britons may have been able to hold the line of the raised Roman road, or they may have compelled the English settlers to use particular areas.

The situation in Lincoln itself was different. Excavations in the Roman forum revealed a fourth-century wooden church and beside it a Christian cemetery. The cemetery must have come later, as it violates the Roman law against burials within the city. Barring one anomalous grave, aligned north/south, the rest, conventionally (for Christians) are oriented west/east, are carbon dated from AD 450 +/-80 at the earliest, then continually to the eleventh century. In contrast to the pagan cemeteries and Anglo-Saxon items obvious in the rest of Lindsey, the city has yielded only the single anomalous burial and a girdle hanger and wrist clasps, probably from the sixth century. All this suggests that the walled area of Lincoln continued to be occupied after the Roman period, as 'a refuge that was both prestigious and secure' (Eagles 1989: 207-8).

As Green interprets it, the archaeological evidence shows that Lincoln was 'able to successfully resist pressure from the invaders and prevent them from encroaching on their chief settlement' (Green 2007: 212). This is contrary to the clear assertion in Gildas that the revolting Saxons had laid low all the *coloniae* with battering rams. This can be contested on the grounds of hyperbole when the western *coloniae* are considered, but the fall of the two eastern *coloniae* of Lincoln and Colchester seems taken for granted. After ravaging to the western sea, the Saxons returned to their homes in the eastern part of the island. Even if Gildas used *coloniae* loosely to mean big cities, the status of Lincoln and Colchester as *coloniae* was so fixed that even the Saxons incorporated this designation into the names they gave them. Perhaps the Saxons simply avoided the walled city in preference for their well-established sites, content to seize the British wealth which surfaces in their grave goods. Or perhaps a very brief period of dominance was soon matched by a counter-attack or resistance by the Britons of neighbouring Britannia Secunda.

I think Green argues very plausibly for the straightforward interpretation that the Dubglas and Arthur's campaign there were intended to be in Lincolnshire by the writer of *Historia Brittonum*, and that there is good reason to imagine that battles were fought there between Britons and Angles at the right period. I do not think it follows that the River Glein and Badon need to be shunted into the same small area. As we shall see, Green's oft repeated assertion that 'it is now generally agreed that he is unlikely to have rode all around Britain fighting' (e.g. Green 2007b:9) is an assumption only, and belies the views of Dark Age authors about what was accomplished by warlords in the period.

As mentioned, Green denies the historicity of Arthur himself, so his Lincolnshire 'Arthur' carries the academic fig-leaf that '*someone* won the battle of Badon ... and thus, to some degree, there *was* a historical "Arthur", even though he may have borne a different name and had his deeds reattributed to Arthur in the ninth century' (Green 2007b: 10). Now, I, like many Arthurian positivists, use 'Arthur' as a convenient name for the historical leader of the Britons at the Battle of Mount Badon, as 'Vortigern' is used as a convenient name for the historical leader who settled the Saxons. Arguing that someone with a different name (of whom no trace persists) lies behind the historical aspect of the legends seems to me to be purposeless moving of the goal posts, though it allows Green the shelter of operating within the current academic orthodoxy. To rely on a second character violates the logical tool of Occam's Razor. Arguments which demand that we must create more Arthurs (in this case a mythical one and a historical Lincolnshire one) ought to lose out to ones which need only the evidence we have to hand. Live to this problem, Green falls back on Ambrosius, an untenable argument as we shall see when we turn to Badon itself.

This is not to say there are not strong counter-arguments. I don't for instance, see why Lindinis, the area of Ilchester, including South Cadbury, would not also take the linguistic route, via *Lindes, to Linnuis. I suppose we must wait for Dumville's definitive edition before we know for sure how representative 'Linnuis', which groups all the most easily confused manuscript characters, is of the likely original reading.

Castellum Guinnion

Historia Brittonum clearly sets much store by the Battle of Castellum Guinnion. Perhaps there was a legend about King Arthur's exploits there or a shrine where the miraculous image of Our Lady was venerated. Unfortunately there were, on Gildas's testimony, innumerable *castella* in Britain, so trying to find this one might be like looking for a needle in a haystack. It might be a village called Guinnion or, given its military context, a fort named after a person called Guinnion. Supposing that it is a Roman fort, the obvious candidate is Vinovium, modern Binchester. This is the identification suggested by the normally level-headed Rivett and Smith in their compendious survey of the place names of Roman Britain. Green, however is adamant they are wrong and that Guinnion cannot derive from Vinovium in the form it is in *Historia Brittonum*. He is convinced that Guinnion is an otherworldly location, based on the word *guin* (white) which for him is generally a signifier of the Celtic otherworld. He even goes so far as to dismiss any physical location for Castellum Guinnion as not sensible and the product of 'copious quantities of imagination' (Green 2007: 208). In the absence of any actual Arthurian legend about 'Cair Guinnion' or plausible explanation as to why Arthur would be carrying the image of the Virgin Mary there, I will stick with Rivet and Smith for the time being.

Binchester is a Roman fort on a hilltop above the point where Dere Street crosses the River Wear. It covers 3.5 hectares and was associated with a sprawling *vicus* or support settlement of 12 hectares (Ferris and Jones 2000: 1). Its function must have been to ensure that the military route to Hadrian's Wall was kept open. It was garrisoned in Roman times by the *Ala Vettonum*, a cavalry unit presumably used to patrol the road.

Excavations indicate that the fort continued in occupation into the mid-sixth century. A large fifth-century courtyard house, presumably the *praetorium* or commander's residence, became more functional, with a smithy and slaughter house, and its fine heating system was run into disuse through lack of maintenance. In spite of this decline in living standards, the site clearly continued to function, with a complex sequence of building works carried out AD 360, the date of the latest coins.

> Like Birdoswald [on Hadrian's Wall], Binchester now forms a northern example of an evolving occupation and material culture across the sub-Roman period. Binchester and Birdoswald match Wroxeter in showing the retention of importance at Roman sites within what became British kingdoms. (Ferris, I and Jones, R 2000: 5)

What is interesting about Binchester is that it is the next fort along the road from Cataractonium (Catterick, the Catraeth of *The Gododdin*). Perhaps the poet used Arthur specifically because he had fought the Saxons in the same area in an earlier generation. As Dark Age battles go, Catraeth is one of the best attested. It is generally held that the Gododdin expedition is historical, that Catraeth is Catterick and that the expedition took place in the late sixth century. In spite of all this, no sign of it has turned up archaeologically, nor is the site interpreted from anything other than its aspect of a Roman fort. Certainly, though, the site appears to have been used in the Arthurian period. A group of brooches from the mid-fifth to mid-sixth century and an early sixth-century urn attest to this, but whether it was a military, let alone a battle site has not been demonstrated archaeologically. The one spearhead which turned up unfortunately 'cannot be closely dated' (Wilson 2000: 25).

Alcock (2003: 142) argues that, though the campaign is plausible, it need not describe a real engagement of the period. The Gododdin could, in theory, have advanced down Dere Street (to the west of the predominantly coastal English settlements). The total distance from Edinburgh is 130 miles by road, less than 10 days for a mixed force of horse and foot. Alcock questions the idea that they would have done this in realty, as Bede describes Catterick as only a *vicus*, and 'recent excavations produced no evidence for Anglian structures or burials'. I am not sure about the logic of this. The importance of Catterick is that it would stop the advance of the Gododdin (on York?), not that it was their destination. It does not follow that the Angles were settled there at this period.

Whether the battles were historical ones really fought by Arthur or not, the fact is that there are some with perfectly acceptable real-world locations and that they fall well within what was considered plausible for a single character's military operations by a Dark Age writer.

So these pointers to the battle locations are by no means as 'historically highly implausible'. Taking for argument's sake the commonly held view that the Caledonian Wood is in lowland Scotland and the City of the Legion in Chester, the battles cover a spread not unlike that which Bede attributes to the Kingdom of Northumbria, both in the (arguably) an-historical early seventh-century reign of Edwin but also closer to his own time. There is no suggestion that Bede or *Historia Brittonum* thought such a widespread area of operations was inherently implausible for an early Dark Age king. If it had been, that would have negated *Historia Brittonum*'s supposed purpose in rationalising a mythological figure.

Bassas

The River Bassas has eluded all but the most contrived attempts to locate it. Instead, investigators have looked for possible locations which are not rivers. If this is a legitimate line of argument, one location sticks out. A poem in the fourteenth-century *Red Book of Hergest* is entitled '*Eglwysseu Bass*'. It is generally assumed to be a Dark Age work and commemorates the death of Kyndylan the

Fair and Elvan of Powys in combat against the English. Each verse begins with the words '*eglwysseu bassa*' 'the churches of Bassa', land of the grave of Kyndylan. The location meant is Baschurch in Shropshire, well within the area of interest of *Historia Brittonum*, the border land of Mercia and southern Wales. The site is dominated by the Iron Age hill fort the Berth of Baschurch, which may have been occupied in the period (Snyder 1998: 161) (James 2007: 170). The River Perry flows past it, a possible 'river Bassas'. Whether the *Historia* means the battle where Kyndylan died or a different one in the same place is moot. Gelling simply wonders (1989: 189) if 'traditions of Dark Age activity there were perhaps current in the ninth century as they were in later times'.

There seems a predisposition to give the benefit of the doubt to the historicity of Cynddylan as a scion of the Powys dynasty, and this in turn is connected with the sub-Roman works at Wroxeter. This city never became an Anglo-Saxon centre, ensuring that its post-Roman remains survived, beside the more spectacular Roman ones. Philip Barker's revolutionary excavations from 1966 opened up the archaeological study of the sub-Roman period as much as those at South Cadbury. He was seen as unusual in paying attention, indeed in even noticing the ephemeral remains of wooden structures which had been built over or into the more impressive Roman stone and brick structures (Pryor 2004: 167). The archaeological record at Wroxeter extends to at least AD 500. At any rate, it was abandoned by the time a burial – radiocarbon-dated to 610 +/-50 – was placed over the main building layers (Pretty 1989: 172). The Wroxeter excavations were often used as providing examples of the kind of Romanised official or military officer some envisaged Arthur to be. But Wroxeter never entered popular consciousness as an Arthurian site. As Pryor puts it (2004: 172) 'if ever a place demanded an Arthur it is surely post-Roman Wroxeter, but his name has never been linked to it.'

The absence of specific legends about Wroxeter in the Arthurian period has made it difficult for historians to construct a narrative around it. It is named Cair Guricon in the list of the cities of Britain attached to *Historia Brittonum* (HB 66a), but not in the main text. Gelling (1989: 187) despairs that 'the history of the region is a total blank for a long time… The obscurity of the sixth century is impenetrable'. What we can say is that 'in Cheshire, Shropshire and Herefordshire there is no archaeological trace of pagan Anglo-Saxons' (Gelling 1989: 196). As the area was to prove very attractive to later expansion by the Mercians, this absence of evidence may itself suggests that the Britons successfully resisted the English here into the seventh century.

The stark contrast between the area dominated by Wroxeter and eastern Britain archaeologically cannot be overstated. Quite simply, no pagan Saxon burial has been found on the west side of the Severn. Indeed, eastwards in the Cotswold area the burials peter out before reaching the flood plain. Farther north there are large Saxon cemeteries around Bredon Hill near the Avon-Severn confluence, but none further west (Pretty 1989: 175). It is (just) conceivable that every Saxon who ventured into the Severn valley was converted to Christianity or forced to assimilate, but wildly unlikely. It is one of the gravest charges laid by Bede that the Britons who St Augustine encountered in this border area had not attempted to convert the English.

Archaeologists can advance various reasons why some areas might have been physically inaccessible to English settlers of the period, but the extensive areas without Anglo-Saxon land holding 'cannot all be explained by highland and woodland … some, like Wroxeter, the Teme valley around Bravonium and Kenchester may be delimiting areas which were too strongly held by British magnates to be accessible to Anglo-Saxon secular domination' (Pretty 1989: 180).

Anglo-Saxons, whether peaceful settlers or warbands, would naturally follow 'the prevailing east/west system of wooded ridges and fertile stream valleys' (Pretty 1989: 172). They would suddenly emerge into an area of very different geography. Not just Wroxeter (Viroconium) but a string of Roman-British centres to the south of it, Bravonium in the Teme valley, Magnis (Kentchester) then Ariconium controlling the lower Wye. All were linked by a major Roman road running north-south through the Church Stretton gap.

> We must assume that the individual polities grew up in the fifth and sixth centuries, some in the Roman towns, others between them … one may propose that in each of the Roman towns down the border … the old public land was taken over, perhaps enclosed as was the baths basilica in Wroxeter, and used as the centre of a small kingdom. (Pretty 1989)

Magnis (Kenchester) was certainly occupied and defended in the fifth century, when its west gate was narrowed and its ditch re-cut. Its ruins were still standing in Leland's time. One of the residents of Wroxeter, presumably of some status, left his name on his tombstone, dated to the last quarter of the fifth century. He was the Irishman CVNORIX MACVVS MAQVI COLINE (Pretty 1989: 172). This may well attest to the use of Irish warriors to aid the defence, if not to an Irish dominated regime at Wroxeter.

When the area finally came under Anglo-Saxon rule, the tribal groupings named there were the Wreocsaete (around Wroxeter), the Magonsaete (Magnis) and the Areosaete (Ariconium). The pattern is familiar as that in the south-west, where the Somersaete and Dorsaete also mark linguistically the areas which resisted the Saxon advance into the late sixth century.

This is good archaeological evidence of what we would expect to find from the *Historia Brittonum*. The Severn valley kingdoms seem to show clearly 'Kings of the Britons' operating together to hold back the Anglo-Saxons. The absence of Saxon remains crosses *civitas* boundaries, with the Roman road as a connection between them. One of two clear geographical connections given to Arthur in *Historia Brittonum* is that he killed and buried his son in Ercing (Ariconium). An alternative name given to the Battle of Mount Agned, given in recensions familiar with the area, Breguin/Bregomium, may hark back to Bravonium. At the very least, traditions known by the writer of *Historia Brittonum* (a local as attested by his familiarity with Ercing and Buelt) provide a very plausible explanation for what is otherwise dismissed as impenetrable obscurity. With the example of Cunorix the Irishman in mind, it is worth remembering that the name Arthur first occurs amongst the Irish operating in western Britain.

12

The City of the Legion

I have singled out the battle at the City of the Legion because *Historia Brittonum* seems clear where it actually was. It appears in the list of the 28 cities, which has usually clear 'British' versions of the names of other possible sites. Caerleon on Usk, for instance, is given as 'Cair Legeion Guar Usic', allowing us to narrow down his 'Cair Legion' as Chester. The writer is aware of Bede and so knows that Bede gave this name, along with English and Latin versions, to the city of Chester.

Snyder (1998: 164) identifies this city as a significant sub-Roman site. It was recently reported that the amphitheatre had been occupied and fortified, perhaps as the base for some Dark Age warlord. There were several phases of work, but unfortunately no datable artefacts to narrow the date from somewhere between the third and the twelfth century (Garner and Wilmott 2008: 25).

Amphitheatres such as that at Chester or Caerleon are often seen as prototypes of the Round Table. This archetypical Arthurian item enters the records in the twelfth-century French and English versions of Geoffrey of Monmouth, written by Wace and Layamon respectively. Both these writers treat the Round Table as a famous object 'which the Britons boast about' (Lawman 11454), which makes it odd that it does not feature in Geoffrey of Monmouth's compendious treatment of the legends. It is clear that a very large structure, much bigger than the wooden disk hanging in Winchester, is what those writers intended.

Interestingly, the refortified Chester amphitheatre is associated with what appears to be an early Christian martyrium, represented by St John's church immediately outside its east entrance. This in turn seems associated with a tethering post, which might have been part of the paraphernalia associated with a public execution of the martyrs Julius and Aaron. Of course this is a chain of speculation any link of which could be open to other interpretation. It is clear, though, that the British warlords of western Britain were Christians, and Gildas is specific on the morale-boosting possibilities the shrines of the martyrs would have for them. A stand at the Chester amphitheatre would make a very plausible and atmospheric Arthurian battle at the City of the Legion.

viii. THE BORDERS OF BRITANNIA PRIMA

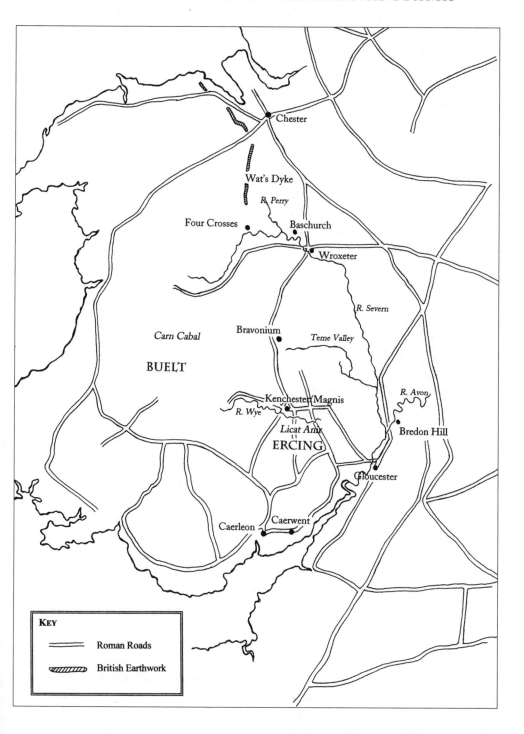

Chester

Wat's Dyke

R. Perry

Four Crosses

Baschurch

Wroxeter

R. Severn

Carn Cabal

Bravonium

Teme Valley

BUELT

R. Avon

Kenchester Magnis

R. Wye

Bredon Hill

Licat Anir

ERCING

Gloucester

Caerleon

Caerwent

KEY

Roman Roads

British Earthwork

Better still, Chester is the only place where unequivocal remains of a Dark Age battle have been discovered. Heronbridge is a riverside site, on the west bank of the Dee, about a mile south of Chester. It was a settlement which lined the main Roman road south of the city, towards Wroxeter. Roman occupation continued until at least AD 350, but a defensive earthwork was built over the top of the remains of some of the buildings, with a dry-stone facing on the front. The age of the earthwork was not clear when excavations began in 1930. Underneath were 'some twenty or more human burials – all apparently battle casualties' (www. chesterarchaeolsoc.org.uk). These skeletons have since disappeared, either rein-terred or destroyed by bombing during the war (Mason 2007) so their own date is uncertain. Fortunately, the story does not end there.

Because Heronbrige was not overlaid by a modern settlement it is ideal for excavation, and the known archaeology of the site showed the potential for fur-ther research. Excavations carried out in 2004 included a specific objective of determining the date and function of the earthwork. The builders had recovered usable stone from the Roman buildings as well as tombstones. Further digging 'quickly located more burials and it soon became very obvious that this was indeed at battle cemetery' (www.chesterarchaeolsoc.org.uk).

The archaeologists had discovered a mass grave pit. Within a 2m x 3m area at least 14 men had been buried. They were aligned west-east without grave goods, which would usually be taken as signifying they were British or post-conversion Saxons, although this is not the interpretation of either 1930 or 2004. The skel-etons of both excavations had extensive injuries. Two were fully excavated and examined by Malin Holst of York Osteoarchaeology Ltd. She determined that they were both well-built men, the elder, in his forties, had been in battle before and that both had been killed by several sword blows to the head. The infer-ence was that they and their companions had been experienced soldiers who had finally met their match. They had died after Roman times but (as carbon dates from the ditch showed) before the area was used for flax manufacture in the eighth century.

Scottish Universities Environmental Research Centre carried out radiocarbon dating on two bone samples. Sample 1 had 95 per cent probability of lying in the range AD 430–640, and 59 per cent of narrowing that to 530–620. The second sample pushed the dates to the later end of the scale, 95 per cent probability 530–660 and 51 per cent 595–645. 'the dating of both battle cemetery and earthwork to the seventh century [would mean] Heronbridge could qualify as the earliest positively identi-fied battle site in England, while Anglo-Saxon fortifications of this early period are virtually unknown' (Mason 2008: www.chesterarchaeolsoc.org.uk).

If the bones had been found at any of the other proposed Arthurian battle sites, they would have been seized on as confirmation of the battle list, perhaps indicating a later date for Arthur in the sixth century. At Chester this did not happen, because we know for certain there was a battle here in the early seventh century. Bede reports that the Britons were defeated in battle at Chester by King Ethelfrid of the Northumbrians. At great cost to his own army, the English ruler inflicted fearful slaughter on the Britons including a deliberate massacre of the British monks aiding their side with prayers. Bede interpreted this victory by the pagan king as just retribution for the Britons' refusal to submit to saint Augustine. Augustine has apparently prophesied this, a prophecy which came to pass 'long after his death' (HE II.2). Augustine died in 604, so the meeting with the Britons must have occurred shortly before this. Ethelfrid's attack is described as coming 'some while after this' (HE II.2) and before the reign of his successor Edwin, who was king by 625. *Annales Cambriae* places the battle, called Gueith Cair Legion, at around AD 613, 97 years after the Battle of Badon. Bede confirms that the City of the Legions or Legacestir is 'more correctly named Carlegion' by the Britons (HE II.2). As this is right in the middle of the carbon dates obtained it would be churlish to argue against the assertion that these bodies are casualties of the attack by Ethelfrid. Their position on the west bank of the Dee, possibly contesting a crossing here where the Roman road from the city met the river, and their lack of any pagan features, would seem to suggest they were British defenders, but analysis of their tooth enamel (Mason 2007) shows they actually grew up in Northumberland.

Where does this leave Arthur? Conventional wisdom (at least since Jackson 1959: 8) is that the battle of the City of the Legion attributed to Arthur is the same as the victory of Ethelfrid, showing a propensity of the writer of *Historia Brittonum* to gather battles from across time and space to aggrandise his chosen figure of Arthur. This might have a grain of plausibility had not Chester been so clearly portrayed as a disastrous British defeat, indeed a massacre. There is no earthly reason for this to be chosen as the ninth battle of the always victorious Arthur and the kings of the Britons. if the writer somehow wanted to set the record straight and record Chester as a victory, he could have placed it during the career of Ethelfrid (whom he calls Aedelferd Flesaur 'the artful') rather than before the establishment of Ethelfrid's Bernician dynasty.

It is obvious that more than one battle can be fought in the same place, especially if that place is of strategic importance. That Chester was important enough for a Northumbrian king to attack makes it more likely it was a location where the English had been checked before. We know for certain that contemporaries had no problem with recording more than one battle at the same place, with no need to conflate them. The Anglo-Saxon Chronicle reports Ethelfrid's battle at Chester (in 605 or 607). In a later passage, it records that in 894 'the Danes … arrived at a deserted Roman site in the Wirral, called Chester. The levies were unable to overtake them before they got inside that fort, but they besieged it some two days' (ASC 894). Though Heronbridge does not confirm the Arthurian battle, it shows clearly that battles were part of the story of that period and that battle sites are there to be discovered and identified by archaeology.

The City of the Legions

Although the writer of *Historia Brittonum* is reasonably clear that the City of the Legion is Chester, it is possible, if he is following an earlier source which includes the name, he might be mistaken in his identification. This is compounded by the conflicting clues given by Gildas, the originator of the almost identical phrase 'City of the Legions'.

When he reaches the time of the Great Persecutions, Gildas breaks off from his narrative to tell us how useful the brilliant lamps lit by the martyrs would have been in his own day if the citizens of contemporary Britain had not been deprived of them by the partition of the island. Let us see exactly what he did write:

> The places of the sufferings and burial of their bodies, were a great many of them not taken away from the citizens by the barbarians' lamentable division, might now kindle no small fire of divine love in the minds of those who beheld them: I mean Saint Alban of Verolamium, Aaron and Julius, citizens of Urbs Legionum, and the others of either sex who in various places stood with the highest courage in Christ's front line. (DEB 10.2)

What *divortio* ('by the division') means and what it implies to the geography of Arthurian Britain is complex. The obvious sense is that Verulamium and the City of the Legions are both in the eastern side of the island, the areas under Saxon rule and that Britons from the unconquered part cannot get there.

Verulamium is the Roman city in the *civitas* of the Catuvellauni beside which the modern town of St Albans, centred on the saint's shrine, grew up. Although according to Dark's analysis it and its hinterland survived as a distinct Romano-British kingdom (Dark 1994: 86) it was surrounded by Saxon settlements. Here Gildas's meaning is clear. The case of the City of the Legions is much more complex.

Although to Bede, *Historia Brittonum* and *Annales Cambriae* the 'City of the Legion' meant Chester, and to the Vatican Recension, Geoffrey of Monmouth and all subsequent Welsh writers Caerleon, this is not the same as proving Gildas meant either. Given that the Saxons did not hold Chester or Caerleon at the time of his writing, it requires geographical gymnastics to place Gildas or his fellow Britons in places where they cannot reach any of these locations.

P.J. Field (1999) offered the suggestion that the actual city Gildas meant was York. Although its usual Roman name was Eboracum, it appears in the *Notitia Dignitatum* as 'Sextae', the home of the Sixth Legion. If it is the true City of the Legions, it is easy to see how its shrines suffered the same fate as Verulamium, both being within the Saxons 'home' territory. Internally to Gildas, Verulamium and *Urbs Legionum* should be in the eastern part of the country under Saxon rule.

That is the only '*divortium*' Gildas has told us of, not a picture of Saxon salients blocking off British enclaves from particular pilgrim routes.

Field thinks Gildas places the emphasis on the saints, rather than the places. I disagree. As Gildas's account of Albans's miracles and martyrdom shows, the examples of the saints still have the capacity to inspire but this is lessened without access to the places. It is surely this deprivation of the places which he emphasises. British place names are just as rare in Gildas as personal names. I conclude that Gildas singled out the saints not because they were uniquely exemplary but because their shrines are significantly hard to access in the present.

It is easy to see how York could be cut off from Gildas's readers in Dumnonia and Demetia. Field errs by suggesting the fall of York is a recent event associated with the settlement of Northumbria after 540. Gildas does not know anything of resurgent Saxons. His '*divortium*' is a longer standing situation.

Urbs is for Field a word denoting a proper city, which Eboracum, a *colonia*, was and Chester and Caerleon (legionary bases) were not. It is from *castra* (camp) that they take their name. He suggests that Gildas was following some sort of official list with his 28 *civitates* and that this would not have included Chester or Caerleon. York was an episcopal see, as it sent its bishop to the council of Arles in 314 at the head of the British delegation.

Green (2007b: 4) seems to have come round to having some sympathy with Field's York theory, having previously rubbished it as 'having no real merit' (2007: 209). Presumably its proximity to Lincolnshire was to its advantage.

I have a couple of observations on Field's theory. Gildas, as we have seen, sets out his hierarchy of settlement at the start of the book – 28 *civitates*, some *castella* and *munitiones* (fortifications) (DEB 3.2). The question is what he means by the other words he used for 'towns'.

Because there are 28 of them, his word *civitas* must be inclusive of all the settlements larger than *civitas* capitals and some smaller. The *coloniae* seem to be at the top. Not only do the Saxons see them as places where the British capable of paying them live, Gildas specifically tells us that their inhabitants include the leaders of the church, distinct from the priests; '*omnesque coloni cum praepositis ecclesiae, cum sacerdotibus ac popolo*' (DEB 24.3). This seems clear evidence that they are the seats of bishoprics, perhaps even metropolitans. It is arguable that *urbes* are distinguished as bishoprics too. Aquileia, an *urbs* he mentions in his story of Magnus Maximus, is a famous ecclesiastical centre; there was a synod there in the fourth century. The connection is made explicit when Gildas calls St Ignatius 'bishop of the city of Antioch' '*antiochiae urbis episcopus*' (DEB 74.1). It would be reasonable to imagine that the shrines of Julius and Aaron had a bishopric attached to them.

It is possible that *urbes* and *coloniae* are synonyms to Gildas. In his 'blurb' (DEB 2) he promises his readers that after the Saxon invasion he will write '*de urbium subversione*' 'the overthrow of the cities'. When we get to the actual passage in the book, he writes instead about '*cunctae coloniae*' (DEB 24.3).

Cities and Legions

So far, Gildas can support the York hypothesis. However, the one aspect Field does not address is the only context where Gildas mentions *urbes* and legions together – the Wall. The only legion in *De Excidio Britanniae* is one sent by the Romans to drive back the Picts (DEB 15). The Romans then instruct the Britons to build the (turf) wall. When this fails the Romans construct a stone wall which runs from sea to sea between the *urbes*, which already happen to be there – the Britons have been cowering in them for fear of the enemy '*tramite a mari usque ad mare inter urbes, quae ibidem forte ob metum hostium collocatae fuerant*' (DEB 18.2). It is reasonable from *De Excidio Britanniae* to see a connection between the *urbes* and the legion.

We know that Gildas is completely off on his dating of the walls. He is honest enough to admit that he doesn't actually know when the saints were martyred, either. 'We conjecture' '*conicimus*' (DEB 10.1) they were killed in the nine years of the Diocletian persecution.

We know that one of the *urbes* on the wall is Carlisle, (probably) *civitas* capital of the Carvetii. That could be seen as a large city, and it could be the seat of a bishop. But it is the only one. If we take the most limited reading of Gildas, that the wall has an *urbs* on either end (and I confess that I read the passage as meaning that all the forts the wall connected from sea to sea were *urbes*) then that gives us Newcastle (Pons Aelius). Newcastle is the only other settlement of any size and it is smaller than the *civitas* capitals. If *urbs*, as Field argues, implies size and significance, the only way Pons Aelius could be an *urbs* would be if it were a bishopric. And the only way it could be a bishopric would be if it had a martyr's shrine.

It is quite possible that Gildas could have seen Newcastle as under Saxon control. We know that Gildas imagined the wall area, particularly its east end, as an area where Saxons operated and settled. We know this because their settlement is a response to exactly the same threats which caused the walls to be built in the first place, attacks by Picts and Scots.

Field suggests that York could be called *Urbs* of the Legions (plural) because of a long memory of its use by IX *Hispana* as well as more recently by the VI. This is surely putting Gildas's memory to the test! It is contradicted by the reference to York in the source closest to Gildas's time, *Notitia Dignitatum*, where its connection to VI *Victrix* is so strong it is called *Sextae*.

Both Carlisle and Newcastle had had more than one legion in them in more recent times. Newcastle had *vexillationes* of VI *Victrix* and XX *Valeria Victrix* under Antoninus Pius. Carlisle, more recently, had *vexillationes* of II *Augusta* and XX *Valeria Victrix* under Caracalla, and they were not the only wall forts with *vexillationes* from more than one legion. Thus, in Gildas a good case could be made for Carlisle – if *urbs* implies size – or Newcastle if *divortium* implied it was held by Saxons, in the only area where Gildas actually connected *urbes* with a legion.

Whether *urbs* actually does imply size or importance is by no means as certain as Field thinks. He starts with the ancient example of Rome as 'the' *Urbs* and works forwards. Dark Age sources and archaeology tell a different story. It is not generally read that the *urbes* in Gildas are at either end of the Wall, but that the Wall links *urbes* along its length. They would thus be only the equivalents of forts. Certainly by the time of Bede *urbs* no longer meant a big city-like town. He sometimes calls Bamburgh a *civitas* or more usually an *urbs*, but as Alcock (1988: 34) points out Bamburgh is smaller than Cadbury/Camelot, Congresbury and Tintagel. Dumbarton is also an *urbs* and a *civitas* to Bede and is of a similar magnitude.

Of course, we may be putting too much weight on Gildas's supposed geographical knowledge. Like many southerners he may have erroneously imagined that York is 'somewhere up North', possibly in the Wall area.

The City of the Legions on the River Usk

Whatever the competing merits of the various Cities of the Legion/Legions as the place intended by either Gildas or the battle list, within 100 years of the composition of *Historia Brittonum*, the localisation at Caerleon had become the standard. The Vatican recension of *Historia Brittonum* explained the battle as being 'called in British Cair Lion', for example. There are archaeologists who adamantly maintain this is the right location. Ray Howell, writing of the late and sub-Roman remains at Caerleon, which we shall turn to in a moment, writes in *Gwent County History* (Aldhouse-Green and Howell 2004: 259) 'it is known that two of the three named early martyrs in Britain, Julius and Aaron, died in Caerleon. A martyrium of the saints in or near Caerleon was mentioned by Gildas in the mid-sixth century.'

He is supported by Jeremy Knight in the same work (Aldhouse-Green and Howell 2004: 274) who is categorical that the martyrium stood at Bullmpre, on the edge of one of the cemeteries across the river from Caerleon, beside the road to Caerwent. The martyrium and the 'territory of the holy martyrs Julius and Aaron' *'territorium sanctorum martirum julii et aaron'* are referred to in a charter *c.*864, part of the collection in the Book of Llandaff. This is, Knight acknowledges (2001: 40) 'a difficult and problematic source 'edited' or rewritten in Anglo-Norman times by the new see of Llandaff for use in territorial disputes with its neighbours of Hereford and St David's. If its date is genuine, then it shows the identification of Gildas's City of the Legions with Caerleon was well established before the Vatican recension made its explicit identification between Arthur's battle and this location. It pushes it back much closer to the writing of *Historia Brittonum* itself. Even if the early dating of the charter is suspect, the Book of Llandaff itself predates Geoffrey of Monmouth, so the identification is clearly independent of his aggrandisement of the city with the shrines. This is supported by the further reference to '*ecclesiam julii et aron*' 'the church of Julius and Aaron' in a charter of 1113 from Robert of Chandos, lord of Caerleon, and again in 1154–58 by the Welsh lord of Caerleon Morgan ap Owain (Knight 2004: 40). Paradoxically, a dedication to St Alban was subsequently added to the church and, with time, the more famous 'proto-martyr' ousted his less well-known colleagues. The site is now known as 'Mount St Albans'.

This site could have been relatively well known to Gildas, if he were based in the *civitas* of the Durotriges, just across the Severn estuary. The twelfth-century saints lives, the *Life of St. Cadoc* and the *Life of Gildas* by Caradoc of Llancarfan, associate Gildas with the Bristol Channel islands of Steepholm and Flatholm, from both of which Mount St Albans is visible (Knight 2001: 41).

The nearest of the sites has to be balanced by Gildas's claim that the *divortium*, the division of the islands with the Saxons, had made the martyrs' shrines inaccessible to the Britons. He had, to be fair, made clear that the estuary of the Severn was now too hazardous for overseas luxuries to be imported up it, so there may be an element of 'so near, yet so far' to the shrine so easily glimpsed from the channel. If Caerleon is the site of an Arthurian battle, this too might be taken as demonstrating it was too dangerous for a pilgrimage.

Is Caerleon really plausible as a location for one of Arthur's battles? Even Geoffrey of Monmouth did not think so. His view of it as King Arthur's base is rather easier to argue. Gwent, the successor kingdom which arose about it has traditionally been considered an area of Arthurian activity. One of the Dark Age kings named in the Llandaff Charters, Athrwys son of Meurig, is sometimes advanced as the 'real' Arthur. His apparent late date (perhaps as late as 605–55, Aldhouse-Green and Howell 2004: 250) rules him out as the victor of Badon and the character referred to in *The Gododdin*.

We know that the Roman remains of Caerleon were still standing, and impressively so, in the twelfth century when the Arthurian connections of the site first enter the written record. The baths were still roofed and a great monument, a tetrapylon or a four-way triumphal arch, stood in the centre of the site, straddling the two main roads (Aldhouse-Green and Howell 2004: 253). Howell refers to Gerald of Wales's identification of this structure as a 'gigantic tower' in 1188 without noting that Gerald was simply looking for confirmation of Geoffrey's '*giganteam turrim*' – 'Tower of Giants' where King Arthur held council. What neither Gerald nor Geoffrey could have been aware of were the Late Roman and Dark Age remains which are only now being uncovered. The tetrapylon stands in the centre of the Roman fortress, but in the fourth century a rather smaller area was fortified, an oval enclosure with the Roman wall at its back and a new embankment across the urban site, with the tetrapylon incorporated in it, presumably as a gate. Geoffrey was specific that the 'Tower of Giants' was at the entrance, although this is unlikely to have been obvious to him on the ground. Howell continues (2004: 253) it is increasingly clear ... that there was considerable activity at the site of the fortress at Caerleon in the fourth century and after ... there is every indication that the barrack blocks stood at least as late as the eighth century when a young woman was buried there at floor level. It was standing and roofed at the time.

Extra buildings built in association with the old barracks are taken as 'implying a considerable population'. Although the II Legion was no longer formally stationed there 'the existence of a late caretaker garrison, possibly of militia status, must now be seen as at least a possibility' given the discovery of late fourth-century military straps (Aldhouse-Green and Howell 2004: 254). Once again the difficulty of dating arises. Roman manufactured objects inevitably date themselves to before the Roman departure in (say) 409. They only date the context in which they are found to sometime after their manufacture. Thus in nearby Caerwent (Aldhouse-Green and Howell 2004: 256), a burial which contained a Roman coin of 335–48 and a late Roman bracelet was radiocarbon dated to 540–770.

Remains at Caerwent, from which the kingdom took its name, show Caerleon was no isolated military base. (White places the martyrdom of Julius and Aaron as possibly here, (2007: 92), but I can find no other argument supporting this.) Lodge Hill camp north-west of Caerleon, which also overlooks the Usk, was possibly reused in the late Roman/post-Roman period, as were undefended but high status sites like Longbury Bank near Tenby. What there are emphatically not are any of the archaeological features diagnostic of Saxon presence. Any Saxons settled in the Caerleon area must have been encouraged (or forced) to conform to the norms of the British kingdom of Gwent. Or, more simply, any attempt to expand westwards into Gwent was resisted and, as the barracks, fortifications and equipment suggest, resisted militarily. Caerleon and its hinterland conform to the pattern we have observed elsewhere in Britannia Prima. Its strategic position linking the Severn Valley kingdoms and those of the west county would have made it both useful as a base for co-ordinated attacks and also a target for Saxon invasions. Its road system would have allowed the king of Dyfed, Vortiporius's father from the generation of Mount Badon, to reach the war-zone from his western homeland.

It remains a possibility, given the archaeological work and the apparent ease of identifying such a site, that Julius and Aaron may still be discovered, in a martyrium in a late Roman cemetery beside either Chester or Caerleon or indeed elsewhere.

Like Shining Beacons

Although the clearest understanding of Gildas is that the shrines of Alban, Julius and Aaron are all cut off from the Britons to whom Gildas writes, subsequent historiography has seen the '*divortium*' as meaning St Albans and the City of the Legion are now separated, one on the Saxon side, one on the British. This would, perhaps, make more out of the sense of divorce or division, that each of the dividers end up with some of the spoils. As we know where Verulamium was – in the east – that would place the City of the Legions in the west (Chester or Caerleon) where it has traditionally been placed.

Dark, though, sees Verulamium as a possible centre of one of the eastern British successor polities. It appears to have been continuously occupied (Snyder 1998: 146). In this case the martyrs' shrines might have been shining out like beacons from enclaves surrounded by Saxons, with the Britons unable to cross the intervening areas.

Andrew Smith argues that this speculation possibly rests on a mistaken premise. Gildas does not say that Verulamium and the City of the Legions are inaccessible, only that the sites of the saints' martyrdoms and tombs are. Alban is from Verulamium and Julius and Aaron are citizens of the City of the Legions. This does not necessarily imply that they were martyred in those locations. A more reasonable inference might be that they were martyred in the diocesan capital, London. Indeed, one of the miracles performed by Alban immediately before his martyrdom was parting the waters of the Thames. The only way this can be squared with the idea that Alban was martyred at Verulamium is to argue that Gildas has a very imperfect grasp of geography and thought that the Thames runs through Verulamium, which it does not. If we accept the possibility that his geography was so wrong, we can then hardly justify historical inferences from the idea that Gildas was familiar with Verulamium and the Thames. If he did not even know which cities stood on the major river, what can we deduce about any other geographical information that he gives? If, on the other hand, all three martyrs died in the same place, London, it is very easy to see how the shrines of their martyrdom would have become inaccessible thanks to the *divortium*, as the Saxons had their homes in the eastern side of the island, and the estuary of the Thames had been rendered unreachable. It does not help with locating the City of the Legions except in as far as it smoothes the way for an identification with either of the western candidates.

Field (1999) also notes the ambiguity but feels sure that Gildas would have mentioned it if they were martyred in different locations. It may be that he thought he was being explicit with his reference to the Thames. Perhaps he was addressing residents of Verulamium and the City of the Legions who could not reach the sites of the martyrdom, rather than, as is generally supposed, readers elsewhere in Britain. Perhaps Gildas was actually writing from Verulamium – a unique example in his text of an actual Roman town name in Briton and a detailed hagiography.

One final wildcard is the fact that by the time of the *Notitia Dignitatum*, the second legion seems no longer to have been based in Isca Silurium (Caerleon), but in the Saxon shore fort of Rutupiae (Richborough) (Knight 2001: 39). This is likely to reflect the situation at the time of the persecution of Diocletian. If this is the meaning of 'City of the Legions' it again raises the possibility of an unproblematic eastern location to be affected by the *divortium*, but provides quite an unlikely candidate for one of Arthur's battles (albeit one firmly in the grasp of his reputed adversaries, the kings of the men of Kent).

13

INVENTING ARTHUR

So far plausible locations for the Arthurian battles have generally been linked to plausible archaeology. This used to be a fairly respectable academic pursuit, and fills many books and articles leading up to the Cadbury/Camelot era. These days, however, the academic consensus is that searching for such explanations is a waste of time. The battle list is not derived from or reflective of fifth/sixth-century reality. This is because Arthur was not a historical figure at all.

Thomas Green and Nick Higham are two of the foremost scholars of the 'Arthurian' period working in the English academic world today. They are, I think, the only ones who continue to use the name of 'King Arthur' in their book titles. Although I disagree with them on many issues there is no doubting their familiarity with the relevant sources and the scholarship around them. For them, the battle list is essentially a work of fiction, reflecting only the concerns of its early ninth-century author.

The advantage of the theory that King Arthur led the Britons in their victorious campaigns against the Saxons has always been one of simplicity. The wars culminating in the Battle of Mount Badon certainly happened, and we have no other name for the victor than the one provided by *Historia Brittonum* – Arthur. It was therefore reasonable to accept this, in default of evidence to the contrary.

Dumville could argue that, with *Historia Brittonum* being 'inadmissable', having no demonstrable claim to be using fifth-century material, there was no good reason to accept the name. We could respond there was equally no good reason to reject it, producing the impasse of the 1970s and 1980s. This should have been the opportunity for pro-Arthurians to press home their advantage but, with the death of John Morris, there were no major pro-Arthurian academics to take up the fight.

The field was left open to the anti-Arthurians. They had three potential avenues of attack:

1   There were no wars between the Britons and the Saxons, or at least not victorious ones. The supposed context did not exist.

2   There were wars, but someone other than Arthur led the Britons in them

3   Arthur was a character from a different (historical or non-historical) context

4   The author of *Historia Brittonum* had a compelling ulterior motive for his story of Arthur sufficiently strong to shake the assertion he only included it because it was real.

The best syntheses of these attacks come from Higham and Green. Their arguments have strengths, certainly, but weaknesses too. Being supportive of the anti-Arthurian consensus, they have not been seriously challenged in the academic field.

Higham starts from the premise that, contrary to the popular perception of a 'Reign of Arthur', the British victory at Badon was followed by Saxon domination. Gildas's *de excidio Britanniae* has always been taken as implying that the author writes from the perspective of a period of British domination. *Historia Brittonum*, on the contrary, says nothing about a British dominated 'Age of Arthur'. In its narrative, the victories of Arthur are followed, without interval, by renewed Saxon attacks by Ida and the rise of Northumbria. It is strange that Higham takes Gildas as supporting his view and rejects *Historia Brittonum*, in spite of the support it could potentially give.

Dumville had fatally weakened the idea that *Historia Brittonum* was the work of Nennius, guilelessly compiling a scrapbook of ancient historical materials primarily from a love of knowledge. He demonstrated that it was a Welsh work of the early ninth century, strongly authored or at least edited to comment on contemporary issues.

Bede had provided a compelling narrative of Dark Age British history. As he saw it, God's providence in the British Isles had worked primarily through the Saxon and English peoples who had settled in the island from the fifth century. He traced a relatively simple path from Pope Gregory's chance encounter with angelic-featured Angle slaves, his commissioning of Augustine to convert these people, a rolling campaign of conversions starting with the kingdom of Kent, through to the major Anglian kingdom of Northumbria and thence to all the other kingdoms of the Angles and Saxons. The role of Irish Christians in evangelising and sustaining the faith among the English was not concealed, but it is through the agency of the Northumbrian Angles that these missionaries were brought to acceptance of the true date of Easter and the supremacy of the Pope.

The native Britons scarcely appear in this providential narrative, except as defeated opponents of the God-supported Angles and Saxons, as semi-barbarians, savage, weak, perfidious and, just as important, shirkers of their responsibility to convert the Saxons to Christianity. Bede took Gildas's condemnation of his contemporary Britons and twisted it to fit this narrative as far as he was able. Certainly Gildas's attacks do add weight to the condemnation, but to him the

Saxons were agents of providence only in as far as the Assyrians and Babylonians in the Bible, chastisers of God's chosen people, not the chosen ones themselves.

Although the political situation had changed by the early ninth century, with Bede's Northumbria eclipsed by the midlands power of Mercia, the basic message still kept is resonance. Bede had shown the Mercians initially under the thumb of the British King Caedwalla, establishing themselves as an independent power under the pagan Penda but then swiftly converting to Christianity under Penda's son Wulfhere. Thereafter the Mercians continued their victorious advance, driving the British ever further westward. Offa, King of Mercia in the late eighth century, extended Mercian power to his giant earthwork, Offa's Dyke, which still substantially forms the frontier between England and Wales.

This is the context in which *Historia Brittonum* was compiled as, it seems, a deliberate riposte to Bede. Using sources Bede did not have, it set out to prove that God had always supported the Britons, with miracles and military victories under Vortimer, Arthur, Outigirn and Urbgen. Lapses, when they occurred, such as the reign of Vortigern, were the exception rather than the rule. The work of British missionary St Patrick in converting the Irish is brought to prominence, leading to the work of the Celtic priests in Britain, a strong counter argument to the idea the Britons had shirked their missionary duty.

Historia Brittonum's Patron

Whose interests were served by this new version of Dark Age history? Higham and Greene followed Dumville in pointing the finger at the king now known as Merfyn Ffrych of Gwynedd. He was the leading British ruler to the west of Offa's Dyke, apparently a newcomer from the Isle of Man. Internally there is nothing in *Historia Brittonum* to support this contention. It mentions King Mermin (as contemporaries called him) once, as a way of fixing the date of the present as the fourth year of his reign (HB 16). Beyond that there is nothing. No place name in mainland Gwynedd, no attempt, in a work full of genealogies, to link Mermin to the earlier Welsh rulers like Bede's Caedwalla or Gildas's Maglocunus, called Mailcunus in the text. Several kings of Gwynedd are given prominence, but this failure to link them genealogically must be significant.

The only ruler who is specifically said to be reigning 'now' is Fernmail of Builth (HB 49). One of the wonders of Britain, Carn Cabal, is located in Builth. None are located in mainland Gwynedd. Even more significant is the fact that *Historia Brittonum's* fifth-century material is effectively an origin myth for Fernmail and his dynasty. He is a descendant of Vortigern, part of his domains, Guorthigirniaun, being, presumably, named for the ruler. His ancestors received their lands thanks to Ambrosius, whose story is told at length. While Vortigern remains a discredited tyrant, his sons are fierce fighters against the Saxons. The

Historia's interest in mid to south Wales is as obvious as its interest in north Wales is not. Fernmail of Builth probably shared exactly the same concerns Higham attributes to Mermin – fears of Offa's resurgent Mercia, desire to show ancient Britons in a martial and providential light – but with much better evidence to support his importance to *Historia Brittonum*. It is just another of many examples of how hypercritical assaults on Arthur stand side by side with uncritical acceptance of Dumville's theories.

Making It All Up

To please his patron, whether a particular ruler or Britons in general, the author of *Historia Brittonum* is seen as inserting Arthur into the narrative as a late fifth-century leader of British kings in their wars against the Saxons. It is a distinctive feature of the author's historical vision that, although Britain in the past was ruled by great kings, it was not they who led the fight against the Saxons in the fifth/ sixth centuries. Instead, when Vortigern was the king it was Vortimer who led the battles. When Ambrosius was king among the kings of the Britons (probably) Arthur led the fight and when Mailcunus was the king Outigern fought the English. Why the author wanted to emphasise this is open to many explanations. Perhaps it was specifically intended to imply that lesser-ranked, non-royal figures like Fernmail of Builth were more part of God's plan for the Britons than kings like Mermin.

Higham does not follow this route, convinced as he is that Mermin was the author's patron. He does not explain why the first Saxon-fighting major king is Cadwallon (Bede's Caedwalla), rather than the rulers of Gwynedd of the earlier era. Instead, he gives two reasons why Arthur was 'invented' to fill this role. The first is superficially plausible. *Historia Brittonum* was presenting a providential history of the Britons as Christian Saxon-fighters and the last thing it needed was the introduction of Ambrosius, the 'last of the Romans', muddying the waters. Ambrosius's status as a Roman had been established by Gildas and reinforced by Bede. He would not fit the requirements for a fighting Briton, so a hero with a solidly British name, Arthur, was used to claim the credit instead.

This sounds plausible. An inconvenient Roman leader would hardly prove the point that God worked through the Britons, or that they had responded militarily to the Saxon invasions. Unfortunately for Higham, *Historia Brittonum* does not support such a clear distinction between the Roman Ambrosius and the British Arthur.

In it, Ambrosius claims, once that his father was a consul (one of *Historia's* words for emperor) of the Roman race, a nod to Bede's 'of royal rank and title'. The author knows, from Bede, and ultimately from Gildas, that Ambrosius should be a Roman, but does everything he can to distance himself from that position.

※

Thus Ambrosius's declaration is contradicted by the earlier assertion, essential to the story, that he is the product of a virgin birth to a Welsh woman. He is a native of Maes Elleti in Glywyssing and later appears as a king among the kings of the Britons. In case readers found his name too Roman, it is also given in British form as Embreis Guledig. In short *Historia Brittonum* seems to be bending over backwards to avoid the implication that Ambrosius was a Roman, and never describes him as one, in stark contrast to Gildas and Bede. As a matter of fact, the author is explicit that Ambrosius was not to be thought of as a Roman. He tells us that Vortigern was under pressure from fear of the Picts, the Scots and a Roman invasion, and also by fear of Ambrosius ('*a metu pictorum, scottorumque et a romanico impetu, nec non et a timore ambrosii*' HB 31) as though these are four distinct categories of enemy.

Equally, it is not clear that *Historia Brittonum* thinks that Arthur is a Briton. In common with all the earliest sources, Arthur has no geographical origin. He is not 'Arthur of' anywhere, nor is he linked genealogically with a particular kingdom. Far from concluding automatically from his 'Celtic' name that he was a Briton, a contemporary reader might just as easily conclude he was an Irishman. All the real Dark Age men called Arthur that we know of were Irish or of claimed Irish extraction. Then there is his title '*dux*'. In *Historia Brittonum*, as opposed to Gildas, this is only used to mean one thing, a Roman general. Usually it is used exactly as it is in the battle list, in contrast to the *reges/reguli* of the Britons. If neither Arthur nor *dux* are words applied to Britons, it is surely just as possible that the *Historia* meant 'then Arthur fought against them in those days, with the kings of the *Britons*' rather than '*kings* of the Britons'. The attempt to cast *Historia Brittonum's* Ambrosius and Arthur as contrasting Roman and Briton is too sharply drawn. They seem to typify a combined 'Romano-British' culture, with elements of each. This is precisely what we would expect to find from Gildas, where tyrants with Roman or impeccably Celtic names seem equally culpable of 'barbaric' behaviour.

That is not to say that I completely disagree with Higham. *Historia Brittonum* has contradicted the possible assumption that Ambrosius was the victor at Badon, or indeed fought the Saxons at all, in favour of the figure of Arthur. Why he has done this is a question which needs to be asked, and which may well have its root in the very purpose which impelled the author to write his history. An obvious reason would be that *Historia Brittonum* had access to sources suggesting that Arthur really was the war leader and wanted to set the record straight. In the current academic climate of privileged scepticism, this is of course not a route which Higham follows up.

Higham looks at the overall structure of *Historia Brittonum* and suggests that the actual model the author used in constructing his 'providential' history is the Old Testament. This has an overarching narrative of God directing his chosen people through thick and thin, via prophets and war leaders. Higham argues that this framework is reiterated by explicit parallels between British and Biblical characters, and implicitly through the use of 'sacral' numbers, with resonances which suggest religious linkage. On this model, Arthur owes his position in the text and the military career ascribed to him to the fact that he follows St Patrick. Patrick is cast in the mould of Moses, a stern prophetic leader, guiding his people via miracles and commandments. The parallel between Moses and Patrick is explicitly stated in the text. The *Books of Moses* are followed in the Bible by the *Book of Joshua*, telling the exploits of Moses's young successor, a war leader who by stratagem and force carved out a homeland for the chosen people in the lands of the pagans. Thus, according to Higham, Arthur is Joshua to Patrick's Moses. The parallel is reinforced by the title '*Dux Belli*' used for Joshua and for Arthur, and linked to the sacral number 12 with which both are connected (Higham 2002: 143).

Higham does not believe there is any historical basis to the Arthurian battle list. This implies that the author is more or less free to make up a satisfying narrative at this point to drive home the Biblical analogy. If this is the case, however, it is astonishing how little use he makes of his freedom. *Historia Brittonum* is not an opaque work where the reader must continually read between the lines to understand its sacral purposes. The Arthur section immediately follows 'Four ways in which Patrick is like Moses', so a few ways in which Arthur was like Joshua would not be too much to ask, if the author saw a connection. True, Joshua is associated with the number 12, as can be seen by a cursory reading of the *Book of Joshua*, where the number recurs. All those references, however, deal with the division of the newly conquered land of Canaan between the Twelve Tribes of Israel. The *Historia* never sees Arthur as a divider or distributor of lands; that function is given to Ambrosius.

Joshua's conquests in the Bible are listed and numbered, and they come to 31. If the battle list was created more or less from whole cloth, Arthur could have been given exactly the same number of victories. None of the colourful incidents of Joshua's career have any parallels in the list. His reliance on heroic lieutenants like Caleb is not hinted at – Arthur is the only person described at Guinnion and Badon, especially odd if material about Cai and Arthur's other heroic warriors was already part of the legendary Arthurian background, as Green argues. Although Arthur fights at rivers, he never crosses them dry footed, he doesn't stop the sun or turn it back, he doesn't go round Castellum Guinnion for six days carrying the image of the Virgin and on the seventh day 'the walls come tumblin' down'.

Arthur's title or description, '*Dux Bellorum*' does not appear in the Bible, let alone applied to Joshua. The version '*Dux Belli*', used instead in the Vatican recension of *Historia Brittonum* is once used, in a passing description of Joshua in the *Book of Judges*. Perhaps the writer of the recension did find it there, though it also occurs in Bede's account of the life of St Germanus, treated at length in *Historia Brittonum*. It is difficult to justify basing an argument on it when it does not occur in the Harleian recension, the earliest version of *Historia Brittonum* we have. In contrast the usual title applied to Joshua is *Iudex* 'judge'. Why the *Historia* did not use this clear title is inexplicable, especially as the writer knew it as a title for ancient British rulers. He uses it in Chapter 8; when judges or kings are spoken of they say 'he judged Britain with its three islands'. This is a clear juxtaposition of judges and kings and would have worked perfectly in the battle list, had the writer ever considered the Joshua/Arthur equation. In short, the list of ways in which Arthur is not like Joshua as far longer than the vanishingly small one in which he is.

The idea that the author of *Historia Brittonum* intruded the figure of Arthur into his text to fill a need for a British Joshua raises the question of where did this figure come from in the first place? Higham's answer is that, searching for a superman, the author fixed on a name connected to supernatural or imposing landscape features in his native land. Here we are on firmer ground as we know for certain the figure of Arthur was being used in this way. The *Mirabilia*, the list of the Wonders of Britain, gives the two examples of Carn Cabal and Licat Amr, within the area of interest to the author of the *Historia* (usually assumed to be the author of the *Mirabilia* too) and of Fernmail of Builth. Higham is sensitive to the idea that these landscape features in turn could take their names from a historical figure. He derives the name Arthur from the Roman *gens* or family name 'Artorius' and suggests that perhaps the Roman military commander Lucius Artorius Castus – who had a peripheral connection with Britain – may have had some unrecorded importance which led to his name being assigned to the features (Higham 2002: 96). This is, to say the least, problematic. We know Lucius Artorius Castus existed, proved by inscriptional evidence, but we know absolutely nothing to suggest to us that his name should be preserved and mythologised in the Welsh Marches over 700 years. He seems a far less likely candidate than a late fifth-century warlord fighting against the Saxons in the border area to have given his name to these features but this simple suggestion is one which Higham refuses to even entertain.

Concepts of Arthur

Thomas Green, in his book *Concepts of Arthur* (2007: 204–5), accepts many of Higham's contentions and specifically that Arthur was placed in the late-fifth century as a Saxon fighter only by the author of *Historia Brittonum*. He offers a different possible source for Arthur, namely mythology. Green argues, perhaps strangely, for the essential historicity of the Arthurian battle list. Though he takes issue with some of the battles, he accepts the reality of a period of warfare between the kings of the Britons and the Saxons. He uses material from the battle list, such as the multiple battles in the Linnuis region, to strengthen his contention that his local Lincolnshire was a site of such warfare, albeit victories assigned to

Ambrosius or some other proto-Arthur. It is the name and figure of Arthur to which he primarily objects.

Green follows Koch (1997) in suggesting that some of the Welsh poems which refer to King Arthur are very much older than the late thirteenth or fourteenth-century manuscripts in which they are preserved, some of them even pre-dating *Historia Brittonum*. While it seems to me, and to most pro-Arthurians, that dating, as Koch does, the reference to Arthur in *The Gododdin* earlier than *Historia Brittonum* and closer to Arthur's own supposed time, considerably strengthens the case for his existence, Green thinks just the reverse. For him, the milieu of the poems – impossibly powered supermen, monsters and animated trees – is in fact the original context. He does not accept the derivation from 'Artorius' but instead connects the '*arth*' element of Arthur's name, meaning 'bear' with the well-attested Celtic bear cult. Arthur was a bear-related god or culture hero, whom the author of *Historia Brittonum* euhemerised into a human warlord and placed in the late fifth century for the sorts of historiographical reasons which Higham advances. Both scholars maintain that this positioning of Arthur in the late fifth or early sixth century was a decision of this author alone, and that all subsequent references to Arthur living in this period derive ultimately from *Historia Brittonum*.

Unlike many anti-Arthurians, who single out Arthur for special treatment, Green at least tries to be even-handed in his charge that historicised mythological figures have been used to pad out the history of Dark Age Britain. Hengist and Horsa, the characters Bede gives to the leaders of the first Saxon settlers in Gildas, are for Green (2007: 205) 'dioscuric horse-gods who were historicised' and (ibid: 9) 'in fact totemic horse gods'. Using material from the continent he argues that they were originally 'protective horse-heads … carved above the crossing gables of houses'. The idea that Hengist and Horsa were 'originally' protective roof supporters who 'later' became euhemerised into real humans, will not stand up to chronological scrutiny. The source of this is that 'in Schleswig-Holstein in the nineteenth century horse-head finials on roofs, which were regarded as protective figures, might be known by the names "hengist" and "hors"' (Yorke 1993: 47 quoting Ward). That is a 1500 year gap in evidence, compared with the 300 years before the Saxons are named as real humans by Bede. Over 1000 of the intervening years included transmission of the Hengist and Horsa story in continental sources of various genres. Schleswig-Holstein stood on the borders of Hanover, whose rulers for 100 years up to the collection of the roof finial folklore had also been kings of Britain. This coincided with the collection and transmission of material about the Anglo-Saxon settlements. Considering the weight of source scepticism placed on *Historia Brittonum*, the uncritical acceptance by Yorke and Green of nineteenth-century folklore as a purer, less tainted source is taking double standards to the extreme.

Green tries to draw Bede into his scepticism about these characters, which is not really supportable. Bede thinks, for instance, there is an inscribed monument to Horsa still visible in Kent. What he doubts is whether these Jutish characters are the leaders of the three Saxon boats (from Gildas). He may also doubt, in the context, that Hengist is really the ancestor of the Oiscings, the contemporary kings of Kent. He euhemerises Woden as an ancestor of current kings. One of the few things Bede knew about the fifth-century barbarian invasions was that (I:14) the Huns were led by two brother kings, Blaedla and Attila, and he may have assumed this was a usual practice. Needless to say Bede's references to them as historical figures predate evidence of their use for carved gables, and Hengist turns up alone in *Beowulf*.

Even if I was prepared to concede that Hengist and Horsa drew their names from tutelary horse deities, this hardly justifies writing them off as non-historical. Incorporating divine elements in names seems a standard Germanic practice. Many of Bede's Northumbrian kings, such as Oswald and Oswy, who as far as I know no-one has doubted as historical, have the even more blatantly pagan 'Os' meaning a type of pagan god, incorporated in their 'Christian' names.

Yorke (1993: 46) was on surer ground arguing that it was common to Germanic tradition to ascribe the formation of new political units to founders who travelled in pairs of kinsmen in small numbers of ships, either of divine descent or divinised after success in battle. The Lombards were founded by the brothers Raus and Raptus, given success in battle by Woden. Even this tradition may simply have resulted in a doubling up of a single leader. Hengist appears without his brother in *Beowulf* and the *Finnsburgh* fragment and the same character seems to be the *princeps* Ansehis who brought the Saxons to Britain in the Ravenna cosmography (Brooks 1989: 59).

I agree that *Historia Brittonum*'s account of the fifth century includes much which is clearly legendary, not to say mythological material. Unfortunately it is nearly all attached to the figure of Ambrosius. Yet Green accepts Ambrosius not merely as historical, but aggrandises him as the victor of Badon and the Lincolnshire 'Arthur'. There is nothing in *Historia Brittonum* to make a modern reader think that Arthur is mythical and everything to make him suppose that Ambrosius is. Only the fact that Ambrosius is named by Gildas proves that *Historia Brittonum*'s picture is based on a real character properly located in history.

Green falls back on the counter argument: Ambrosius is named in *De Excidio Britanniae*, therefore he existed, Arthur is not so he didn't. This argument from silence proves nothing at all. No women are named by Gildas. Nobody from the generation of Ambrosius's children is named. We hear of the good king who was Vortiporius's father, the uncle of Maglocunus, the fathers (!) of Aurelius who died young in civil war. In Gildas's present, he does not name the two youths killed by Constantine or the handful of good rulers, at least one of whom is more powerful than Maglocunus. In the past he does not name the Proud Tyrant or Ambrosius's father, important though they are in his scheme of history, nor the tyrants who succeed Maximus, let alone the Saxon leaders. These are all people whose names we can feel sure Gildas knew, but he preferred not to name them. In the whole of his book only eight Britons are named. Five are contemporary tyrants and three are saints martyred in the great persecution. This is simply not a book teeming with named individuals therefore one cannot infer that anyone not named in it did not exist.

The medieval fiction that Gildas deliberately left out Arthur's name because of a quarrel is wide of the mark. It would be harder to explain its presence if he had included it. The names are given only when they specifically relate to the present. The three saints are named because in the present Britons can't get to their shrines. The tyrants are named because of their contemporary impact. Why is Ambrosius named? For exactly the same reason, to castigate his present day grandchildren for not following their grandfather's example. I suspect that the grandsons are named, among the tyrants, with the similarly named Aurelius being the most likely.

Central to Green's argument is the idea that the Welsh Arthurian poems are of ancient origin. The three which most inform his view are *The Gododdin*, with its brief reference to the hero Guaurddur not being Arthur, *Pa Gur* in which Arthur, challenged by the doorkeeper Gleuluid, reveals the fantastical group of warriors who accompany him, and *Cat Godeu*, a battle between trees, presumably magically animated, in which Arthur is fleetingly mentioned. Green accepts that these poems pre-date *Historia Brittonum* and that it is from such a background that the author has drawn and historicised his Arthur character.

The debate about the priority of the poems has raged for over a century (Jackson in Loomis 1959) but usually it has been pro-Arthurians who have wanted them to represent a closer link to the Dark Age Arthur. I have generally been wary of accepting these arguments, since I can imagine the pressures which would incline a historian engaged in long and painstaking work on obscure Welsh texts, to err to the feeling that they are early and important rather than late and derivative.

To be fair, I also accept Koch's early dating of the Arthurian verse in *Y Gododdin* and the idea that it assumes the same story as *Historia Brittonum*, that Arthur is a character from before the Cattraeth expedition in the (?) sixth century, and that fighting many foes at sites such as Roman cities are common to both Arthur and Guaurddur.

It certainly seems true that *Historia Brittonum* is aware of a pre-existing stratum of poetic material. The *Mirabilia* indicate this but more so the reference to the famous British poets working in the generation after Arthur. Those he names include Neirin, believed in the middle ages, if not earlier, to be the author of *Y Gododdin*, and Taliesin, supposed author of *Cat Godeu*. Although Green makes a conventional distinction between the 'real' Taliesin who wrote works praising sixth-century ruler Urien of Rheged, and the author of *Cat Godeu* and other mythological poems, accepting the earliest dates for the latter pushes them far closer together, certainly to a point where *Historia Brittonum* could know them as a single body of work.

Man and Superman

It surprises me to find *The Gododdin* reference used to support a mythological Arthur. The poem has no obvious mythological component. It appears to refer to a historical event and the characters in it are written of as though they are ordinary humans. Arthur would be unique in the poem as a mythological hero. Green argues that *The Gododdin* reference concerns the mythical Arthur by following Oliver Padel's idea that its comparison between Guaurddur and Arthur is between man and superman. 'Arthur is implicitly portrayed as superhuman, not human, in *Y Gododdin*', (2007: 14) 'a military "superhero", someone whose heights of valour not even a man who killed 300 could compare' 'a "superhero" to whom not even the greatest living warrior could compare' (2007: 51, quoting Koch). 'Arthur is presented as an unrivalled paragon of martial valour and is thus used to form a highly unusual comparison by rendering explicitly inferior the honourand of the *awdl*.'

Putting aside that the only 'superhuman' feat mentioned in the verse is the slaying of 300 men, attributed to Guaurddur, you can only wonder what the poet thought he was doing by making the comparison. Certainly there are poems in which the writer compares the person being honoured to a mighty hero of history and legend, but I cannot think of a single example where the writer compares the person being honoured *unfavourably*. This would be a peculiar 'compliment' and never occurs elsewhere in *Y Gododdin*. I think the poem can be read in other and more plausible ways.

The most obvious reading is that Arthur is someone you may have heard of, while the equally impressive Guaurddur is someone you haven't. Guaurddur fought and died in a superlative way the poet celebrates, even though to the listener he is not a universally famous character. It almost goes without saying that Arthur was famous. *Historia Brittonum*, *Pa Gur* and *Y Gododdin* expect you to have heard of him without prompting. Geoffrey of Monmouth and the inscription from his tomb at Glastonbury both state his fame explicitly.

It may be that Arthur's fame rests on his superhuman military prowess, but this isn't necessarily the aspect *Y Gododdin* wants the listener to recall. After all, the men honoured in the poem are all warriors but only Guaurddur is compared with Arthur. Guaurddur is notable for other things than his fighting ability. He is an extremely generous man. If we can include later material in the picture of what constituted the concept of Arthur, then Arthur is also famed for his generosity. In the Triads he is more generous than the three generous men. In the *Life of St Illtud* the saint is attracted by his generosity. We don't have to assume that Guaurddur is less generous than Arthur. He may be just as generous, but from more limited resources. There may be some black humour here, as Guaurddur generously serves the ravens with ample food.

In *Culhwch and Olwen*, we find out that Guaurddur is a hunchback. Although, in looks, height and physical stamina Guaurddur can't compete, in the extremity of battle he takes down 300 men. All of these are I think are more supportable than the idea the comparison is an inherently impossible one between man and superman.

The large number of enemies killed by Arthur, by Guaurddur or by the early Saxon leaders of the Anglo-Saxon Chronicle would not have evoked scepticism in their readers. They were part of the standard repertoire of feats that heroic but real warriors were expected to accomplish. The Bible had plenty of examples for comparison. The idea that Arthur must be mythical because he has killed 960 men 'single-handedly' is no more than an anachronistic modern gloss. This can be demonstrated with reference to the entirely contemporary writings of Sidonius Apollinaris. Sidonius was the Bishop of Clermont Ferrand in Gaul. A Gallo-Roman aristocrat, he wrote poems to celebrate public events and copious letters. In 474 Clermont was besieged by several thousand Goths. The situation would have been desperate had not a young noble called Ecdicius come to the aid of the citizens. Afterwards Sidonius wrote to Ecdicius to thank him. He relived the noble's incredible exploit how, with a '*comitatus*' of just 18 mounted companions 'fewer than your table normally has guests' he was able to cut his way through 'thousands' of Goths and put them to flight without any loss (Sidonius. Apollinaris Epist 3.3.3-4).

> at the mere mention of your name and the sight of your person a well-seasoned army was so utterly astounded that the enemy generals [*duces*] in their amazement could not realise how many were their followers and how few were yours. The whole army was at once withdrawn to the brow of a precipitous hill, and, though previously employed in a storming assault, was not deployed for an encounter after sighting you.

Sidonius then goes on to recount the exuberant welcome given to Ecdicius from the perspective of an eyewitness, as indeed he was. Some of the relieved citizens:

> kissed away the dust which covered you, others caught the bridle that was thick with blood and foam; some turned back the pommels of the horses saddles, which were bathed in sweat, others, when you wished to free your head from the skull piece of your helmet, unclasped the bands of pliant steel; some entangled themselves in disentangling the fastenings of your greaves, some counted the dents on the edges of swords blunted with slaughter, others by forcing in

their envious fingers measured the holes made by blade and point amid the rings of the cuirasses.

One hundred years later, Gregory of Tours thought this was insufficiently heroic and (2.24) reduced the number of Ecdicius's companions to 10.

This should teach us to be cautious about dismissing Arthur's feats as 'superhuman'. Doubtless hyperbole played its part in Sidonius's letter but the siege and the relief by Ecdicius and his horsemen were facts and their achievements no less 'fantastic' than those attributed to Arthur in *Historia Brittonum*.

14

LOST IN THE WOODS

The presumption that Arthur is essentially mythological has its most serious repercussion in the battle list. As we have seen, most of the battle sites are obscure and subject to various interpretations, based on whatever regional theories the author in question holds. One battle site however is pretty clear. It is the battle the author of *Historia Brittonum* takes pains to give in both the Latin and Welsh form – the Battle in the Caledonian Wood. This is, almost indisputably, in Scotland, most likely in the forest region between the Antonine and Hadrian's Walls.

The author tells us the battle is '*in silva Celidonis*' – 'in the Caledonian Wood', then adds his translation, a gloss as it is technically called, '*id est Cat Coit Celidon*' 'the battle of the wood of Celidon'. Why he does this is not clear. Many of the other battles could do with being glossed in this way. The most reasonable inference is that he expects his readers to have heard of Cat Coit Celidon – that it has some degree of fame.

In classical times the Caledones had been one of the principle tribes north of the firths of Forth and Clyde. The Roman General Agricola fought against them. By the fifth century the tribal name was no longer in use. The northern tribes had become known collectively as Picts. As a place name, Celidon seems to have been creeping southwards and seems to indicate the forested area between Hadrian's Wall and the Antonine Wall. However vague this might be – the chances of actually pinpointing a battle site in this wide area are remote – it at least shows that the *Historia* intended Arthur's theatre of operations to extend far from South Wales, where his wonders are located.

For *Historia Brittonum* it is obvious why Arthur would be fighting Saxons in this area. Hengist's son Octha has come down from the north so battles should be expected there. Archaeology, however is not able to detect Saxon settlement in the area until later, linked with the establishment of the Anglian Kingdom of Bernicia. It is possible that *Historia Brittonum* is wrong. The Celidonian Wood may be a battle of a later era attributed to Arthur by accident or design. Or not all his campaigns were against the Saxons. Although Gildas rails against the Picts and the

Scots, with the arrival of the Saxons they drop completely out of his narrative. Is it credible that such a threat simply vanished? We would surely expect wars with these longstanding foes to continue.

My view is that there is no reason to look for evidence of settlement to confirm military activity. If Arthur battled against a marauding band or thwarted an invasion then his victory by itself would account for the lack of settlement evidence. The history of Britain is full of invasions, from Caesar to Harald Hardrada which would not yield evidence of settlement. If Harold had beaten the Normans in 1066 there would have been no evidence of their presence in Hastings and accounts of the Duke venturing so far from his stamping grounds of Brittany and the Vexin would seem equally outlandish.

Although a physical location for the Battle of the Caledonian Wood is perfectly plausible for a historical Arthur to have fought in, Thomas Green takes it as the clearest example in the battle list of his contention that Arthur is a god. He believes this battle to be the same as the mythological battle of animated trees in the poem *Cat Godeu*. He argues this by the process of creeping certainty, by which the proposition is re-enforced by continual repetition. First he asserts that (2007: 64-65) Godeu is the animated trees of 'the famed *Coed Celyddon*', (quoting Bromwich 1978: 540). From the possibility that the fighting trees are from Celidon, he is able to state: 'it is generally agreed that the trees magically animated for Arthur's battle were those of *Coed Celyddon*, "the Caledonian Forest".' Therefore this is Arthur's battle 'which is mentioned in no other "historical" source' (2007: 67). By the end of the book, it has become (2007: 207) 'given that Cat Godeu is an Arthurian battle which looks to have involved the trees of Coed Celyddon'.

Those equations are possibilities, not 'givens'. No Arthurian positivist would join the 'general agreement' that the Battle in the Caledonian Wood involved animated trees. It is conjecture only that Arthur has anything to do with *Cat Godeu*. There is just one reference to him in the poem, as someone to whom druids prophesy. The argument that no other historical source mentions the Battle of the Caledonian Wood means nothing at all. If *Historia Brittonum*'s battle lists are dismissed then we have no names for the battles of the British resistance other than the siege of Badon Hill; we would only have Gildas as a source. But Gildas tells us that the Britons held out in forests, that the first Saxons were settled to defend against attacks by the Picts, and that there were battles other than Badon. This is as good as anything we are going to get from the period. Battle names given in the Anglo-Saxon Chronicle cannot provide support. They post-date those in *Historia Brittonum*, and the chronicler knows nothing of wars in Scotland during the period.

If the Battle of the Caledonian Wood and *Cat Godeu* are really the same, it is a puzzle why the author of *Historia Brittonum* didn't say so. He could just as easily have written '*in Silva Celidonis, id est Cat Godeu*' if he wanted to make that connection. The equation of Celidon with Goddeu is extremely contentious and is not supported by evidence; it has the effect of robbing the battle list of its one certain geographical anchor point, rendering the rest of the list more hazy.

Arthur the God

I agree with Green that the reference to Arthur in *Y Gododdin* harks back to an established body of tradition. I take the simple view that Arthur is a character not unlike the other Dark Age (sixth-century?) Britons fighting the Saxons commemorated in the poem, and that the body of tradition is exemplified in the *Historia Brittonum* battle list. For Green, both *Y Gododdin* and the battle list hark back to an earlier stratum, evidenced by poems like *Pa Gur* and *Cat Godeu*, in which Arthur was actually a Celtic god.

It is Dumville's dictum that history can only be written from contemporary sources. Thus a work such as *Historia Brittonum* can only, as far as he is concerned, be used as evidence for the early ninth century, irrespective of the fact that it purports to preserve the history of an earlier era. This is quite a depressing reflection of the historian's craft. Is it really true that in 300 years' time Dumville's work will only be valuable in as far as it allows future historians to find out about the silver jubilee of Elizabeth II, and the origins of the winter of discontent and the rise of Margaret Thatcher? The history of Alexander the Great would be very meagre if we could not construct a narrative from works written 300 years after his death.

Green follows Dumville's presumption but in my view opens up even more problems with his contention that Arthur was a Celtic god. My theory, that Arthur was historical, supposes only that a few names of people who flourished in a period of 40 years at the turn of the fifth/sixth centuries, a period when written sources are few in number, left no contemporary trace but may have been somehow preserved over 200–300 years, reappearing in the first written works we have to cover their period – Bede and *Historia Brittonum*. Hardly, I think, an incredible or even unlikely proposition.

Green, on the other hand, would have us suppose that the names of British gods somehow passed through 300 years when Britain was part of a literate pagan society, which left us abundant evidence of the names of its gods, only to emerge 400–500 years later in the self-same texts. The only way Green can make this plausible is to suggest there was a deliberate taboo against the use of the name of the mythological Arthur, only broken by the Irish in the seventh century (Green 2007: 196).

Green argues that the name Arthur derives from the Welsh word '*Arth*' (bear) and therefore harks back to a pagan bear cult. That may or may not be the case, but it is dubious that this has any bearing on its use in the fifth or sixth century. Are the dog names of Cuneglassus, Caninus and Maglocunus (to say nothing of

Cynric, Cynon and many others) indicative of a dog cult and what would it mean if they were?

The example of Maglocunus makes it abundantly clear that quasi-divine names did exist outside mythological contexts in fifth/sixth-century Britain. We know for an absolute fact that there was a Romano-British deity named Apollo Cunomaglus. He was worshipped at Nettleton Shrub, Wiltshire, where an altar bearing his name was discovered. Yet we also know for certain that an actual Christian ruler of Britain, a former monk, went by the all but identical name of Maglocunus. There is no indication he abandoned his faith when he left his monastery. Gildas is explicit that the tyrants do not sacrifice to pagan gods, though he is happy to accuse them of just about everything else. The only one he calls 'bear', Cuneglassus, is surrounded by Christian holy men.

This shows how dangerous it is to argue simply from derivations of British names. If Maglocunus had stayed a monk, or lived a life of private virtue, Gildas would never have named him. 'Mailcunus' might then have appeared for the first time in *Historia Brittonum* as a great king of Britain just after Arthur, and as part of a linked series of Arthurian entries in *Annales Cambriae*. I don't doubt that Green would then have used his name and the proven existence of Apollo Cunomaglus to put him down as 'mythological', possibly connected with Cei's dog-headed adversaries in *Pa Gur* and his cousin Cinglas (Blue Dog) in the Harleian Genealogies. Here, though, we have proof that a mythological name does not prove a mythological character.

Argument from names is, unfortunately, one Green frequently employs. Arthur's wife is stated categorically to be a figure of mythology solely on the basis of her name. The first time she is mentioned (2007: 30) she is 'Arthur's fairy wife Gwenhwyvar (sacred enchantress)'. Then (ibid: 56) 'Gwenhwyvar (white/sacred fairy enchantress)', then (ibid: 59) 'Gwenhwyvar (white/sacred/otherworld fairy/ enchantress)' and finally (ibid: 62) 'Arthur's fairy wife Gwenhwyvar.'

Now, Guinevere is never treated as a fairy enchantress in any source of any sort whatsoever. She appears in stories by writers who were happy to make Arthur's sister an enchantress called Morgan le Fay, have his best knight brought up by fairies in an underwater castle, have his arms and armour made by elves in Avalon and have him guided by a prophetic enchanter and a Lady of the Lake. Despite this, Guinevere is only ever treated as a real human being.

It is true, and has been argued since the early days of modern Arthurian scholarship, (e.g. Loomis 1927), that Guinevere figures in stories such as her abductions to the otherworld and perhaps her giant father Ogfran which have a mythological basis. This is by no means the same as proving she is at base a 'sacred otherworld fairy enchantress'. Gildas and Owain son of Urien appear in those stories too, without being mythological.

Guinevere is treated in this way by Green because she is tarred by association with Arthur, already assumed to be mythological, but also on the more dubious grounds (in which Green follows Ford 1983) that the name element '*Guin*' is a pointer towards an otherworldly origin. This is hardly supported in the numerous names of Celtic deities we have from inscriptions or classical sources. And even if it were true that otherworldly items have a tendency to be described as '*Guin*', it cannot be true that all things so described are otherworldly. It is just a Welsh word for fair or white and appears frequently in the names of real historical characters.

What Sort of Book is *Historia Brittonum*?

By focusing on the Arthurian battle list and associated material, Green creates a very misleading picture of the nature of *Historia Brittonum*. He gives the impression that this is the work of an arch-rationaliser, who misses out mythological or legendary features to create a more plausible historical version of Arthur than reliance on *Cat Godeu*, *Pa Gur* or the Book of Joshua would have given him. I see nothing of this. Before he gets to Arthur, *Historia Brittonum* presents a fifth-century Britain where mystical things often occur. Examples of this include the Tyrant Benlli's castle being destroyed overnight by fire from heaven, the building material for Vortigern's tower disappearing three times due to the prophetic worms buried underneath it, Ambrosius Aurelianus being conceived by a virgin, Vortigern being killed when, after three days of prayer, St Germanus called down fire from heaven which completely destroyed his fortress (or he was sucked into the ground) and St Patrick talking to an angel in a burning bush. And these happen to characters, generally, that *Historia Brittonum* has encountered in fully rational guise, in Bede. Why he couldn't think of anything similar to do with a 'Brittonic Superhero' or Joshua figure is extraordinary and a question which both Green and Higham avoid answering. The author even claims to have witnessed wonders for himself. It defies belief that, given a pre-existing body of mythological Arthurian material including (at the very least) magic battling trees, voyages to the otherworld and a cast of supermen he was able to make such limited use of them.

If the band of supermen led by Arthur in *Pa Gur* was an integral feature of Arthurian mythology, as Green argues, what happened to them in *Historia Brittonum*? Instead of anonymous 'kings of the Britons' *Historia Brittonum* could have included any number of Arthur's companions. *Historia Brittonum* is no Gildas, reticent of including names. On the contrary, all the indications are that the author grasped at names wherever he could. In a far from exhaustive list, he names (from Bede) Vortigern, Hengist and Horsa, Germanus, Octha and Ambrosius, and adds from his own sources Benlli, Catel Durnluc, Guoyrancgon of Kent, Ebissa (Hengist's cousin), Guorthemir, Cateyrn, Pascent, Faustus and St Patrick, not to mention the ancestors including the mythological ones of Hengist and Fernmail of Builth. He even names Vortigern's interpreter, Ceretic. That is, in a few pages, more than twice the number Gildas names in a whole book. We are looking at a man seemingly determined to include just about every name he knows. Why not Cei? Why not Bedwyr? If they are Arthur's inseparable companions, why has he separated them here? Green usefully includes a table showing where Arthur's companions are mentioned, (2007: 133) which demonstrates absolutely that there is no connection between *Historia Brittonum*, *Annales Cambriae* and the concept of a mythical Arthurian warband. There are no names, other than Arthur, in common between the sources and the concept is foreign to the 'historical' ones, unless we are to suppose that the 'kings of the Britons' are these people euhemerised, a great leap considering that the kings of the Britons did fight back against the Saxons even if, in Green's theory, Arthur did not.

Is Arthur Unique?

The big question is whether *Historia Brittonum* is unique in its treatment of Arthur. If the author generally takes mythological characters and places them in spurious historical contexts to give weight to his historiographical aims, then the idea that this is what happened with Arthur would carry a lot of weight. If, on the contrary, the general practice of the author is that exemplified in his treatment of Ambrosius – mythological stories are attached to historical characters properly located in time – this would give more credence to a historical Arthur position.

There are certainly legendary or mythological characters in the early chapters; Brutus/Britto who gave his name to Britain, characters from the stories of Aeneas and Noah, Partholon, Nemet and Mil, from the Irish *Book of Invasions*, and so on. But these characters are in the expected mythological era. Once the Romans arrive, we meet Julius, Dolabella, Claudius, Constantinus, Maximus and so forth, all clearly drawn from Roman history. Lucius could be one of the mythological Lluchs, but we know he is a misplaced king of Edessa the author found in Bede. Likewise Belinus is definitely a mythological character, worshipped as Apollo in Gaul, but we know *Historia Brittonum* has mistakenly detached his name from that of King Cunobelinus.

Even if Hengist and Horsa are 'dioscuric horse gods' plucked from their proper context supporting roofs in Schleswig-Holstein, *Historia Brittonum* has no reason to think that. Bede had already historicised them. Did Bede do the same with Vortigern? His name is so plausible that it is used as a convenient short hand for the Proud Tyrant – an apparently historical character – in Gildas. But was Vortigern real? Did Bede find the name in the mythology of the dioscuric horse gods? Did he find it separately, in its own mythology, perhaps in a context of disappearing towers, wizards, prophetic worms and virgin births? Did he fuse those mythologies or did someone earlier than him provide this unique insight into British mythology?

Disregarding the question of how Bede got Vortigern's name, what about *Historia Brittonum*? Does *Historia Brittonum* have Guorthigirn and his wizards in a mythological package which he attached to the similarly named Vortigern to give him a fifth-century context or have he and Bede latched onto the same mythological character, *Historia Brittonum* agreeing with Bede's historical context?. What about Guorthemir? He shares with Arthur the fact he is a previously unattested Saxon fighter, with tutelary power over the island. They share the motif of having a given number of battles – four in Guorthemir's case (Higham would probably see this as 'suspiciously sacral'), the same proportion for names to numbers in Arthur's battle list. Is Guorthemir a mythological figure plucked into a historical context or is he part of the Vortigern or Hengist and Horsa mythology? Benli? Catel? These characters are part of a foundation myth of Powys, certainly, but have they come to *Historia Brittonum* as mythological characters who he slips into the time of Germanus for his own purposes, or are they already assigned to that time?

Green does not answer any of these questions. By concentrating on the academic hate figure of King Arthur, he avoids the implication of his theory. To engage with it would be to acknowledge that the author has access to a vast amount of hitherto unsuspected Celtic mythology and fortuitously makes the same decisions as to where to place it in real history as Bede does. The argument loses all credibility once the context of Arthur is considered. Ambrosius, Patrick, Octha and Mailcunus come to *Historia Brittonum* from external sources which have already located them in the fifth/sixth centuries. The mythological components of the English genealogies are attached to characters of the sixth and seventh centuries mainly contextualised by Bede.

After Arthur there are two more fighters against the Saxons who just might be mythological characters. These are Outigirn and Urbgen. They are treated similarly to each other, with many of the same words, and to Arthur. Outigirn might have featured in mythological songs by any of the famous poets named by the *Historia* as flourishing in his time, but we have no evidence on this.

Double Standards in the Dark Ages – Urien Rheged

Frequently it strikes me just how unjust the treatment of Arthur is. Other characters from *Historia Brittonum* allocated to the same time period are not only given the benefit of the doubt, but are often made significant components of historical theories. In *The Reign of Arthur* I gave the example of how the *Historia's* claim that Maglocunus (from Gildas) was an ancient King of Gwynedd is accepted unthinkingly by writers who will not even deign to put Arthur in their indexes. An even worse double standard is that applied to the *Historia's* character Urbgen, more familiar from the later form of his name, Urien.

Urien, in Welsh legend, appears alongside various characters who (to say the least) share names with mythological figures. He is husband of Modron (the Celtic deity Matrona) who in turn is mother of Mabon, the deity Apollo Maponus and a leading character in a heavily mythological section of *Culhwch and Olwen*. If this were not bad enough, Urien is also brother of both Arawn, ruler of the otherworld and the god Lleu. These characters are placed in pre-Roman times in the *Mabinogion*. Urien's son owns of a flock of ravens at war with the magical men of gigantic Arthur. In the romances, 'Uriens' is Morgan le Fay's husband and hails from the enchanted land of Gore, scene of one of Guinevere's abductions.

Urien/Urbgen immediately fails the Bede test. Bede had never heard of him or the attack on the Northumbrian island of Metcaud attributed to him by *Historia Brittonum*. Urbgen is given superhuman qualities 'his military skill and generalship surpassed that of all the other kings' (HB 63). Most of his story shares words with the battles of Guorthimir, Arthur and Outigirn. The phrase '*tribus diebus et tribus noctibus*' 'for three days and three nights' which Higham and Green use to demonstrate the borrowings of *Annales Cambriae* from *Historia Brittonum* occurs in the account of Urbgen's career, not in the Arthurian section. Urbgen and his sons are shown besieging the Island of Metcaud for three days and three nights, when an evil character called Morcant slits his throat. I have absolutely no doubt that if this material had been applied to Arthur in the chapter 56 battle list, Green would have pounced on it as clear evidence of a mythological attack on the otherworld given spurious historical placing.

Despite this overwhelming evidence, Urien/Urbgen gets off very lightly in the historical vs mythological debate. I've never read a *Concepts of Urbgen* or *Urgben*, *Mythmaking and History*, which argues he was a mythological character pulled randomly into the affairs of sixth-century Northumbria by *Historia Brittonum*. He escapes all of this because he appears in some of Taliesin's poems. The circular reasoning here is evident. If Taliesin's poems about Urien are separated from all the others, such as those featuring animated trees, on the grounds that Taliesin and Urien were real characters then inevitably both characters look more historical. This is exactly the process that I and other Arthurian positivists take and Green attacks so vehemently – if you separate historical from legendary material then the historical material looks more historical, but is there any warrant for making such a separation in the first place?

The potential early dating for some of the mythological Taliesin material which Green supports means that, regardless of any possible historical kernel at the heart of the Urbgen story, by 830 the Taliesin corpus was already leaning heavily towards the mythological material. *Historia Brittonum*, if Green's view of his practice is right, might have just seen Urien as yet another unlocated mythological superman and put him in his book where it suited his historiographical purposes.

Unlike Arthur, Urbgen/Urien really is a character adrift in time and space. The Taliesin poems suggest that Taliesin and Urien are contemporaries, or Taliesin is slightly younger, post-dating his death and aware of his son's military career. The supposed contemporaneity between poet and subject is not to be wondered at. Poems attributed to Taliesin and Neirin, not to mention anonymous ones, show Welsh poets as adept at thinking themselves into different historical periods. *Historia Brittonum*, though, thinks that Taliesin flourished a good 30 years before the death of Urbgen. Geoffrey of Monmouth thinks Urianus is even earlier, a (younger?) contemporary of Uther Pendragon in the fifth century. He also doubles up as the name of a prehistoric king of Britain, reigning between 390–55BC and as Urbgennius, one of Arthur's nobles. Urbgennius is from Bath, and Urianus from a northern Mureifensium (Moray?). The poems think he is from Reget, and that he was the lord of Catraeth. Reget was not a place Bede or *Historia Brittonum* were confident in locating. Bede had heard of Catterick, but his construction of the history of Northumberland makes it impossible that Urien was lord of it in the late sixth century.

Annales Cambriae, for all its supposed reliance on *Historia Brittonum*, knew nothing of Urbgen's military career. Instead it claims Run son of Urbgen baptised Edwin of Northumbria 110 (?) years after Badon. This supports *Historia Brittonum*'s chronology for Urbgen, but contradicts Bede's version of the event.

I have no problem with the idea that Urbgen was a real sixth-century king. I do think, though, that his historical reality is as weak (or as strong) as Arthur's. I don't see any merit in assuming (as Green does) that Urbgen 'really' fought the Battle of Brewyn as Taliesin claimed. If Bregomion and Brewyn are the same battle (quite a weak suggestion) then 'Taliesin' was just as capable of attaching a mythical battle associated with Arthur to Urien as the Vatican recension was of doing the opposite.

Personally I do not believe that Urbgen was a mythological character. He is, though, the only other possibility in *Historia Brittonum* for arguing that a 'mythological character' has been assigned a pseudo-historical role in the sixth-century wars between Briton and Saxon.

Was Arthur Historical?

If Arthur were symptomatic of *Historia Brittonum*'s general practice of plucking mythological characters from their fictional context and placing them, according to whim, in the early Dark Ages, then Green would have a strong case. However, if, as it seems, Arthur would have to be a unique instance of this practice and that elsewhere *Historia Brittonum* has only embellished the stories of characters already located in the fifth/sixth century, then the case becomes much harder to argue.

My own view is that *Historia Brittonum* takes characters already established in time and embroiders them into its narrative. No matter how wild and legendary its stories about them, we can generally pin down the historical origins. Vortigern,

Hengist, Ambrosius and Germanus all have their chronological position established in Bede.

Granted, Arthur is almost unique in having folkloric stories about landscape features attached to him, but the catch is in the 'almost'. The other person is Illtud, and I have never seen anyone argue that Illtud is a famous superhuman character, capriciously made a cleric in sixth-century Wales to satisfy *Historia Brittonum's* desire for a providential history of the Britons.

The implication of the mythological Arthur theory as argued by Higham and Green is that a connection between Arthur and the fifth/sixth centuries is a product of *Historia Brittonum* alone, followed by all subsequent writers. This is severely weakened by the fact there is no alternative chronological placing for Arthur. *Historia Brittonum* is, however popular, not the final arbiter of history. Just because the author decided to locate his mythical character in the fifth/sixth century should leave it possible that other historical placements for him would exist. Green's own research demonstrates that attempts to historicised the legendary Finn MacCool by Irish writers resulted in him being placed in various periods. The only alternative time period for Arthur Green can come up with is a piece of 1881 folklore about Arthur fighting Danes in Cornwall. This is simply a mistake and no more a variant location in time than Malory having the knights of the Round Table fight the Saracens in the Holy Land. Arthur is either fixed in the fifth/sixth century or nowhere. This would argue for a prevailing assumption that Arthur lived in that period, rather than one created from whole cloth by *Historia Brittonum*.

The only counter evidence is Arthur's association with Manawyddan Son of Llyr in *Pa Gur*. Manawyddan really does seem to be a Celtic deity, as evidenced by his appearance in Irish legends as Manannan son of Lir. The Four Branches of the *Mabinogi* place him to just before the reign of Cassivellaunus (the adversary of Julius Caesar?). I think this is far more plausibly explained by bards giving long life to a heroic semi-divine character, so that he could interact with the historic Arthur, rather than that Arthur and the rest of his men have been shifted forward in time from an originally pre-Roman context.

In conclusion, while the idea that a substantial, coherent and early mass of legendary material underlies the general picture of Arthur emerging in the early middle ages has merit, I do not think that the contention that *Historia Brittonum* historicised this figure our of whole cloth is supported by the evidence. Far more plausible is the view, general until the 1970s, that Arthur was a real character to whom legends of various types gradually adhered.

15

THE SIEGE OF BADON HILL

One of the most puzzling omissions from the pantheon of Arthurian sites is that of his greatest battle, the siege of Badon Hill. This is particularly odd, given that of all the sites associated with King Arthur, it is the only one which all experts agree is real. Gildas started off his book by outlining the historical subjects which he would be covering. He would, he promised, address the memorable victory won 'in our time by the will of God'. He did not disappoint. He described the revolt of the Saxons, the resistance under Ambrosius Aurelianus, the period when Saxons and Britons struggled, first one side then the other gaining the upper hand. This lasted up to the year of the siege of Badon Hill, almost the last and certainly not the least of the victories over the invaders. Gildas struck home the immediacy of the battle which had ushered in a generation of peace between Britons and Saxons by pointing out it was fought in the very year that he was born, almost 44 years before.

Bede, while trying his hardest to argue his thesis of divine providence working through the English people, had no option but to record the battle as a great victory by the Britons. He even went so far as to date it quite precisely, ensuring thereby that it entered the standard English historiography of the Dark Ages. *Historia Brittonum* made the battle of Badon the culmination of Arthur's 12 victorious battles, the one in which he alone triumphed, not sharing victory with the kings of the Britons but overthrowing 960 men in a single charge. *Annales Cambriae* makes no mention of the other 11 battles, or indeed of any other secular events leading up to it, but faithfully records the battle of Badon, in which Arthur carried the cross of Jesus three days and three nights on his shoulders, and the pagans were put to flight.

There is no doubt about it, the siege of Mount Badon was the rock against which the inexorable Saxon tide finally broke, a British Stalingrad where the invaders met their match, where decades of peace were won by struggle and sacrifice. And to cap it all, the only name given to its victor in all the ancient sources was Arthur.

Some anti-Arthurians dispute this, claiming that Gildas and Bede ascribe the victory to Ambrosius Aurelianus. This is not the case. Both writers are clear that Ambrosius was the leader who initiated the resistance, but that the warfare lasted quite some time. For Bede, Ambrosius gave the Britons their first victory over the English, as distinct from their last at Badon, which took place 44 years after the Saxons arrived. In Gildas it is clear that another generation has elapsed. Gildas, born 43 years ago at the time of the battle, is a contemporary of Ambrosius's grandchildren. It is in the time of Ambrosius's child(ren) that the siege itself was fought.

So why is there no monument on top of Badon Hill? Why isn't it a tourist site like the fields of Hastings, Bannockburn, Bosworth or Waterloo? For the prime reason that nobody knows where it is.

Where is Badon?

As we saw earlier, the most plausible scenario from Gildas is that Mount Badon was a fortified location held by Britons and besieged by the Saxons, but that the victory was won when other Britons involved in active resistance raise the siege. Logically a location which would fit this scenario should be somewhere in the disputed area contested by Britons and Saxons in the fifth and sixth centuries. It should be placed in such a way that a victory there would have repercussions all through the invading Saxons. As the reaction of the Britons to the Saxon revolt was to *retreat* to high fortified hills, amongst other defensible locations, Badon must therefore have been a British site, which formed an insurmountable obstacle to a Saxon advance. Whether it was actually a fortification is disputed. The fact that it is called a hill, rather than a *castellum*, or a *receptaculum*, even a *civitas* or *urbs*, would argue not; the fact that it was besieged suggests on the contrary it was at least defensible, if not actually fortified. The most reasonable conjecture is that it was the same sort of feature as the high fortified hills Gildas had only just mentioned, features which we have connected, at least since the Cadbury/Camelot excavations, with the re-fortified Iron Age hill forts.

Gildas had always believed that trusting in fortifications rather than in God was doomed to failure, and it is not a course followed by Ambrosius and the resistance, who took the fight to the enemy. We should probably see Arthur as leading the forces which relieved the siege, presumably shattering the attackers in the process.

We can assume that Gildas knew where *Mons Badonicus* was. The most northerly named location (presuming that not to be Mons Badonicus, for the moment) was Verulamium, home of St Alban. All the other named locations – the Thames and Severn estuaries, the Demetii, Dumnonia (presuming this is the right location) – have tended to push Badon into this southern area.

The Battle of Bath

The first clear location given is by Geoffrey of Monmouth. He places the siege at Bath. The waters are somewhat muddied by John Morris's edition of *Historia Brittonum*. He agreed with Geoffrey's location (Morris 1977:112), and incorporated passages into his text of the *Historia* which reinforced this identification. Because the edition was published posthumously, with no indication of the criteria Morris used for preferring these readings to that of the Harleian Manuscript, his basic (and oldest) text, it is very difficult for most historians to support these insertions. They seem to derive from sources which post-date Geoffrey and do not place the Bath material where Morris does.

Bath was an important Romano-British spa centre. Even after the abolition of the pagan cults, its hot baths continued to be visited, albeit in increasing levels of decay. Bath itself though was not a defensible site. When the Wansdyke was built, it was deliberately sited, indeed detoured, to by-pass Bath to the south. *Mons Badonicus* is not, though 'a hill called Badon'. It is a hill belonging to or connected with Badon (assumed here for argument's sake to be a place name). Bath is ringed by defensible hills. The most obvious of them is Solsbury Hill, which is topped by an Iron Age hill fort.

We do not know the British name for Bath. Its Roman name was Aquae Sulis, the waters of the goddess Sulis. Bath appears to be the Germanic word '*bath*' making it odd that Gildas should have used it (if that is what he means by Badon) in preference to a Roman or British name. Of course the name could be a coincidence. Eforwic sounds a perfectly Anglo-Saxon name 'boar-wic' but we know that is actually derived from the Roman, and before that British, Eboracum. For Geoffrey the connection was more obvious. Both old English (*Bedum*) and twelfth-century Welsh (*Vaddon*, mutated from Baddon) used the 'th' sound instead of the 'd' sound, making a much clearer identification.

Although Geoffrey's campaign culminating in Badon is fanciful, it is not an unreasonable objective for a Saxon force. Victory here would separate the *civitates* of the Durotriges and the Dumnonii from those in Wales. The Saxons' capture of Bath, recorded in the Anglo-Saxon Chronicle as having taken place after the Battle of Dyrham in 577, did have just such drastic consequences. If the Saxons had overextended themselves for one last push, hoping for re-supply from plunder or by sea, then defeat here could be catastrophic, with the kings of the Durotiriges and the Dobunni being able to pincer them.

Whether a fifth- or sixth-century siege had been fought at Solsbury Hill would have been an ideal archaeological research project for the archaeologists of the 1960s. The founders of the Camelot Research Committee had included the Somerset Archaeological Society and the University of Bristol, and went on to include the Somerset County Council. That fact that it was ignored as an Arthurian location then and is still ignored now is strange. It is as if a Somerset strategic plan to focus on the Arthurian locations of Glastonbury and Cadbury has meant dropping other Arthurian sites which might compete. Granted we do not know that Badon was at Bath, but we equally do not know that Glastonbury was Avalon or that Cadbury was Camelot. Bath was being hailed as Badon 60 years before Arthur was ever connected with Glastonbury and 400 before he was connected with Cadbury.

Bath itself saw domestic building and occupation 'well into the fifth and possibly the sixth centuries' (Cunliffe quoted by Snyder 1998: 151). The temple and bath complex itself was frequently re-cobbled, sealing datable coins are various intervals. 'The archaeologists believe that the chronology of this sequence extends the occupation of the temple precinct at least to 470, and very likely into the sixth century and beyond' (Snyder 1998: 150). These dates bring Bath within the ambit of a possible Saxon siege at the right time, if no more than that.

In Bath there is no interpretation of the Arthurian connection at all. The Roman Bath Museum, the Abbey Museum and the Building of Bath Museum are all silent on the transition from Roman to Saxon Bath. The Romans are typical 'Mediterranean colonists' – toga and tunic wearers fossilised somewhere between Pompeii and Constantine. It is a typical high profile tourist site and would, I imagine, benefit from some sort of Arthurian connection.

It might be argued that Badon is not a famous Arthurian location in the way that Camelot and Avalon are. These are timeless locations which speak of mystery and romance. That is certainly true, but the real analogy is with Tintagel. Both Tintagel and Badon/Bath appear for the first time in Geoffrey of Monmouth. Malory did not mention the Battle of Badon (as a Wars of the Roses writer, he concentrates on British Civil Wars rather than invasions). Tintagel's fame as a tourist destination comes not direct from him, however, but from Tennyson's *Idylls of the King*. Tennyson also covers Badon. In *Lancelot and Elaine*, Lancelot tells Elaine's brother about the campaigns of Arthur (from the battle list):

> and on the mount
> of Badon, I myself beheld the king
> charge at the head of all his Table Round
> and all his legions, crying Christ and him
> and break them; and I saw him, after, stand
> high on a heap of slain, from spur to plume
> red as the rising sun with heathen blood.

The Battle of Badon Hill is also referred to in passing in that touchstone of modern Arthurian fame, *Monty Python and the Holy Grail*.

Solsbury Hill is owned by the National Trust and is part of their 'Bath skyline' properties. The Trust refer to it only as 'an Iron Age hill fort'. An independent tourist site (City of Bath) breaks the silence 'Solsbury hill, 600ft high has traces of a circular camp supposed to have been used by the Saxons in their siege of Bath'. It adds 'featured in one of Peter Gabriel's songs.'

Neither the Saxon siege nor Peter Gabriel is interpreted on site. The Gabriel connection, however does account for a disconcertingly large web presence for the hill, including such sites as the (for me very disappointing) 'explanationsolsbury' (www.solsburyhill.org): 'It's about Gabriel's departure from Genesis'. Equally disconcerting is the large number of websites alluding to 'The Battle of Solsbury Hill'. This was 'fought' in 1994 by eco-warriors protesting against the building of the Batheaston by-pass. The protests attracted the druids, neo-pagans and others seen at similar protests from Twyford Down to Seahenge, including one identified as 'John Pendragon' (www.guardian.co.uk). Arbib's introduction to his anniversary collection of photographs contains the resonant phrase 'We fought for Solsbury Hill' (quoted on resurgence.org) along with images reminiscent of First World War trench warfare. He gives a long list of reasons why Solsbury Hill was so significant and should have been spared, but never once plays the Arthurian battle site card. Historic battle sites are often used as reasons for opposing development, such as that proposed at Tewksbury, and Arthurian motifs often chosen as symbolic of an indigenous 'pagan' culture to be protected from modernity but at this ideal site these did not come together.

The Battle of Badbury

As with Camelot, the site of Badon has been contested, but without the aid of the 1960s archaeologists Bath was unable to prevail. Badon/Bath was the accepted equation until modern times, even after the discrediting of Geoffrey of Monmouth. When the challenge came it was not from archaeologists or from source critics, but from philologists. It seems likely that Bath was a Germanic name and therefore unlikely to have been the source of Gildas's '*Mons Badonicus*'. There is no Welsh Caer Vaddon or Mynydd Vaddon, and logic would suggest that a site of a British victory would fall in the next Saxon thrust westward. Unless the place name was utterly expunged, it could have survived in an English form such as (for argument's sake) Badbury.

There is in fact a Badbury in the land of the Durotriges, Badbury Rings in Dorset. It fulfils the same strategic logic as an attack on Bath and is well within the supposed ambit of Gildas's knowledge. It even appears in the Anglo-Saxon Chronicle as the site of later Saxon activity. In the annal of 901 it appears as *Baddanbyrig*, specifically near Winbourne, confirming this is the site. Badbury Rings is in fact an Iron Age hill fort, spectacular, relatively isolated and unsurprisingly often picked by Arthurians as 'the site of Mount Badon'. It is owned, like Solsbury Hill, by the National Trust, as part of their Kingston Lacy estate. 20 years ago I picked up a leaflet which alluded to the Arthurian connection, but the modern Trust seems to have swung in behind academic orthodoxy to deny it. Their website calls it only 'an Iron Age hill fort' (kingstonlacy). The writer does seem to be aware of some fantastical battle associations but rather fumbles this: 'Lord of the rings, ... [Badbury was] home to our ancestors, its deep ditches defending against invaders.'

The National Trust, like its competitor organisation English Heritage (the Trust is an independent charity while English Heritage is a Government body) does not capitalise on Arthurian associations at its sites and, again possibly as a matter of policy, has decided to place all its Arthurian interpretation on one site. In the case of the Trust this is Alderley Edge in Cheshire, connected to the myth of Arthur and his knights sleeping in a cave awaiting the hour of his country's greatest need.

In general, in historical Arthur material, it is neither Badbury nor Bath which are most commonly cited as the real Badon. Geoffrey Ashe championed Liddington Castle (Ashe 1982: 116), another Iron Age hill fort, not unlike Cadbury/Camelot in overall appearance, near Swindon. The name was not a problem. Liddington is near the village of Baydon, and even nearer to another Badbury. This would serve quite well to explain why it is a 'hill in the Badon area' rather than a hill called Badon. The primary considerations for Liddington were strategic. It dominates the Ridgeway and is far to the east of the other two sites; Saxons approaching along the Ridgeway would have no option but to take Liddington. If it was successfully held against them they could make no progress further westward. The Anglo-Saxon Chronicle preserves an impression, if nothing more, that the expansion of the West Saxons had not proceeded westward as far as Badbury Rings or Bath by this time.

Liddington has not been extensively excavated. Ashe (1980: 134) reports 'a trial excavation in 1976 uncovered traces of work on the top rampart in the fifth or sixth century, suggesting re-use' but nothing on the scale of Cadbury. It does not appear as a 'significant site' in Snyder's comprehensive list (Snyder 1998). This is not a major problem, since it would explain why Gildas only referred to it as a hill, while at the same time being defensible enough to withstand a siege.

Although Liddington is sufficiently windswept and imposing to appear in photographs in many Arthurian works (for example Snyder 2000: 70), it is not interpreted as an Arthurian site. On the summit is a monument which declares 'Liddington Hill. The hill beloved of Richard Jefferies and Alfred Williams'. Jefferies writes about his experiences there in *The Story of my Heart* (1883). Whatever you feel about these authors, they are hardly in the same recognition league as King Arthur. It raises the terrible spectre that in 100 years the only monument on Solsbury Hill might be one to Peter Gabriel's moment of conversion.

Clearly we are back in the familiar '12 battles' territory of reminiscent place names combined with strategic conjecture. Bath, Badbury and Liddington all work with Gildas, as do other candidates, but without clear archaeological work there is nothing at present to separate them. The best additional piece of evidence we have is that *Annales Cambriae* thought there was a second battle of Badon, 149 years after the first one. This would be in the region of AD 665. The second battle could be the final one, in which the Saxons finally overcame the obstacle which had checked their advance, or a battle coincidentally fought by Saxons in the same place. At the outside it could be the scene of an eastward British counter-thrust.

The late seventh century is a period well covered by Bede and by the Anglo-Saxon Chronicle. The first Battle of Badon shows up the limitations of the Chronicle as an unbiased source. The compiler knew as well as we do, from Bede, that there had been a Battle of Badon. He knew more or less its exact date, as given by Bede (44 years after the arrival of the Saxons during the period when Marcian was co-emperor with Valentian – a synchronism the Chronicle takes from Bede). Yet Badon is resolutely ignored in favour of the story of continuous and uninterrupted Saxon victory. It does record the conquest of Bath after the Battle of Dyrham in 577. If this is the second battle of Badon, then this section of *Annales Cambriae* is out by 90 years or so from the Anglo-Saxon Chronicle. This is possible. *Annales Cambriae* is a list of years, starting at its own 'year one'. We do not know for sure when this was, and there are ample opportunities for events to be wrongly placed amongst its sparse entries. Its dates are nothing like as established as they are often taken to be.

Annales Cambriae synchronises the second battle with 'First Easter celebrated among the Saxons' which must be earlier than 665. It cannot, though, be pushed back to 577, when the Saxons were still pagans. The nearest battle to the date (675 according to the Chronicle) is that at Bedanheafod, which happens to mean 'Bedan-head', a perfectly appropriate place name for a hill in the Bedan area. It was fought between the West Saxons and the Mercians, so within the area that we could expect Gildas to know. But unfortunately, even if Bedanheafod is the same as the second Battle of Badon, we do not know where it is. The famous editor of the Anglo-Saxon Chronicle, Plummer, opted for Great Bedwyn. This is itself in the river valley but its head or hill is topped by the Iron Age hill fort of Chisbury. It stands at the eastern extremity of the Wansdyke, where the Savernake forest would make cross-country progress difficult. If the Wansdyke was already in existence, failure to turn the flank would have left the Saxons unable to advance. Alternatively the Wansdyke could have been built after the victory, specifically taking the impregnable site as one of its flanks.

About all we can say is that it is unlikely that Bedanheafod is either Bath or Badbury Rings, as the Chronicle includes and names both sites. It could equally well be Liddington, if Plummer's Bedwyn location is not supported.

Needless to say there are many more potential Badons, with Badbury not being an uncommon place name, not to mention a variety of names beginning with 'b' both in modern Britain and in the Anglo-Saxon Chronicle.

Thomas Green, as mentioned above, argues for a Lincolnshire Arthur/ Ambrosius and accordingly finds a Badon substitute at Baumber, known as Badeburg in the Domesday Book (Green 2007: 4). There was a small fortified Roman town at nearby Horncastle, and an Anglo-Saxon sword pommel dated *c*.450–500 AD was found there. Baumber fares reasonably well against the measure of a second Battle of Badon. Bede knew nothing of the Mercian and West Saxon Wars recorded in the Chronicle. What he does record is that in the eight years before 678, Egfrid King of Northumbria had seized Lindsey from Wulfhere of Mercia. This could well give a battle of Baumber in the period. Knowledge of a second Badon would come to *Annales Cambriae* via a Mercian source, during the tenth-century period of rapprochement between Gwynedd and Mercia.

On the minus side, if Mount Badon is at Baumber it would be the most northerly place name in Gildas, though most modern thought makes him a southern writer. Most arguments in favour of a southern Badon are based on strategic considerations. It is relatively easy to see how a siege of a strong point along the Ridgeway or in the Thames Valley or an abortive Saxon thrust as far as Bath would lead to a generation in which the Saxon advance was curtailed. This is a very difficult case to make with the Lincolnshire Badon. Why would a British victory there, spectacularly eastward though it would have been, have cowed the Saxons south of the Humber? The counter-argument, how would a victory at Liddington Castle, say, stop the Angles of Lindsey, will not hold. Wherever we locate Gildas, he still needs a victory which secured peace for tyrants in Dumnonia and Demetia.

It is odd, given his contention that Arthur is mythological, that Green entertains the idea of a historical Battle of Badon, so rooted in the Arthurian tradition. He does this by the circular reasoning that, if you exclude all the texts which connect Arthur and Badon, you are left with no texts which connect Arthur and Badon. He sees this as a conclusive argument that Arthur and Badon were not traditionally connected, reiterating:

> Outside [*Historia Brittonum* and *Annales Cambriae*], Arthur is *never* associated in the whole body of pre-Galfridian literature with Badon… Arthur [is] not linked with Badon but Badon is in fact not linked with Arthur… The only instance of Arthur being portrayed as a historical defeater of Anglo-Saxons and victor of Badon' is *Historia Brittonum* and its derivative *Annales Cambriae*… no contemporary or near-contemporary source makes any mention of such a figure' as Arthur at Badon… It is worth noting once more in this context that Arthur is *never* associated with either the Saxons or Badon in the vast majority of the material… it is *only* present in those sources which are directly derivative of *Historia Brittonum* chapter 56 … [other than in *Historia Brittonum* 56], Arthur is never made to fight the Germanic invaders, nor is he placed at Badon… He is never connected in this material in any way with either the Saxons or Badon. (2007)

This is the exact opposite of the situation as I read it. In all sources, pre- or post-Geoffrey, whenever the victor of Badon is named he is named as Arthur. The dominance of Camlan, Arthur's last battle, in the poetic tradition has no bearing on this. Badon was significant to Gildas as marking the start of the period of peace with the Saxons and civil war amongst the Britons. Doubtless with the benefit of hindsight the tragedy of Arthur's end became more significant in the overall picture of British decline and Saxon advance. The Battle of Waterloo looms larger in the literary traditions of Napoleon than the battle of Austerlitz, after all.

While the case for Arthur being the victor at Badon is as strong as we can reasonably expect, the case for Green's preferred leader, Ambrosius, is small, still less that he did so at a battle in Lincolnshire. This concept never appears in later material at all. It is simply not correct to say (Green 2007: 31) that 'Gildas does indeed assign Badon a victor – Ambrosius Aurelianus'. Gildas does not make this explicit at all. The period of wars ebbing and flowing between Britons and Saxons could be of any duration from a few years (the *year* of Badon is the significant thing to Gildas) to a generation. Those of us who take the longer option do not, as Green accuses us, base it on supposed section breaks in its manuscripts, but on the fact that Gildas's generation, 44 years later, sees the adulthood of Ambrosius's grandchildren, men who have forgotten his example. It follows a generation of good Britons, exemplars of moral rectitude, peace with each other and, most importantly, war with the Saxons, and therefore contemporaries of the Badon period.

No subsequent Dark Age writer, including Bede and *Historia Brittonum*, read Gildas as attributing Badon to Ambrosius. Bede makes Ambrosius give the Angles their first defeat, a reasonable inference from Gildas. This is followed by the to and fro victories and ends with Badon, but not a Badon where Ambrosius leads.

Historia Brittonum is a key text in this respect as it is the first to cover both Ambrosius and Arthur. As noted earlier, the author does all that he can to distance himself from any implication that Ambrosius led at Badon. This is part of a consistent pattern of contradicting Gildas. Whatever Gildas says about Ambrosius's parents he is explicit that Ambrosius is not a king. He is an ordinary man '*vir modestus*'. And whatever he says about Badon, he is quite clear that Ambrosius initiates the fight against the Saxons. Nennius's Ambrosius is definitely not a *vir modestus*; he is a prophetic wonder child and king of the kings of the Britons, and he never fights the Saxons himself. The author seems to consciously set himself against Bede not by setting up a rival leader at Badon, but by denying Ambrosius any role in resisting the Saxons.

Bede has even more need to distance Ambrosius from the battle since he thinks there are 44 years between the Saxon arrival and the battle. In Gildas it does not seem anywhere near as long, even if Ambrosius is an infant when his parents die. We really don't know anything about Ambrosius's career from Gildas. He rallies the survivors of the Saxon revolt, '*duce Ambrosio Aureliano ... vires capessunt, victores provocantes ad proelium'* 'led by Ambrosius Aurelianus, [or 'with Ambrosius as their leader' or, technically, with Ambrosius as their *Dux*] the men gained strength, calling out the victors to battle'. It is not 100 per cent clear that Ambrosius was a war leader, or even, at a stretch, that he was not a religious leader. Germanus, after all is '*Dux*' at the Alleluia victory. Any reader of Gildas would have been reminded of the more famous Ambrosius, St Ambrose the Bishop of Milan. Ambrosius's importance is in rallying and inspiring the Britons. This is not the same as making him a superlative army commander or a king. He might have been any or none of those things. He may have been the equivalent of the man in front of the tanks in Tiananmen Square. It is his action in standing up to the Saxons which sets him apart. The fact he is a '*vir modestus*' an ordinary man compared with the last Roman the Britons had looked to for help, Agitius 'a man of Roman power' counts against him being a warlord or great king.

The deduction that Ambrosius won the Battle of Badon needs a lot more support from its proponents. It is equally possible to argue that Vortiporius's father or Maglocunus's uncle are responsible. Maglocunus's uncle and his soldiers are the only military figures of the previous generation spoken of with approval by Gildas. Although we cannot tell whether their bravery and fierceness in battle relate only to their battle against Maglocunus, it is more likely that Gildas means they were brave and fierce in battle against Saxons since he considered fighting civil wars reprehensible. Vortiporius's father is compared to Hezekiah, who was the Judean king who stood up against the Assyrians, the analogy Gildas explicitly chose for the Saxon revolt. Hezekiah holds out in Jerusalem until the army of Sennacherib besieging him is destroyed by God. This is an explicit siege analogy and Badon is the only explicit siege in Gildas. Of course either of those unnamed characters could have been Ambrosius, and I am sure there are other characters we could argue for. I simply want to point out that Ambrosius as the victor of Badon is a speculation as much as any of the other candidates, not a given from the text. The fact that all subsequent writers thought that Ambrosius and the victor of Badon were different men even when, like the author of *Historia Brittonum*, they set out to aggrandise Ambrosius, must count for something.

It might be argued that the very fact that Ambrosius was named at all by Gildas indicates that he was particularly famous and hence strengthens his possible connection with the victory at Badon. There is some circularity in this, as part of his fame comes from the fact he is mentioned by Gildas. Certainly he appears famous in Bede and then in *Historia Brittonum*, but the author of *Historia Brittonum* was still unable to point out any contemporary wonders connected to him. He certainly is not in the league of Arthur, specifically described as famous on many occasions. A few people are in Gildas arguably because of their fame – Magnus Maximus and Agitius for example. But the number of people unnamed or unmentioned in spite of their fame is much more striking. Constantine the Great, Constantine III, and St Germanus are not in the book at all, though we might expect them to be named if Gildas was in the business of name checking. Perhaps the Proud Tyrant was, like his Saxon allies, deliberately unnamed, but how can we explain Vortiporius's good father? The two superlative youths killed by Constantine? One of the most clearly famous characters in the whole book is 'the elegant master of almost all Britain' (DEB 36.1), who taught Maglocunus, but is nevertheless not named. Being named or not must mean something more than fame in *De Excidio Britanniae*.

Incidentally, although I argue for quite a gap in time between Ambrosius and Arthur on the basis of Gildas, this isn't clear in *Historia Brittonum*. Green is wrong to say (2007: 204) that *Historia Brittonum* separates Ambrosius from Badon as 'dubious understanding of fifth century chronology ... meant he had already associated him with the corrupt reign of Vortigern'. Gildas establishes that some people who saw the 'desperate ... blow to the island' of the Saxon revolt also lived to see the 'unlooked for recovery' under Ambrosius (DEB 26:2). So those events took place within one lifetime. Ambrosius's parents were killed in the revolt, leaving open the possibility that he was a child at the time as *Historia Brittonum* has it. According to *Historia Brittonum*, the revolt started under Hengist, when Ambrosius was a child. Arthur fights Saxons led by Hengist's son Octha. The last time we see Ambrosius in the main narrative he is *'rex inter omnes reges Brittanicae gentis'* (HB 48), 'king among all the kings of the British race' generously bestowing the region of Buelt on Guorthegirn's third son Pascent. The next time the kings of the Britons appear, in this same generation, they are accompanying Arthur in his wars. That means that *Historia Brittonum*, far from having dubious notions of chronology, follows Green's proposed scheme in making, almost certainly, Ambrosius still alive and ruling at the time of Badon, having led a recovery in the lifetime of those who saw the revolt. *Historia Brittonum*'s contribution is to place a non-royal ruler (Arthur) in the forefront of the resistance.

For those interested in a more detailed understanding of the chronology of the events recorded in Gildas and their reflection in archaeology, I have included an appendix with my thoughts on the subject.

16

THE STRIFE OF CAMLAN

Where was King Arthur's last battle? His Waterloo comes with a readily accessible package of images. The trusted companion hurls the sword into the lake. A mysterious hand grasps the word, brandishes it and then disappears beneath the water. A boat-load of pre-Raphaelite ladies arrive to carry the mortally wounded king off to Avalon. But what was the battle even called?

Just as we probably have Tennyson to thank for the popularity of Tintagel as a modern tourist location, it is probably his contribution which has made this so obscure. His 'last, dim, weird battle of the west' deliberately defies location. Arthur and Modred fall back to the farthest bounds of Britain 'Lyonesse / a land of old upheaven from the abyss / by fire, to sink into the abyss again' (*The Passing of Arthur*). This is the supposed land to the west of Cornwall now represented only by the Scilly Isles. Tennyson is clearly telling his readers this battle site is no longer to be found, sunk beneath the waters of the Atlantic.

This is Tennyson's innovation, for his own poetic purposes. For many people (Ashley 1998) *The Passing of Arthur* is the definitive account. I personally prefer Malory's version, on which it drew heavily. Malory, following his French source, places the last battle at 'a downe besyde Salesbury and nat farre from the seesyde'. Visitors to Salisbury Plain would doubtless be disappointed to find no nearby lakes or seas, and archaeologists working there have tended to have too much on their minds with its prehistoric remains to go looking for Arthur.

In *Hengeworld* (2000), the archaeologist of Stonehenge, Mike Pitts, does investigate a suggestion that a skeleton found there in 1923 is King Arthur. Pitts identifies the suggestion as originating with Geoffrey of Monmouth, who has Ambrosius, Uther Pendragon and Arthur's heir Constantine of Cornwall all buried there but not Arthur. The radiocarbon date made any of these a possibility (Pitts 2000: 318) but what would probably have been seen as a newsworthy find at, say, Glastonbury, is here only a footnote to the study of 'Life in Britain 2000 BC'.

According to Geoffrey of Monmouth, Arthur's last battle was fought against his rebellious nephew Modred on the River Camblan in Cornwall. He dated this

ix. HADRIAN'S WALL

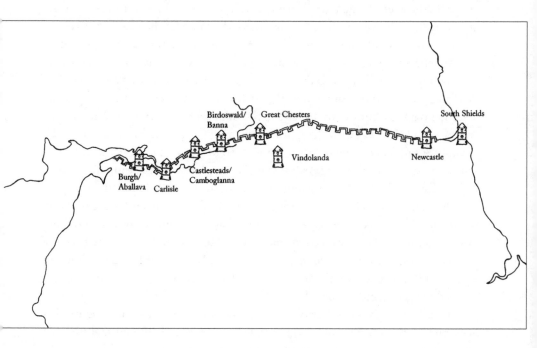

to AD 542. These ideas did not originate with him. The '*Gueith Camlann* [Strife of Camlan, in Welsh], in which Arthur and Medraut were slain', is an entry in *Annales Cambriae*, 21 years after Arthur's victory at the Battle of Badon. As with all the battles though, having a name is not the same as proving a location.

Slaughterbridge

The Slaughterbridge 'battle site' at Camelford is unique in Britain. It is an Arthurian site with a good provenance (apparently the site intended by Geoffrey of Monmouth) which is interpreted on site as Arthurian and which also uses academic archaeology to give some measure of support to it. It is a shame it is not better known. The site features an 'Arthurian Centre' with various interpretative techniques, primarily graphic panels and an audio-visual presentation, to tell a combined story of the historical Arthur and romance features such as the Knights of the Round Table and the Grail quest. The centre features Arthurian souvenirs; children's toys of medieval castles and knights and an imaginative Arthurian castle play area. Instead of turning the historic site into an over-interpreted theme park, the centre is located beside the road. The visitor is then encouraged to follow a trail through the battle site, culminating in a sixth-century inscribed memorial stone (often called the Arthur Stone) in its atmospheric location beside the River Camel. Although the general interpretative thrust is positivist 'visitors can walk through the fields where King Arthur and Modred met for their last battle' (www. arthur-online.co.uk), the debates and uncertainties of the issue are still presented.

That the Slaughterbridge battle site ought to be a very fertile one for archaeological investigation is apparent. There is, for instance, the inscribed stone. 'The interim picture of this site is this: the Arthur stone was erected as a memorial beside a road that runs across the site in the sixth century' writes resident archaeologist Nick Hanks (www.slaughterbridgedig.blogspot.com). It was moved a couple of times before being placed in its current 'grotto' in the eighteenth century. I presume calling it 'the Arthur stone' is a riposte to the version in Tintagel. There have in the past been various readings of the stone including the names of Merlin and Arthur. These seem more wishful thinking than anything else. Apart from an A and an R in general proximity, I have been unable to read anything like either name. The most recent transcription on the centre's website (Okasha 1993) reads *Latini ic iacet filius ma[...]ri* apparently 'a son of Latinus'. Although it is hard to imagine a more Roman name than Latinus, the same name appears carved in Ogham along one edge.

The blogspot gives another two examples of pre-modern archaeological discoveries on the site. Leland in 1538 wrote 'by this ryver Arthure fought his last field yn token wherof the people fynd there in plowing bones and harneys'. As recently as 1864–67 a 'scimitar shaped sword' and a 'gold collar and spearheads were found', although the sword might be connected with a nearby English Civil War location.

The evidence from the Slaughterbridge battle relics is quite persuasive, but is unfortunately confounded by the idea, reported on the site, that there was another Dark Age battle there in 823. I have seen this presented in various places (significantly by Ashe 1971: 150), including the Arthurian Centre's own website and leaflet. On investigation this turns out to be something of an own goal by Cornish partisans. The Anglo-Saxon Chronicle does indeed report a battle at 'Gafulforde' in 823 involving the men of Devon and Cornwall. Presumably at a period when Anglo-Saxon roots and sources were all the rage, it became useful for Cornish antiquarians to claim this site was in their county rather than the obvious conclusion it was in Galford in Devon. Arguing that the Battle of Gafulforde was at Slaughterbridge has effectively muddied the waters for an Arthurian identification of the site. No datable ninth-century material has been found at Slaughterbridge, in contrast to the indisputably sixth-century inscribed stone.

The Slaughterbridge site is home to a considerable archaeological presence. It is regularly used by the University of Winchester for training digs and participates in the National Archaeology Week, also known as the Festival of British Archaeology, promoted by the Council for British Archaeology. It was even part of Time Team's 'Big Dig' in 2003, perhaps the source of the programme's Arthurian imagery.

There is a summary description of the Slaughterbridge training excavation project (Hanks: slaughterbidgedig) which in its statement of significance tells us that it is 'one of the sites reputed to be of King Arthur's last battle'. This is a very refreshing moment of clarity in a discipline which has taken every opportunity in the last few decades to ignore Arthurian connections, even though the training project is not specifically intended to investigate it. Its successes have been in recovering the ornamental gardens of which the relocated stone formed a part.

There is also an allied 'Tintagel Environs Survey Project' looking at the wider context. Its premise is that, if it is 'assumed that the sub-Roman occupation of Tintagel was seasonal, then other sites in the area may produce similar wares from some peripatetic ruler' (Hanks).

It is hard not to see the Slaughterbridge work as some measure of a riposte to the archaeology and interpretation at Tintagel. Both Tintagel and the Cornish Camel location are from Geoffrey of Monmouth, but the archaeological work at Tintagel has taken great pains to distance itself from a prime reason why a visitor might be visiting the site. Slaughterbridge has turned to archaeology to support and enhance its reputation. Although I have some reservations about the mixing with Grail Quest and mystical materials in the Arthurian Centre, I feel this is a far more honest and constructive approach to interpreting the site for those interested in the Arthurian connection. Has anything actually been found on the site to vindicate the Arthurian connection? Unfortunately not: 'Work has only just begun on the first trench on the battlefield' (Hanks).

Camlan and Avalon

We do not know the names borne in Roman times by the vast majority of places in Britain. This is often difficult to appreciate, as we do know the names of the towns. But most rivers, hills, villages, hill forts and so on though they may bear names which can be derived from Celtic originals, do not enter the written record until many centuries later. Disproportionately the place names of Roman Britain are those found on roads covered by itineraries, or those under the military command of the late Roman *Dux Brittaniarum* or *Comes Litoris Saxonici*. There might have been very many Camlans. The prevalence of Cam/Camel river names, such as the famous river at Cambridge or the 'Arthurian' one at Cadbury attest to this. There is even an actual Camlan in mid-Wales. There may have been many Avalons, as there certainly were in Gaul, but the name ('orchard') is unlikely to be found on a main road or occupied by troops. It is therefore quite possible that a disproportionate weight has been placed on the two places known to have had these names in the Roman period. Camlan may derive from *Camboglanna* ('crooked glen') and Avalon is related to *Aballava*. Camboglanna and Aballava are the names of nearby forts on the west side of Hadrian's Wall. These names have been of great significance to authors trying to prove a 'northern Arthur'.

Aside from the expected excesses of 'Postcode Arthur' theories centring on the Scottish border, there is actually quite a respectable tradition of academics arguing for a northern milieu. The first reference to Arthur is in *The Gododdin*, after all, and no one doubts its northern focus, an expedition from Edinburgh to Catterick. There is a logic to the wars of the resistance to the Saxons being fought in the north. As Gildas tells us, the Saxons were first settled specifically to combat the threat of the Picts and the Scots. There is also the slight similarity of Arthur's title in *Historia Brittonum*, '*Dux Bellorum*', and that of the commander of the Hadrian's Wall garrisons, the *Dux Brittaniarum*. Even in the early romances, Arthur is shown in the company of distinctly northern heroes and as likely to hold court in Carlisle as Camelot.

In spite of this, I have not been able to track down any excavations on Hadrian's Wall with a stated intention of searching for Arthurian connections. Similarly I could not find any locations where the possible Arthurian connections are interpreted on site. The Roman context of the still impressive stone fortifications has understandably dominated the interpretation. Signs show legionaries and occasionally auxiliaries of the Trajan/Hadrian period and re-enactments are usually by groups such as the Ermine Street Guard, in uniforms similar to those depicted on Trajan's Column.

This makes what actually turned up on site all the more interesting. Very frequently in 'historical' Arthur works the concept of the northern Arthur is illustrated by a photograph of the Roman remains at Birdoswald Fort. They are undoubtedly photogenic, always a good excuse for an Arthurian connection to be made, but more to the point they were in the past wrongly identified as those of Camboglanna (e.g. Morris 1977: 140). This turned out to be based on a mistake in *Notitia Dignitatum*. Excavation recovered inscriptional evidence showing that Birdoswald was probably Banna, while Camboglanna was the next fort to the west, Castlesteads.

Unfortunately Castlesteads was destroyed, landscaped away to create fashionable surroundings for an eighteenth-century country house. Excavations in 1970 revealed the shape of the fort. It is not absolutely clear which 'crooked valley/bank' its name refers to. It stands to the north of the River Irthing, which takes a sharp south turn here. On place name basis, though, it would be churlish to ignore the fact that the stream which runs directly to the north of the fort (so close it has now eroded away all traces of the north wall) is called the Cam Beck. It turns sharply to the south-west, to join the Irthing, and its valley is steep and spectacular.

As luck would have it, even if Birdoswald wasn't Camboglanna, recent excavations found intriguing evidence of the Arthurian period there. Tony Wilmott, now senior archaeologist with English Heritage, directed excavations from 1987 to 1992. As with Barker's work at Wroxeter, Wilmott paid close attention to the traces of timber structures overlaying the obvious Roman remains. He interpreted several phases of timber construction, giving an estimated terminal date of 520, though possibly even up to a century later. 'There is no evidence whatever of a phase of abandonment, however brief, within this sequence' (Wilmott 2000: 14).

Over the top of the conventional Roman military buildings, within the standing walls, there was a large timber hall, together with smaller support buildings. It was nothing like a Roman building, let alone a Roman military one. It looked very much like the kind of chieftain's hall you might expect to find at Yeavering or South Cadbury:

> the presence of a hearth at one end of a long spacious building, and the loss of high quality objects near the hearth has distinctly similar echoes, with implications of high status individuals enjoying the best seat ... in its cultural setting generally, the settlement at Birdoswald should be set beside other fortified centres of the period as listed by Leslie Alcock (1988, 27); the reoccupied hill forts of the west country such as South Cadbury, sites on hill-tops or promontories, using natural features of defence ... as one of a patchwork of early post-Roman fortified places, it is hard to think of a better location than Birdoswald. In these terms, it is a stone-walled promontory fort, defended on the north side by a linear barrier, the wall, and beyond that, by a marsh ... it commands a river crossing, and a fertile river valley. (Wilmott 2000)

This is as near as an archaeologist publishing in 2000 could get to saying that what he had found was an Arthurian site. Francis Pryor had no such qualms about helping him out 'if one is looking for a job description for an early fifth century [I think he means sixth-century] Arthur like figure, the post Roman commander at Birdoswald would be an almost perfect match' (Pryor 2004: 202).

Ken and Petra Dark had earlier argued, from the study of pollen samples, that the wall forts had been abandoned and then refortified. The more recent publications contradict this, and Wilmott specifically rejects this interpretation. Occupation was continuous from the late Roman period, although it took on a distinctly more local colour (Wilmott 2000: 16).

The late Roman context was characterised by blocking the gates. The north gate has not been recovered; it is under a modern road. The south gate was completely blocked in the fourth century and a ditch cut in front of it. The east and west gates were narrowed and at least half the mile castles on either side of Birdoswald had their gates narrowed to prevent carts and herds passing. The garrison was asserting its economic dominance over the area (Collins 2004: 127-9).

Contrary to what is often suggested, the *Limitanei* – the border troops stationed at the northern forts – were not part-time soldier-farmers, housing their families

inside the barrack blocks (Wilmott 2000: 17). They were professional soldiers who
expected to be paid by the government. When the this ceased in the early fifth
century, the garrisons would have had to survive by other means. They continued
to collect tax revenue, presumably in kind, from the local population in return for
protection. As Wilmot puts it this relationship 'might have been coercive, symbiotic,
or a little of both' (2000:17).

The evidence for this is in the pollen analysis. The area immediately around
the fort had been cleared in Roman times, and continued to be kept clear at least
until the early seventh century. A few trees remained but the area was used predominantly for pasture. In spite of this, the evidence from inside the fort showed
wheat, barley and hay, most of which must have come from over 10km away
(Collins, R. 2004: 126–7). The diversity of the garrison's diet 'suggests that external contacts continued or developed, and contradicts the once popular theory
that the "Dark Ages" marked a severe recession and decline of economic and
social networks. People in the fifth–seventh centuries did not "revert" to Iron Age
modes of subsistence and trade' (Stallibrass 2000: 73).

As Wilmott sees it, the *Limitanei* of Birdoswald were hereditary soldiers, whose
ancestors had been locally recruited and who therefore can be assumed to have
a shared ethnic and cultural background to the local population. In addition,
they were 'hereditary possessors of Roman military tradition' (Wilmott 2000:17).
When the Roman central government ceased to supply them, they had no reason
or inclination to abandon their livelihoods and take up farming. Birdoswald was
inland and safe from attacks from the sea, it held the high land which dominated
the area of cultivation and could therefore secure supplies. They had no need to
abandon their posts.

Wilmott's evocation of the lifestyle of the successor soldiers at the fort would
not have seemed out of place in the Cadbury/Camelot era (2000: 17–18):

> If securely located, they might themselves become a self-sustaining community
> based around a hereditary commander. It is even possible … the leader was
> the recipient of personal oaths of allegiance in the manner of the late Roman
> *bucellarii* (Liebeschutz 1986; 1993) … this … would be entirely consistent with
> the architectural affinities of the latest timber buildings at Birdoswald which
> so closely recall the hall buildings on such sites as … South Cadbury … these
> buildings are generally interpreted within a Celtic (in heavy inverted commas)
> heroic tradition as the feasting halls of powerful individuals surrounded by war
> bands within the kind of society described … by Higham, but as Dark (1994,
> 178-81) has pointed out, many features noted as typical of such recrudescent
> heroic celticism, such as feasting, panegyric poetry, bands of retainers, and
> aisled buildings are not inconsistent with late Roman culture.' What the sol-
> diers seem to be doing is adapting features of the culture of their neighbours in
> their hill forts to the north, creating a hybrid culture 'more closely reminiscent

of a sub-Roman society revolving around the hall of a warleader, while maintaining a social and cultural legitimacy based on Roman antecedents.

The Men of the North

Although there is nothing like the thorough investigation of Birdoswald's post-Roman story at other wall sites, there is sufficient evidence to show it was not an isolated case. Bede confirms that Hadrian's Wall was still a significant feature in his own time 'this famous and still conspicuous wall ... eight feet in breadth and twelve in height' (1:2).

Great Chesters, to the east of Birdoswald, also blocked its south gate in the fourth century. (Collins 2004: 128). South Shields was not abandoned. Its blocked south-west gate was unblocked and provided with a new timber gatehouse. Unusually burials were preserved here, along the road leading to it and dated to the first half of the fifth century. Though not abandoned, South Shields seems to have come to a possibly violent end shortly after, with bodies buried in its courtyard house. Vindolanda was repaired, possibly in the early fifth century, and a Christian tombstone of early sixth-century design, to a man named Brigomaglos, erected there. There was also an apparently similar tombstone found at Castlesteads (Willmott 2000: 15).

What does all this imply? We can be reasonably sure that post-Roman British kingdoms formed in the north, some out of the *civitates* of the Brigantes and the Carvetii or sub kingdoms within them, some from generally un-Romanised tribes north of the Wall. The Gododdin derived from the Votadini and the poem of that name refers to the Novantae and possibly the Brigantes too (Dark 2000b: 85).

We know from Bede and *Annales Cambriae* that Elmet was a long surviving British kingdom, and the names of Deira and Bernicia are British ones, reflecting 'polities of which we know almost or absolutely nothing' (Dumville 1989: 221).

North of the Wall, the kings of the Britons acted in ways we might expect from our experience with the southern sites. They refortified the old hill forts of their ancestors, like the Mote of Mark (Dark 2000b: 85). South of the Wall, however, they acted in a completely different way. There are no refortified hill forts between the Wall and the Mersey. Instead they reoccupied or, as at Birdoswald, they continued to occupy the Roman fortifications. And not just any fortifications but, with the possible exception of Manchester, they only occupied forts of the command of the *Dux Britanniarum* (Dark 2000b: 84–5). For Dark the inference is clear. The local kings and aristocrats did not built hill forts because they were co-operating in a joint defence system organised in a reformed or (Wilmott might argue) continuing command of the *Dux Britanniarum*.

the most probable explanation is that one or more local ruler(s) wished to recreate the dux's command in a 'sub Roman' form. [This suggests] that political authorities existed in the fifth and sixth centuries capable of organising military activities across large tracts of what had been the Roman North, and that political fragmentation did not accompany the end of Roman rule in this part of the diocese. (Dark 2000b: 84-5)

The Wall ran across the boundaries of two *civitates* and it required support from forts to the south and to the north. We can be pretty sure, although Dark does not spell it out, what the intention of the *Dux's* reformed command was – to resist the Anglo-Saxon incursions.

As Dumville (1989: 219) puts it

Anglo-British relations in the fifth, sixth and seventh centuries were of course largely characterised by hostility … English aggression is a constant theme in Anglo-British relations, talk of treaties, and of continuity of institutions and population between British and English rule, cannot wish that away. On the British side Welsh heroic poetry leaves us in no doubt of the sixth-century northern hostilities between Briton and Angle. Bede stresses the savage vigour of Aethelfrith of Bernicia and, in return, of Cadwallon of Gwynedd who (Bede thought) wanted to extirpate the entire Northumbrian people … the overall pattern [is] of continuing Northumbrian aggression and expansion. It would be perverse to pretend that the result of such expansion was business as usual for the Britons, if under new management.

The archaeological record is what we would expect from Gildas. There is military activity at the forts in the early fifth century, corresponding to his attacks by the Picts and the Scots. It is presumable to this course the destruction and abandonment of South Shields is to be attributed. If we follow Gildas, we would expect to see Anglo-Saxons introduced, as mercenaries, into the north-eastern quarter of Britain where they could be of most use shoring up the defences against the Picts. And so, as Dumville points out, we do, from York to Catterick, in association with major military centres (1989: 215). The continuing presence of garrisons at forts like Birdoswald would not contradict this. Liebeschuetz (1993: 274–75) explains it was normal practice in the late Roman military for regulars to be kept on in garrison duties while federates were employed for the duration of the campaign when a large expeditionary force was needed.

Placed in these strategic positions, the Saxons would be in a position to do grave damage to the military infrastructure should they revolt, as Dumville points out. Crucially this early settlement was not sustained. Saxon remains in the region are limited. 'to judge by the burial evidence, the Anglo-Saxon physical presence in Bernicia, including Yeavering, and in Elmet in the fifth, sixth and early seventh centuries was minimal' (O'Brien 1999: 185). The wall area and most of the *civitas* of the Brigantes formed a Saxon-free area. Late Anglo-Saxon traditions placed the founding of the Northumbrian kingdoms no earlier than 547, Bede's date, calculated from a regnal list. 'Kingship in Deira is visible only from the 560s ... on the face of it the fifth century and much of the sixth were largely lost to Anglo-Saxon historical memory in Northumbria's early Christian period' (Dumville 1989: 219). They had, it seemed, faced a catastrophic reverse and unbeatable resistance.

Arthur of the North?

Dark never mentions Arthur in his books, and Dumville's role as 'Arthur's assassin' is well noted. But it is clear that their interpretation of the archaeological record of the sub-Roman North reveals exactly what we would expect in our search for Arthur.

According to *Historia Brittonum*, the Arthurian battles begin with Octha, son of the leader of the original Saxon settlers coming down from the north to lead a Saxon attack. Arthur fights against them, with the kings of the Britons, but he himself was the *Dux* in the battles. The kings of the Britons, whether derived from Celtic tribes or Roman institutions, have joined together under a single war leader. Some of the battles are fought exactly where we would expect them to be, in the Caledonian forest north of the Wall, near the River Glein in Bernicia. Perhaps Castellum Guinnion is Binchester, or perhaps it is a small structure like a mile castle on the Wall. The occupied forts show traces of Christian activity and unlike the west a mixture of secular and religious activities. Perhaps the River Dubglas is just across the Humber in the Linnuis Region. The British period of unbroken victory ends, of course, with the arrival of Ida in Bernicia.

A death of Arthur at Camboglanna makes excellent sense in this scenario, either beaten by a new wave of invaders or, as tradition from the time of Geoffrey of Monmouth has it, killed in a civil war. Gildas is quite clear that civil war among the Britons was endemic, as a new generation which had forgotten the Saxon threat arose. The unity of the British kings and the warlords of Birdoswald and the like might well have been a very fragile thing, needing an outside threat to keep it viable. Although Geoffrey thought the Battle of Camblan was in Cornwall, he did make Arthur's adversary Modred the son of the king of Lothian, the later name for the lands of the Gododdin. An interesting coincidence, if nothing else, is that the garrison of Banna was principally composed of the first cohort of the Dacians. They had originally been raised in what is now Transylvania. The *Notitia Dignitatum* accidentally recorded them at [C]Amboglanna, one of the reasons for the confusion of the neighbouring sites. In Geoffrey of Monmouth, one of Arthur's allies is Aschillus king of the Dacians, and he is one of the named commanders killed fighting alongside Arthur at the Battle of Camblan (HRB XI: 80).

✂

Here is an archaeological scenario which makes sense in the context of Gildas, of *Historia Brittonum* and indeed of some later Arthurian materials. None of the writers, except Francis Pryor, made the Arthurian connection, but then neither did they go out of their way to deny it. It seems that freed from the pressures of a West Country tourist industry, and out of the shadow of the Cadbury/Camelot dig, everyone was able to take a step back and evaluate the evidence as it stood.

Arthur of the Britains

I do not want to suggest that these discoveries vindicate the idea of a completely northern Arthur. The evidence from Britannia Prima is very similar. There are several British kingdoms which have united to confront the Saxons militarily. Indeed they have been even more successful. The province was a totally Saxon-free zone.

We don't know what the late Roman military establishment of Britannia Prima was. There were Roman forts, but no officer in *Notitia Dignitatum* is given the job of running them. This may be a scribal oversight or it might indicate a change in policy, giving over the responsibility for defence against the Irish to native Britons. Without a *Limes* system of frontier defences, the Britons re-occupied existing fortifications, but in this case Iron Age ones as well as Roman ones. They put up their own linear earthworks and managed their own system of provisioning them. In the same way that the un-Romanised Gododdin and the Novantae seem to support the Romanised Britons, so the un-Romanised Dumnonia and Vendedotia seem brought in to the same defence system.

Alongside the *Dux Britanniarum* there was a *Comes Britanniarum* (Companion or as later ages would term it 'Count' of the Britains). The *Comes* led the mobile reserve forces which would move swiftly along the roads to support the *Limitanaei* or deal with any irruptions that occurred. Although the *Comes* had the senior title to the *Dux*, he was not his commanding officer. Both reported to the *Magister Militum* in Gaul. This was the post held by Aetius and gives a reason why Britons might appeal to him. Without aid from the continent, the Britons would have had to appoint their own *Magister Militum*, a supreme commander to coordinate the military response. Britannia Prima and Secunda must have held together. They did not fortify against each other and neither of them seems to have let the Saxons settle within them.

We have other indications that the two provinces did co-operate. Five work parties working on Hadrian's Wall proudly recorded their origins. Two were from the '*civitas Durotrigum Lendiniensis*', that is the people from the South Cadbury/Ilchester area. Another was formed of the Dumnonii (Davey 2005: 127). I have already mentioned the Cohort of the Cornovii, from the Wroxeter area, stationed in Newcastle.

⚮

When it came, the Saxon revolt was not confined to the north and the east. It spread across the island to the western shores, laying low all the *coloniae*. It is likely that Vortiporius of Demetia's father (likened to Hezekiah as the Saxons are to Hezekiah's adversaries, the Assyrians) took part in the resistance. At the least the victories culminating in the siege of Mount Badon secured peace for the ruler of Demetia and for the Constantine of Dumnonia, indicating the resistance was not confined to Britannia Secunda.

The *Magister Militum* might be a Roman, like Aetius, and this could be the role assigned to Ambrosius. More commonly in this period, the Romans opted for generals of more warlike barbarian origin, like Stilicho and Odoacer. An Arthur with an origin in Ireland (from his name) or the un-Romanised west (tradition) would fit this pattern.

Arthur as *Magister Militum*, co-ordinating the military response of the kings, and the *Comes* and *Dux* of the Britains makes sense of the archaeological evidence and of the *Historia Brittonum*. It also explains the confusion over his exact status. Was he a king or not? Civil authority at this point would be different from military authority. This might be the force of Gildas's claim that in the Badon period kings and public officials kept to their station. In military matters the military officers would be superior to kings (Aetius commanded kings against Attila) while in the social sphere they might be less prestigious. Maybe this is why Arthur was remembered as 'Arthur the soldier' in south-east Wales.

It could be that *The Gododdin*'s comparison 'though he wasn't an Arthur' refers to rank or status; Guaurddur took out huge numbers of Saxons 'though he wasn't a general'. The only other place in *The Gododdin* where the same comparison is made ('though he wasn't...' '*cen ne bei...*') is used in exactly this way, to tell us about Uruei's father 'though he wasn't a Guledig' (B2.28).

17

THE RETURN OF ARTHUR

Interest in King Arthur is arguably just as strong now as it was in the 1960s. There is an ever-growing number of Arthurian fictions. Those for adults tend to aim for a Dark Age idiom while those for children, exemplified by the current television series *Merlin* seem to stick to the high medieval era of the romances. That makes the reversal of fortunes King Arthur has suffered in the archaeological world all the more extraordinary.

Avalon, Tintagel, Camelot, Camlan: the Arthurian spin given to Glastonbury, Tintagel, Cadbury and Slaughterbridge is atypical. It surprises me how capriciously Arthurian sites are presented to the public. This ranges from the rare 'full-on' Arthurian experiences at Camelford and the Arthurian emphasis at Tintagel, to the far more usual 'nothing'. Fairbairn (1983) trawled the country for Arthurian sites, using evidence from folklore associations and medieval romances. Of the 155 British sites in his comprehensive survey, the vast majority have not been investigated for their sub-Roman archaeology, and have no on-site interpretation of their Arthurian connection at all. The region with the most, Wales, was, as we have seen, distinguished by no mention at all of Arthur on the Cadw website.

There are only four Arthurian sites on the English Heritage website, Tintagel, the Arthurian Centre at Slaughterbridge, a Neolithic henge dating from *c.*2000 BC called King Arthur's Round Table (English Heritage Property. 152), and 'Arthur's Stone', an 'atmospheric Neolithic "dolmen" burial chamber' (English Heritage Property. 330). The habit of naming prehistoric monuments after mythical heroes, including Arthur, is covered at length by Higham (2002). As it happens, the Arthur Stone site is quite possibly the tomb of Anir, a son of 'the Soldier Arthur' who killed him and buried him there, one of the Wonders of Britain in *Historia Brittonum*, and thus one of the very earliest 'Arthurian' sites. At the site, an interpretation board explains the Neolithic origin of the tomb and goes on to cover its legendary association with Arthur. Its somewhat garbled account, illustrated with a line drawing of Dark Age warriors, is that it marks the site of one of Arthur's battles, where he killed his son, clearly identifying it with the tale of Arthur and Mordred. This board places the Arthur Stone in the tiny minority of Arthurian sites so presented to the public. Archaeologists do not use the name Arthur in the titles of their books or even in their indices. Higham and Green do, to give them credit, have Arthur's name prominently displayed in their titles and cover imagery, but lay readers are bound to find their *a priori* assumptions that Arthur is fictitious unsettling.

Alongside this has been, I think a less than creditable attempt by publishers to fill the vacuum. Most claims to 'reveal' king Arthur seem to be blinkered partisan attempts to tie Arthur to the authors' home territory, ignoring any post-1960s scholarship while decrying academics for ignoring their chosen early modern source material. Cadbury/Camelot era texts like John Morris's *Age of Arthur* are resolutely reprinted.

The reprint of Alcock's *Arthur's Britain* (as an 'Archaeology Classic' from Penguin) did give the author the opportunity to review his ideas in a new introduction and bibliography. Alcock has clearly repudiated many of his Cadbury/Camelot arguments. He has abandoned the idea that South Cadbury was a campaign base for the defence of Dumnonia against the Saxons in the Thames Valley. He now sees it as a permanently occupied political and administrative centre, descendant of the *civitas* capital of Ilchester.

He obviously remained aggrieved at the way the debate had swung and the role of Dumville in this. He writes more than once about how his use of the written sources has been 'sometimes less than scrupulously attacked by Dr David Dumville' (Alcock 2001: 405). He gives an example where Kathleen Hughes had challenged his view that the *Annales Cambriae* went back to a contemporary source. She said there was no evidence of this but softened it with a footnote (1980: 73 n.41) saying that while it was not impossible the fifth- and sixth-century annals derived from contemporary Easter tables, 'it is much more likely that they are based on the calculations of an eighth- (or perhaps seventh-) century scholar.'

Alcock then quotes Dumville's version of this: 'there is no question, as Dr Hughes has made clear' of them deriving from a contemporary source. Alcock notes acidly (2001: 392) 'the modern historian may well consider that source criticism needs applying to the writings of Dr Dumville as much as to *Annales Cambriae* and the *Historia Brittonum*'.

Archaeology has, in the intervening years, added 'richness and complexity' to our knowledge of the period but there are some areas where it simply cannot go. 'It is axiomatic, for a start, that archaeology cannot prove the historicity of Arthur, except through the unlikely discovery of an unambiguously inscribed memorial stone, or some personal object like the signet ring of the Frankish king Childeric or the well-known Alfred jewel' (Alcock 2001: 404). Even artefacts as obvious as the Voteporix stone are sometimes considered insufficiently clear. The meticulous analysis of the written sources is necessary, but he regrets the fact that the historians engaged in this refuse to draw wider inferences from their work, such as producing broader syntheses of the evidence (Alcock 2001: 407).

By this I suppose Alcock means there is nothing like his own book, which addressed both archaeology and history to present a single narrative of the period. I agree that it is a problem that there is no attempt to present this new think-ing clearly to the general public. This is particularly galling as the interest in the period was clearly stoked up by archaeologists and historians in the first place. Given that there is a demonstrable public appetite for the subject, why are the academics not queuing up to satisfy it?

Perhaps there is a feeling that too many of the professionals had their fin-gers burnt by the excessive reliance on unhistorical sources of the archaeologists of the Cadbury/Camelot era. Even so, the public is in no way served by this refusal to engage. The visitors 'in tens of thousands' (Alcock 1972: 9) enticed by the Camelot Research Committee to support the excavations, paid in large part for the work at South Cadbury. They were repaid, 25 years later, by a highly technical report which refused to discuss the myths or the Arthurian period at all. As this was an English Heritage publication, they had in fact paid for it twice over, through general taxation. The Arthurian excavations were covered in an obscurely printed supplement which equally failed to mention King Arthur and Camelot. Hutton speaks for all the aggrieved members of the public:

> right up to the present, visitors to public libraries, Glastonbury and Tintagel, look-ing for information upon King Arthur, will find the books of Ashe, and that of Alcock which is in a new paperback edition. Dumville has never addressed the general public on the matter, preferring so far to write only for his colleagues. None of the textbook-writers who have followed him have provided any full explanation for the academic rejection of the historical Arthur. (Hutton 2003: 56)

Francis Pryor is one of the very few professional archaeologists to tackle the subject, albeit in a subtitle to his *Britain AD*. He writes warmly of the archae-ologists of the late 1960s, and more recently, who were prepared to challenge the all-pervasive orthodoxy of the previous period. He notes the sheepishness with which they had previously kowtowed to the prevailing explanation of mass Anglo-Saxon invasions evidenced by changing pottery styles, exemplified by the great J.N.L. Myres. To do otherwise he acknowledges would have meant 'profes-sional suicide' (Pryor 2004: 133). I am not at all convinced that the situation is any better now. Belief or not in Arthur is part of a package, dominated by fashion not by new research. It would be next to impossible for a British academic to get funded or find an a supervisor for his PhD if his thesis was to prove or argue for a historical Arthur. No tenured academic has argued this in print for decades.

Dumville's work on the written sources is absolutely invaluable. There are very few places where I disagree with his detailed critique, but Dumville is treated with exactly the same awe and reverence as Myres was a generation ago. His pronouncements are never challenged even when, as with his connection of *Historia Brittonum* to the court of Merfyn Ffrych, they are so ill founded. No academic has commented on the inordinate time it has taken Dumville to publish his edition of the *Historia Brittonum*, on which his criticism rests, or broken ranks, as was done heroically to end the monopoly of the Dead Sea Scrolls, by publishing a single manuscript edition and translation of the Harleian manuscript which contains the best exemplar of it and the *Annales Cambriae*.

As the existence of Arthur has neither been proved nor disproved in the 30 years since Dumville first opened the attack, one would expect, given a perfectly free intellectual and academic field where various schools of thought contend, that we would find at least some academic material entertaining the idea that Arthur refortified Binchester or that factual material underlies the Arthurian battle list. The fact that there are no such works (excepting Pryor's *Britain AD* at a pinch, though he rejects all aspects of the background picture offered by Gildas and *Historia Brittonum*) demonstrates all too well that avoidance of professional suicide by breaking ranks is still the name of the archaeological game.

Scepticism quite rightly has its place in history. To advance our understanding of the past, old assumptions need to be challenged. I certainly agree with most historians and archaeologists that the positivism of the Cadbury/Camelot era was overstated. The relative value of written sources was not adequately considered and connections between them and the archaeological finds were made too quickly. With King Arthur this scepticism has become wildly unbalanced. Degrees of proof which are impossible in the Dark Ages are demanded and finds consistent with the Arthurian legend are distanced from them by ignorance and mental gymnastics.

Many times in my research I have been exasperated by the double standards applied to King Arthur. We have to demonstrate his existence beyond all reasonable doubt before we can speak positively about him. Yet in fairness a hypothesis which has been accepted for 1200 years and which has never been disproved hardly needs such treatment. Instead it ought to be expected that archaeologists and historians who decide to remove Arthur from the picture in their works should explain why. This should require rather more work from them than referring to a journal article from the 1970s which apparently disproved his existence.

It is time to reclaim the Dark Age history of Britain from 'the nameless dead' (as Charles Thomas puts it) and instead examine and reinstate the traditional names, Arthur amongst them. In each generation the paralysing grip of academic orthodoxy needs to be broken. It is just as important now for historians and archaeologists holding broadly positivist Arthurian views to publish them as it was for sceptical voices to be raised against Cadbury/Camelot and *The Age of Arthur*. Given the great public interest in King Arthur it is imperative that accessible works on the excavations of Cadbury, Tintagel and Glastonbury, which address the Arthurian connections with something other than contempt be published. Historians like Dumville need to present their counter arguments to the general public as Alcock and Morris did in their heyday. Only once such lively debate and engagement with the public has been generated will we be assured that the next item inscribed with the letters ART discovered at an Arthurian site will be properly interpreted and understood.

Digging for Myths

So, what has half a century of archaeological investigation revealed? The propensity of archaeologists before Dumville to connect sites with the glamorous locations of later legends was never going to work out happily. Camelot and Avalon had all their resonance from the realm of myth, not history. We have a firm foundation in the work of Gildas. The archaeological record justifies and I would say confirms his picture of Saxon invasion and British resistance. Looking for locations he actually mentions, the *coloniae*, the City of the Legions, Badon itself, would be more profitable.

The Arthurian material in *Historia Brittonum* is perfectly consistent with what archaeology has revealed. It shows the kings of the Britons co-operating in widespread resistance to the invaders, and provides us with names of the battles and just importantly for us names their war leader, Arthur. Of course the battles and the war leader had names and nothing has been found, either in archaeology or historical research to disprove the versions given in *Historia Brittonum*.

The anti-Arthurian camp takes disengagement with Arthurian material to bizarre and unbalanced lengths. *Historia Brittonum* can only be used to give insight into the court politics of Merfyn Frych, *Annales Cambriae* can only show the ecclesiastical preoccupations of tenth-century St Davids or the dynasticism of Hywell Dda. Gildas is not even allowed to illuminate his own time, rejected instantly if his testimony about the world he actually lived in fails to support whatever fashionable notion the archaeologist subscribes. Even when he supported as far as possible the archaeologists' interpretation at Tintagel, he got less mention in the official publication than a jar of Shippam's Paste, which amused the archaeologists so much they included the same anecdote about it twice (complete with 'geddit!!' exclamation marks and two index entries).

The existence of Arthur is in no sense 'disproved'. On the contrary there is a very good balance-of-probability case in his favour. It infuriates me that belief in a historical Arthur is lumped alongside pseudo-archaeological views such as extraterrestrial origins, lost civilisations and radical re-dating schemes. There are very strong evidence-based counter-arguments against these positions. Arthur by contrast is simply not in this league. There is nothing to disprove *Historia Brittonum*'s position, nothing indeed to disprove the ideas that he was conceived in Tintagel and buried at Glastonbury, yet these beliefs are treated as equally ill-founded and fanciful.

It is worrying just how convoluted, how complex, the arguments against Arthur are. Faced with the mass of evidence, opponents are forced to imagine an unknown British god called Arthur (with a convenient taboo against naming him), or landscape features named after other Arthurs of earlier history or mythology whose importance to the inhabitants is nowhere attested. These chimerical Arthurs have left legends which have, for inscrutable reasons, been attached to a military figure of the fifth or sixth century who, if he existed, cannot possibly have borne the name Arthur. Whatever name he had must, despite his importance, have become irretrievably lost. The author of *Historia Brittonum* has for his own purposes of creating a synthetic (and effectively false) history of God's purpose for the Britons, uniquely put this composite figure in a narrative which otherwise only features major figures already placed in this time period. All other references to Arthur as a historical figure derive from this single source. The counter-argument, that Arthur was a real person who fought the Saxons at the Battle of Mount Badon, and who later attracted legendary tall tales, has the advantage of simplicity and requires fewer unknown steps and sources.

On the level of Schliemann and Troy, the legends proved surprisingly reliable predictors of the age and type of structures discovered by archaeologists at Arthurian sites. This is all the more surprising as the actual sites visible when the legendary identifications were first made often gave no clue to the fifth/sixth-century remains discovered. Often the legends provided the spur for intensive excavation which might not have been forthcoming at less famous sites.

Hutton (2003: 42) notes there is something slightly unbalanced in the academic treatment of Arthur. As evidence from Tintagel during the 1990s piled up demonstrating that it had been a defensible residence of the ruling house of Cornwall, inhabited by women around about the year 500, all involved tried frantically to distance themselves from the fact these conclusions had been pre-empted by the literary tradition.

The Arthurian legends have often pointed archaeologists correctly in the direction of real finds. That, however, is not their prime utility. Rather they have the rare gift of imbuing sites with the factors of recognition, empathy and emotional engagement they might otherwise lack. In the past 30 years, however, there has been such a backlash against the Arthurian myths by the archaeological community that sites are unable to capitalise in what could be very effective tools to attract and interpret to the public.

The Importance of Myths

In the wider world of archaeology, the casual dismissal or ridicule of the Arthurian legends would be unacceptable. It often seems as if the delight some archaeologists take in ridiculing belief or interest in King Arthur is directly related to the significance he has to the wider public. This is very far from archaeological best practice, which considers the cultural importance of a site or artefact along with its physical remains. The intangible heritage of story, tradition and written history is accorded value. When preparing an archaeological statement of significance for the Bloody Tower at the Tower of London, it is just as important that the site is associated with the imprisonment and murder of the Princes in the Tower as it is as a gateway in Henry III's curtain wall. It does not matter whether the details of the Princes' story are true or not. Whether they were imprisoned there, or murdered, is not really the point. The site has been associated with the story, and the story embodied in great literature and art, for so long that it has a significance of itself.

The insensitivity and derision archaeologists pour on the Arthurian legends is actually quite shocking. It is inconceivable anywhere else in the world that the archaeological community would be so dismissive of the beliefs of the indigenous population. The archaeology of the settlement of New Zealand by the Maori, for example, is always these days presented with an eye to the Maori traditions. Where the two views diverge this is addressed with sensitivity.

Compare and contrast. King Arthur's burial at Glastonbury/Avalon has been an important British tradition for centuries, but this view is treated as a hoax. And who can doubt that the major significance of the site is not that it is a gothic ruin, a dissolved monastery, a Church of England place of worship, even a burial place of some Anglo-Saxon kings. In these aspects it is hardly unique. It is the identification of the site with a mystic Avalon which makes it a modern pilgrimage destination.

It is readily appreciated by archaeologists working in non-western cultures that 'indigenous traditions of knowing the past should be respected, not eradicated' and that 'archaeologists are not the only people with a legitimate and genuine interest in the past' (Gazin-Schwartz and Holtorf 1999: 18). In their study, *Archaeology and Folklore*, Gazin-Schwartz and Holtorf and their contributors argue strongly that the same attitude of respect and indeed humility should be displayed to western myths. Collective identities are often connected with the folklore of archaeological sites (Gazin-Schwartz and Holtorf 1999: 17) and if the concept of Camelot is not deep within our collective identity, then nothing is.

All these strictures on multiple viewpoints, of tolerance and understanding would hold true even if the Arthurian legends flew in the face of all external historical evidence. Are people not allowed to visit sites connected with figures of literature, like 221b Baker Street, just because the figures are literary creations who never inhabited the real world?

Meeting the Myth-seekers

There is little appreciation of what it is visitors are seeking at Arthurian sites. Smiles (1994: 45) sees Arthur as part of a family of patriot heroes, defenders of the island against outside evils. He occupies a combined figure of both Celtic and English king, a fitting icon for Britain as a whole. Without, strangely, mentioning Arthur at all, Smith (1999: 112) highlights Geoffrey of Monmouth's role in providing a unifying mythical past not peculiar to any one of the British nations. The concept of a lost golden age which could dramatise the 'atmosphere and picturesque uniqueness of the people's past and the events and personages which compose it' (Smith 1999: 66) is bolstered by archaeology in a composite process of ethnic mythmaking.

We can certainly see the archaeologists of the 1960s and 1970s working in this idiom, fostering a comfortable form of ethnic past, but in the intervening years a gulf has opened between the archaeologists and their ethnic community, who seek a golden age of virtue and heroism 'when men were "heroes" ... models of virtuous conduct, their deeds of valour inspir[ing] faith and courage in their oppressed and decadent descendants' (Smith 1999: 65).

Archaeologists around the world have stopped thinking of the wide variety of values placed on ancient sites as being wrong, and those dealing with Arthurian sites in Britain need to catch up with this. A visitor may go to Stonehenge because it features in the Arthurian legends, rebuilt by Merlin and a burial place for Uther Pendragon. They are not 'wrong' any more than a visitor to whom the site has importance as the place where Tess of the d'Urbervilles was arrested, a landscape Turner painted or somewhere where religious feelings for the land or the heavens were (re)awakened by neo-pagans of the nineteenth and twentieth centuries. We aren't wrong, we have simply started at a different place. That we have trekked to the Tintagel peninsula, to the top of Glastonbury Tor, to the mouth of the River Glen shows something of the value we place on those locations. We pay admission charges, buy the guidebooks, even the excavation reports and we do not expect our interest and commitment to be devalued just because it is not the same as the particular one espoused by current academic fashion. Why are we wrong because our interest has been sparked by one reason and not another?

If I visit Tintagel because I think Arthur was conceived there, Liddington because I think he fought there, Glastonbury because I think he was buried there, am I less worthy to have the site interpreted to me than someone whose interest is in Earl Richard's castle, or the Iron age or the Church of England? It reminds me of the old joke about the couple motoring through the Irish countryside. They stop and ask a villager the best way to get to Dublin. His scratches his head and answers, 'Well, I wouldn't have started from here.'

This seems entirely the attitude embodied by the excavation report on Tintagel, the graphic panels at Glastonbury and the website of Colchester. If we are coming to these things because we have been excited by *The Once and Future King*, *The Mists of Avalon* or *The Age of Arthur*, we are wrong. We should have started out with an interest in early Christian settlement hierarchies, chantry chapels or Boudicca's rebellion. Then the archaeologists would have come out to meet us.

Rahtz, although he frequently presents myth and archaeology as a dichotomy, acknowledges that there is a spectrum from potentially true, though probably not, to completely impossible, on which any theory can lie. Equally there is a spectrum of response to the myths, in his case those of Glastonbury, ranging from absolute belief to absolute scepticism (his own position 'they are not true but are wholly the product of medieval and later invention... The myths are an important record of what people believed, but should not be confused with what actually happened') (1993: 42). He goes on to enumerate different classes of believers, from those who see the myths as exaggerated or garbled versions of real events, through those who think it is their affirmation which is important to our cultural heritage, not their historical reality, those who wish to suspend their disbelief in the interests of a satisfying visit, those interested in the symbolic truths to those 'very common' at Glastonbury (Rahtz 1993: 43) cynically using it to make money. Very little appreciation is shown at any of the Arthurian sites of this broad visitor spectrum, and the appropriate ways of interpreting to each type of tourist.

There is no doubt that a lot of the public's interest in the archaeology of those sites springs directly from the mythical associations. 'Every once in a while myth triumphs conclusively over reality' writes Fairbairn (1983: 9) 'say the words King Arthur ... and you will conjure up a vision of knights and maidens, quests and adventures, good and evil'. The idea that such things can be directly encountered at an archaeological site would always be appealing. Selwyn (1996: 2) argues that it is precisely the fact that contemporary tourists are seeking out a 'pre-modern "Other" which is in some way more whole, structured and authentic ... than the everyday world they inhabit' which leads to the creation of the 'mythical structures or tourist myths, and the imagery associated with them' (Selwyn 1996: 3). In this sense the visitors are simply reiterating or reaffirming the power of the myth which drew attention to the site in the first place, the 'universal human tendency to desire narratives that in some fashion assist one to make sense of one's position in life, or to confirm one's value system, or simply to provide reassurance that the world and its events are charged with meaning on a human scale' (Levitt 2006: 277).

The norm in the last 30 years has been for archaeologists to ignore or swiftly dismiss Arthurian associations. By not engaging with the Arthurian material, they reject an important tool for interpreting the past to a wider audience. They deprive their sites of a narrative and emotional context which could have been used to make meaningful connections with the public.

There is a feeling that the public are so irredeemably wedded to myths that there is no point engaging with them;

the public is not interested in other forms of reality supported by academic research. There is no mileage in suggesting that a typical monarch in sixth-century Britain ... would have been a short, wary-looking young man with bad teeth, bad breath, body lice and a suspicious temper' (Thomas 1993: 126).

Myth Busters

There are many ways archaeologists can engage with myth other than dishonest acquiescence in views they cannot support. There is a clear worry that engagement with myths and legend is a betrayal of the scientific method just to pander to the preconceptions of the visitors (South 1997: 54). Some have, as we have seen, responded by avoidance. Others (Michlovic 1990: 103) rise to it as a challenge to their presumed monopoly on interpretations of the past.

I, as I hope I make clear in my books, am every bit as committed to communicating the truth of Dark Age British history and Arthur's possible role in it as any academic historian or archaeologist. It is an important part of my professional life as a historical interpreter to show how ideas about the past come about and pointing out where such ideas have been proven wrong. I am not about trivialising or falsifying history to support irrational ideas. Most of us who support a positive stance on Arthur are not 'Arthur nuts', credulous wishful thinkers fleeing from objective reality.

The public enjoys the spectacle of 'myth-busting' (Hutton 2003: 37), and this is a function many archaeologists are happy to perform. Despairing of the 'strange miscellany' of books of 'dubious value' available on Glastonbury, Rahtz set out to help the discerning reader disentangle myth and history to arrive at 'the closest approach to truth that historical and archaeological scholarship is able to provide' (Rahtz 1993: 10).

Is the best an archaeologist can do with a myth to bust it? Even Charles Thomas admits 'it would be a grey world if ever the Thought Police outlawed all but academically-approved writings about a past we never knew, a country where none but the nameless dead may dwell' (Thomas 1993: 128). These myths have been valued for 900 years, in the case of Arthur. Gazin-Schwartz and Holtorf (1999: 13) argue that under those circumstances, the question of accuracy is moot: 'it is part of that tradition whether or not its origins are in literature or commercial invention'. 'Post-structuralism and multiculturist theorizing [have raised the question of] who can speak for whom in histories and history' writes Berkhoffer (1995: 3). 'Is academic knowledge superior to other forms of knowledge?' ask Gazin-Schwartz and Holtorf (1999: 18).

Examples of how both mythical and archaeological perspectives can be accommodated at single sites are easily obtainable from non-western sites. For example at the Hatzic site in British Columbia, important both to the origin myths of the indigenous population and to pre-historians, the archaeological investigation and the spiritual significance of the site to the local population were consciously given equal significance in the interpretation of the site.'When native interpretations differed from academic ones, *both* perspectives were presented' (Pokotylo and Brass 1997: 160).This is the sort of approach envisaged at Tintagel, with occasional storytelling, but could clearly be applied elsewhere. It provides one answer to the question posed by Renfrew and Bahn (2004: 576) of how to deal with the fact that the beliefs of druids and aboriginals are not supported by archaeological evidence. It hardly requires the acceptance of 'post-processual relativistic positions' to acknowledge the existence of myth as a separate strand of information. Selwyn is adamant (1996: 20) that relaxing distinctions in what he calls a 'postmodern way' is dangerous to heritage tourism, running the risk of confusing the issue of what is 'authentic' – the specific quality heritage tourists seek.

Much of the disjunction between archaeologists and the public arise from a misconception of what sort of evidence can possibly be retrieved by archaeology. 'Questions that arise from a consideration of a great mass of hard archaeological finds ... are not quite in the same category as questions that may be given shape by considering later literary or mythical attributions' (Thomas 1993: 86). Archaeologists need to be clear on exactly what they have to offer to 'a cultural group already in possession of a sufficient and valid version of their own history' (Layton 1989: 14). Levitt proposes an alternative vision (2006: 273) where future archaeologists are honest that there is very little they can add in confirmatory substance to cherished myths. As Alcock and the Camelot Research Committee stressed at Cadbury, they were not expecting to find personal relics of Arthur (Alcock 1972: 193). 'Current technology can demonstrate that the inhabitants of fifth-century Tintagel ate apples, pears and celery, but cannot, as yet, reveal their names, identities, loves and lusts' (Radford and Swanton 2002: xii).

The New Bards

While there are certainly areas of myth which archaeology will never be able prove, equally there are areas which it will never disprove. It is a mistake to regard myth and archaeology as easily definable opposites, and the only possible reaction to them as belief and disbelief. Rüsen's study of a Highland myth in *Studies in Metahistory* (1993: 4) identified four possible responses.The first, the traditional, was to follow the legend, repeating it to renew its validity.An example might be simply narrating the story of Arthur's conception on site at Tintagel. Christopher Morris's response would be characterised as 'critical', refusing to narrate or follow the story, stating that 'it is merely a "myth" or "legend" devoid of any evidence or binding validity' (Rüsen 1993: 4). Rüsen's two other responses are more useful for interpretation.The 'exemplary' response is to follow and narrate the myth, as an example, in this case the sort of function the site might have had, the society it typified, and hence its validity. The 'genetic' response would be to retell the myth as an example of change. It is disbelieved now, because of these circumstances.

Rahtz condemns Arthur as representing the trivialised personification of the past. I say there is nothing trivial about it. It is the humanisation of the past, wrestled from the grasp of the nameless dead. It is the suggestion of a narrative, of human motivations and actions to allow us to make sense of trends and movements. It is not trivialising but investing sites with weight, engaging the public with their significance.

What I would like to see is archaeologists of potential Arthurian sites acknowledging the Arthurian element. Even if they completely disprove the validity of the Arthurian connection (the remains date from a later period or serve a different purpose) this needs to be explained. Desk-based research needs to cover whatever the range of Arthurian material relating to the site might be, not just a few secondary sources. Where competing positions exist they should be addressed. Any archaeologist who starts with an *a priori* assumption that there is no historical Arthur should read Dumville's 1977 article and précis what they think are salient points in it regarding their site, not just footnote it as a complete explanation. Every archaeologist dealing with sub-Roman Britain should read Gildas (not just a single chapter) and where they disagree with his view explain why (and not just because they imagine him to be a boring old whinger).

Arthurian archaeology should be scientific, it should engage with the public, it should be published both in academic and popular form. The pioneering spirit of Cadbury/Camelot has its legacy in the current golden age of popular archaeology, with *Time Team*, *Big Dig*, *Meet the Ancestors* and the popularity of heritage tourism.

Archaeologists must recognise the importance of King Arthur and the Arthurian legends as enduring images and ideas which hold weight with the public. We aren't misguided or trivialising in wanting to invest them with the weight we do. So much great art and great literature has drawn on them and embellished them that it is hardly surprising that these characters and themes evoke recognition and response.

Good interpretation needs to meet the visitors at a site. It can lead them to different conclusions if that is necessary, not refuse to engage with them from the start. This is not about trivialisation or dumbing down. Of course there sometimes does come a time when the archaeologist needs to correct misapprehensions or mistakes. We are the experts and the public expect us to tell them 'what really happened'. They expect accurate and well-founded answers. 'Certainly in the nineteenth century people said Arthur was born here. Interestingly, the earlier sources only said he was conceived here. They didn't say exactly where he was born. Perhaps the Victorians were just trying to gloss over this aspect.' Even this approach requires a degree of humility, of work in progress or partial evidence partially understood. Think how many visitors to Tintagel have had their 'erroneous' views on Arthur's conception debunked because it *was* a Dark Age monastery.

Hutton, one of the leading exponents of taking the evidence to the audience, sees a dual function of the historian as practitioner of a bardic art. There is a scientific element, testing and evaluating theories, using the methods with the best chance of recovering knowledge of the past. Equally there is a responsibility to advance opinions about the nature of the past which speak to the present 'to craft that information for an audience in such a way as to turn it into stories with the carrying power of myth' (Hutton 2003: 37).

Whatever the archaeologists may feel about the utility of myths to their work, it ought to be appreciated that these myths are valuable means of attracting the public and their money.

Archaeologists and interpreters must engage with the public. Fleming (2002: 69) applauds his colleagues who write in a popular style and in popular media as being the counter-attack in the battle against 'pseudo-thinking'. Arnold exhorts serious scholars to 'engage rather than withdraw, and provide resources, access to information for the interested general public … present lectures … making effective use of the internet' (Arnold 2006: 179). The heritage industry is in the forefront of 'making history more accessible, popular and democratic [and] historians more accountable' (Selwyn 1996: 8). At present only Christopher Snyder has really entered the fray, with a coffee-table illustrated Arthurian book for the general reader supporting his academic work (Snyder 2000).

Telling a Different Story

It is always difficult to decide which stories to tell at a historic sites. Picking any one of the numerous eras and perspectives inevitably 'privileges' the one chosen over those rejected. To tell the story of the man buried in the tomb raises that story over that of the patron who commissioned the monument, the craftsman who carved it, the pilgrim who visited it, the reformer who smashed it and the antiquarian who restored it. In making those choices we pick stories of significance, unusually connected with the site, rather than common ones, because the former are simply better in terms of narrative. This is very rarely the tack followed at 'Arthurian' sites, where common narratives like 'Iron Age hill fort' or 'Roman camp' are frequently chosen over the unusual, exciting or resonant Arthurian connections.

Much of the interpretation of the British Dark Ages is characterised by the gendered presentation which Jones and Pay (in Gathercole and Lowenthal 1990) detected at Jorvik, the Viking experience at York. It was a time of masculine warriors, with women, when encountered at all, their helpless victims. Spector (in Peucel and Hodder 1996: 485) believes this is because western academic knowledge has been dominated by white, western, middle-class men. This is undoubtedly true on the archaeological side of Arthurian investigation, but the subject has a much broader appeal, with clear opportunities for alternative perspectives. A very large proportion of those interested in the legends are women. The seminal retellings of the legends in recent times have been those of Rosemary Sutcliffe (1963), Mary Stewart (1979) and Marion Zimmer Bradley (1983). Bradley's original feminist perspective on the tales has led to a new genre in which the female characters have generally become portrayed as strong warrior protagonists in the story of Dark Age Britain.

Assimilating this perspective would highlight the spindle whorls at Tintagel, which led to the rejection of the monastic hypothesis. This would lead to Geoffrey's depiction of the site as a fortified refuge for the late fifth-century Duchess of Cornwall. Identification of the site as a royal court of the ruler of Cornwall, still culturally attached to the Roman world might lead to a mention that, according to Geoffrey of Monmouth, Queen Guinevere, a descendant of a noble Roman family, had been brought up at the court of the Duke of Cornwall (HRB IX.9). There is no reason why the site on Glastonbury Tor should not have been suggested as a residence for Morgan le Fay, associated with the site by Gerald of Wales. The Abbey was where, in 1191, the monks claimed to have found the bones of Queen Guinevere and where, 90 years later, Queen Eleanor of Castile, a noted patroness of Arthurian romance, had wrapped and reinterred the supposed bones of her predecessor. At Cadbury, we could find that the name Camelot had first appeared in a romance whose subject matter was provided by Countess Marie of Champagne. It epitomised the reckless, even slavish devotion a knight was expected to have for his lady in the culture of 'courtly love' encouraged by Marie and her mother Eleanor of Aquitaine. There is plenty of scope for narrative approaches such as Spector advocates (Preucel and Hodder 1996: 423).

Interpretation of King Arthur and the elite of society, male or female, is also a narrative choice which can be challenged 'by emphasising that our investigation of the past owes as much to people who lived and died in poverty and obscurity as it does to potentates and warrior chieftains' (Levitt 2006: 273). The South Cadbury Environs project provides a needed balance to the elite coverage of the hill fort.

Glastonbury

Handled well, the 'Whodunit' approach could work here. Instead of being given the establishment line, visitors could be introduced to the discovery of unusual skeletons in the graveyard in the manner of a classic detective story. The evidence for the 1191 discovery, the 'crime scene', witness statements, possible suspects could be available on request. Further clues could be encountered on site, leading the visitors to draw their own conclusions.

Tintagel

English Heritage obviously responded to public concerns about the presentation
of the site (Thomas 1993: 131). Thomas advised that future presentations should
contextualise Arthur as 'a twelfth-century literary figure, not an archaeological
concept' (Thomas 1993: 131). This is more or less what the site chose to do with its
various interpretative techniques. Geoffrey's story, as the earliest written evidence,
is a reasonable point of departure. However, instead of following the Arthur route,
to swift dismissal then an unconnected move to the sixth century, the interpretation could move instead to the background implied by Geoffrey. This would
introduce the visitor to the concept of an independent Dumnonia, one of several
competing kingdoms in Britain AD 500, the decline of Roman culture and the
rise of the western kingdoms, typified by the imported pottery and Latin inscriptions at this most un-Roman of settlements. The threat of the Saxons, Gildas's call
for British unity, and the history of Dumnonian tyrant Constantine would bring
the visitor neatly back to Arthur.

Cadbury

Cadbury is all but uninterpreted these days. It is clear that the first piece of interpretation it requires is a popular book, comparable to Cadbury/Camelot (Alcock
1972) bringing the story up to date. Instead of pointing readers to the all but
unobtainable Dumville article (1977), this would directly tackle the issue of the
linkage or otherwise between the archaeology of the site and the literary evidence. On-site interpretation would begin with the concept of Britain in the
fifth and sixth century, the collapse of central government while regional and
rural identities remained strong. The literary evidence from Gildas for the flight
to defended hill sites and the eventual British counter-attack would provide a
strong narrative. The visitor would discover that 300 years later, Arthur was being
named as the leader of the British kings in their wars of resistance, and be asked
to consider for themselves if he could have been connected with the works at
Cadbury. The denouement of this type of exposition could be Leland's identification of the site as Camelot.

Revealing King Arthur

So, have we revealed King Arthur? It is remarkable how much the search for
tangible remains behind the Arthurian legends has revealed about his period.
The Glastonbury find pointed towards the importance of west/east burials
without grave goods as archaeological indicators of Arthur's Britons. Cadbury

Castle showed the refortification of hill forts as a significant feature of the British kingdoms, and spurred more research which explained their context and development. The wealthy regional kings revealed at Tintagel, at once un-Romanised yet in close contact with the Roman Empire, opened a window on the Arthurian courts. The battle list, discredited for 30 years, illuminated the surviving provinces of Britannia Prima and Britannia Secunda and their resistance to the Saxons. Perhaps most strangely, the haunting myths of Arthur's last battle and mysterious end drew us to the evidence of how British kings had united under the successors of Roman military institutions to secure their survival and independence. For knowledge and understanding of this formative Dark Age, these traces have revealed far more than any inscribed stone or jewel could ever do.

We have shown too how important it is for those who reveal the past to be receptive to new ideas, to challenge established ones and to communicate to all of us whose heritage they guard. The King Arthur we have revealed is a figure in whom both myth and history meet. These are not conflicting visions but complementary ones, engagement with which can win both hearts and minds so that we not only understand, but feel, the importance of our common past.

THE YEAR OF THE SIEGE OF BADON HILL

Since writing *The Reign of Arthur* I have been asked by many enthusiasts what I think about the dating of Arthur and how I interpret or decide between the competing Dark Age dates. As with all Arthurian scholarship, the lynch-pin must be Gildas, the only author from the period in Britain whose work survived. Gildas is usually presented as a sixth-century writer, largely on the basis of his *Annales Cambriae* dates, and other data in his work are squeezed to fit them. I propose a different methodology. I will look at what sorts of dating systems Gildas might have used and then look at his *De Excidio Britanniae* itself. This will give a very rough impression of the sort of chronological framework in which Gildas seems to think he is writing. In this I follow Dumville (in Lapidge and Dumville 1984: 61). As Dumville writes 'it is of course possible that Gildas knew no temporal era, that he lived in a chronological fog. But, in my view at least it is foolish to start from such a presupposition.'

Firstly we have to divest ourselves of our notion of 'the date'. Gildas was not using an acknowledged universal dating system which could equally well be used to assign a 'date' to the present or to past events. He might have known for certain that he lived in year x of the reign of the ruler of the Durotriges, but to date the life of the prophet Jeremiah or the last days of the reign of Tiberius, two individuals mentioned in his book, he would have had to deal with other dating systems then work out how those systems related to his own. Some Dark Age writers were fascinated by this sort of question, Gregory of Tours and Bede for instance write extensively on their calculations. Gildas, however, does not and we simply cannot take for granted that he has anything like a universal dating system in his mind by which to order the events he describes.

Officially, in the Roman Empire, the date was the name of the two consuls appointed for that year. The jobs were only honorific by the fifth century but the dating convention persisted. It was not a case of remembering that, say, Aetius was consul for the third time in the year 446, but that the year which we call 446 was, to a Roman contemporary, Aetius Consul III. Gildas was familiar with the concept. He does, after all, refer to Agitius as '*ter consule*'.

In the non-Roman world, the year would generally be expressed as 'x of the king', the year since the accession of the current ruler. This is the system which even the very Romanised Gregory of Tours generally used, living as he did under the barbarian Frankish kings.

Christian writers had worked on chronological systems which took a longer and more universal view of dating. They sought to place historical dates within a wider narrative of salvation. The Anno Domini system, dating from the birth of Christ, was the innovation of the writer Dionysius Exiguus in the year of the consulship of Probus Junior. He described that year as AD 525, the name we still give it. This was not the only system he used. Dionysius combined the 19-year Easter cycles with his AD dates, and used cycles as the system for dating before he moved to AD (Sims-Williams 1983b: 36).

Gildas, understandably, also sees the Incarnation as a watershed between the two periods of history. He decides not to concern himself with 'ancient errors before the coming of Christ in the flesh' (4:2) '*ante adventum Christi in carne*'. We might take this as equivalent to our BC/AD divide, but closer examination of the text shows that this was not exactly how Gildas thought. Before Dionysius, many Christian writers had seen the division between the old and new dispensations not as Jesus's conception or birth (very little actually changed then), but the year of the Passion. This is Gildas's view. He says in his narrative when, in an incredible ornate sentence culminating in the word '*Christus*', the light of Christ penetrated the gloom of Britain 'this happened first, as we know, in the last years of the Emperor Tiberius' (8) '*tempore, ut scimus, summo Tiberii Caesaris*'. This dating system, 'after the Passion' was used on the continent in the sixth century, forming the backbone of Gregory of Tours' *History of the Franks*.

Dionysius composed his AD system not as an alternative to the post-Passion system (they were after all very similar), but against the prevailing Christian dating system, the 'era of the Martyrs'. This took the Great Persecution by the Emperor Diocletian as the end of the old era of the suffering Church and the beginning of the new one, the triumphant Church. Gildas certainly knew about this. He talks about the evangelisation of Britain 'right up till the nine years persecution by the tyrant Diocletian' (9:1) '*usque ad persecutionem Diocletiani tyranni novennum*'.

Gildas named very few Romans in his book, far fewer than the tiny number of Britons. It cannot be a coincidence that the three he did name were those associated with contemporary dating systems: Tiberius (after the Passion), Diocletian (Era of the Martyrs) and '*Agitius ter consule*' (the consular system). I think that these markers are used to give a historical flavour to his self-styled history. Can we go further than this, though, and deduce that Gildas knows his own 'date' according to any of those systems, or the dates of any other events depending on them?

Remember, none of the dating systems are truly universal. Knowing about them does not imply that, for instance, Gildas knows how many years he lived after the Passion, after the Great Persecution or who the consuls of the year were. He was explicit about the difficulty he faced. He knew about the Great Persecution from 'church history' *'ecclesiastica historia narrat'* (9:2). The works of Eusebius and Orosius, for instance, give those details. Gildas did not have corresponding insular texts and must have relied on continental sources. He had to guess at the relationship between them and events in his own land. Thus he did not even know if the stories of the martyrdoms of Alban (which he knew well), Julius and Aaron even belonged to the Great Persecution 'in the time (as I conjecture) of the same persecution' *'supra dicto ut conicimus persecutionis tempore'* (10:1).

As a side note, it is quite likely that Gildas was wrong in his conjecture. While the continental sources stressed the horrors inflicted in areas under the direct sway of Diocletian and his co-Augustus, at that time Britain was ruled by Diocletian's junior Caesar, Constantius Chlorus. Constantius was not particularly noted for his persecution of Christians. His son Constantine would convert to and decriminalise the religion. If Christianity was already established in Britain we would expect it to have already seen its first martyrdoms, say in the Persecution of Decius. Gildas's inability to get a date for something which he cared so much about and could even look to history books for context puts his 'dates' of the arrival of the Saxons and the Battle of Badon in perspective.

Whatever his familiarity with the 'historic' dating systems, Gildas could not have been entirely adrift with no notion of wider time keeping. He and his community would have observed the moveable feast of Easter and the other celebrations which depended on it. This is a deduction based on known Christian practice rather than internal to the text, to be sure, but one we can be pretty certain of. After the Great Persecution, Gildas noted that Christians resumed celebrating the feast days (12:2) *'dies festos celebrant'*. The Penitentials attributed to him also mention the Passion as the occasion for an annual celebration.

At the very least, observing Easter would have meant following the 19-year Metonic cycle, at the end of which the sun and moon are roughly back to the same position. We can be assured, though, that Gildas was not part of a self-sufficient community forced to fall back on its own rough and ready calculations. He wrote directly to bishops and priests of the wider church, referred to priests going abroad for advancement and was quoted with approval by late sixth-century Irish clerics as a correspondent. The Irish Church and those in contact with it in the British Isles used an 84-year cycle, the Augustalis. This is specifically noted by Bede (II.2) as the 'stubborn practice' of the British Church in the sixth century. The Church in Britain and Ireland continued to accept modifications to the calculation of the date of Easter ordered by Rome through to the mid-fifth century, but did not accept the full revised 532-year cycle finalised in 457. Gildas showed no knowledge of or interest in competing Easter systems, so a reasonable guess is that he used the 84-year system and would have been able to locate himself somewhere within the cycle.

Finally, Gildas had his own age to use as a yardstick. Counting birthdays is not a universal preoccupation, but it is a Roman one. Gildas uses the word *'anniversarias'* (17:3) to apply to the regular annual attacks of the Picts and the Scots. I believe, as does the current translator and most other readers of Gildas, that Gildas clearly dates the siege of Badon Hill to 43 years and one month before the present based on the fact he is just beginning his forty-fourth year (26:1). 'That was the year of my birth, as I know, one month of the forty-fourth year since then has already passed' *'quique quadragesimus quartus (ut novi) orditur annus mense iam uno emenso'.* Knowledge of personal age and dating events by it certainly existed in Gildas's Britain. The fifth-century British cleric, St Patrick, also uses it. His *'Confessio'* is even lighter in datable material than *De Excidio Britanniae*, but he also uses his age to 'date' an incident; he was 'taken captive when I was nearly 16.'

A Chronology from Gildas

I believe it is possible to construct a rough and ready chronological framework from *De Excidio Britanniae*. In this I agree with Dumville that the historical narrative is basically sequential. 'Especially unhelpful, it therefore seems to me, is,' he writes, 'the old theory – periodically revived – that Gildas misplaced the letter bearing the *gemitus britannorum* to "Agitius"' (Lapidge and Dumville 1984: 61). Equally I do not believe that Gildas's reference to Badon being the year of his birth is confusingly worded or has some other meaning. Arguments that the narrative overlaps different chronologies, or which force dates to be reread or reordered always derive not from the text but from Procrustean attempts to make *De Excidio Britanniae* fit dates from outside sources. As these dates from Bede, the Anglo-Saxon Chronicle or *Historia Brittonum*, seem less well founded that Gildas's own history, this is putting the cart before the horse. Instead, I propose to show what sense we can make of Gildas's text in its own right.

As a building block for his chronology, let us take the first period of time Gildas mentions, the *'bilustrum'*. This is the space of time for which Gildas stayed silent before publishing *De Excidio Britanniae* (1:2) *'spatio bilustri temporis'.* A *lustrum* is a five-year Roman liturgical period and a *bilustrum* is two of these, a decade. Gildas goes on to describe this decade as 'no short time' (1:15) *'non parvo, ut dixi, temporis'.* By this, we can deduce that when Gildas refers to events separated by or lasting for 'a short time' or similar phrases, he is thinking of something less than 10 years as, by definition, a *bilustrum* is 'no short time'.

The next mention of a *bilustrum* is at the end of the Great Persecution. The persecution passed relatively quickly, the 'whirlwind' subsiding before it had lasted a *'bilustrum'* (12:1) *'igitur bilustro supra dicti turbinis necdum ... expleto'.* In addition to this, Gildas is explicit on how long the Great Persecution actually lasted, nine years of the reign of the tyrant Diocletian (9:1) *'usque ad persecutionem Diocletianai tyranni novennnum'*. The *bilustrum*, therefore, marks the watershed between a duration Gildas would consider not short (10+) and one which he would (up to nine).

The longest period Gildas specifically refers to is the three centuries for which, according to their prophecy, the Saxons will live in this land (2:7) *'ter centum annis'*. As the Saxons are still in the Island as Gildas writes, they must have arrived more recently than 300 years ago. That this is a specific period, not just a generally long time, is clarified as the prophesy says that for half that time, 150 years, they will repeatedly lay it waste; *'centum vero quinquaginta, hoc est dimidio tempore'*. In isolation we might imagine the period of devastation lasting up to the siege of Badon. In context, however, this would justify the complacency of his contemporaries. As Gildas needs the Saxon threat to hang over Britain, he must believe he is writing within the 150 years that the Saxons will devastate, hence the Saxons arrived less than 150 years before this time. Gildas's age links Badon to his own time by 43 years, so the very longest before Badon that the Saxons have been in Britain is 106 years. Is this too long?

Are there any clearer indications of what Gildas considered a long time? He imagines a long period of history before 'the coming of Christ in the flesh' (4:2) and the coming of the Romans to Britain soon after. 'Ever since it was first inhabited' (4:1), he writes of Britain, not dwelling on the 'ancient errors' (4:2) and the 'long past years when dreadful tyrants reigned' *'vetustos immanium tyrannorum annos'*. These are clearly vast and indefinable periods of time, comparable to our idea of 'prehistory'. It is with the 'times of the Roman emperors' (4:6) *'temporibus imperatorum Romanorum'* that we enter the period of time defined by the dating systems we have examined, beginning with the reigns of the emperors Tiberius and Diocletian, as noted above.

In contrast to his vagueness about the dating of Alban, Julius and Aaron, Gildas provides a brief but highly circumstantial account of the reign of Maximus. Maximus begins his tyranny 'at length' (13:1) *'tandem'* after the restoration of Christianity. This is actually in our year AD 383, after the Edict of Milan in AD 313 which ended the Great Persecution. Gildas refers to the two legitimate emperors (13:2) defeated by Maximus. Maximus's triumph is short lived and he is executed 'without delay' *'nec mora'*, in our year AD 388. Such is the detail given about Maximus that we can be sure Gildas derives his material from the 'Church history' *'ecclesiastica historia'* (9:2) he referred to earlier. Maximus featured, for instance, in the history of St Martin of Tours. It would be incredible if this detailed history had come to Gildas without a dating framework – regnal lengths of the legitimate emperors or consular dates, imbedded in it. This would presumably allow him to know that his *'tandem'* covers 70 years.

From Maximus to Gildas

The most difficult calculation, but the most vital to us, is to discover how many years separated Gildas from the death of Maximus. Historians' calculations vary from 100 to 200 years afterwards, a huge difference. This is largely because the next part of his history is riddled with well-known errors, like the dating of the northern frontier defences and the withdrawal of Roman troops from Britain. These huge errors, however, do not mean that Gildas does not have an opinion as to the amount of time which has elapsed. He gives a lot of references to the passage of time and duration of incidents, far more than in the earlier part of the book.

After Maximus, the Island groans for 'many years' (14:1) '*multos annos*' under the attacks of the Picts and Scots. The Romans then return and construct the turf wall, but when they leave the Picts and Scots return to plunder 'year after year' (17:3) '*anniversarias praedas*'. The stone wall is built but again the attacks resume. Desperate, the Britons appeal to Agitius, a man of Roman power, calling him '*ter consule*' (20:1) 'consul for the third time'. This appeal was obviously of some significance to Gildas, as he promised to write about the letter to Agitius '*de epistolis ad Agitum*' in his 'blurb' (2:1). The appeal is of course rejected, the Britons are gripped by a notorious famine but some fight back, 'meanwhile' (20:2) '*interea*', that is at the same time as the rejected appeal, defeating the invaders who had plundered the land for many years '*per multos annos*'.

Why did Gildas mention Agitius twice? He does not seem to know who he is or what his position was. Agitius does not respond nor does he appear as a claimed ancestor by later British dynasties. I believe he is mentioned specifically because Gildas knows him from the date. '*Ter consul*' is not a title Aetius (no other potential Agitius could be addressed as *ter consule*) would have used year after year. Aetius Consul III was, instead, the official Roman way of describing the year we call AD 446. Even if we allow an appeal to Aetius '*ter consule*' to be made after he had relinquished the annual post, an extended duration would take us no further than AD 453, year Aetius Consul IV. That seems unlikely, as Latin had different ways of referring to people who had previously held the consulship.

What is interesting is that only 58 years actually separate year Aetius Consul III from the last year of Maximus. If Gildas knows this, that is if Gildas has sufficient dating material to place Maximus and Aetius *ter consul* relative to each other, then we can make another calculation. Gildas has identified three long periods, many years, year after year, within this time. These run from the death of Maximus to the building of the turf wall, from the turf wall to the stone wall and from the stone wall to the native defeat of the Picts and Scots while the appeal to Agitius was made. On average there would be three 19-year periods (allowing next to no time for the periods of recovery). Even if two of the periods were only of 10 years duration (the shortest time Gildas considers no small time), the longest would only be 37 years. If Gildas is prepared to accept 'many years' as

referring to an average period of 19 years, this give us another building block for
our putative chronology.

After the British victory there is a respite for a little while (20:3) *'parumper'* and
the Irish are shortly to return *'post non longum temporis'* (21). We already know
that 10 years is no short time for Gildas and that the upper limit of what he
would consider a short time is nine years. In this period a very swift plague (22:2)
robs Britain of its fighting men *'in brevi'* reinforcing the notion of its closeness
to Aetius. It is after that short amount of time that the three Saxon ships arrive,
giving an *Adventus Saxonum* of AD 455. Obviously 'a short time' could mean less
than this, and the count could start as late as AD 453. So the range, from the shortest short time (one year) after the earliest date (AD 447) to the longest short time
(nine years) after the latest date (AD 462) is 15 years. For argument's sake I will
take the average – between 454 and 455, as the sort of date Gildas is imagining. A
longer period implied by *'Interea'* could push the date later, but by no more than
nine years.

In the familiar story, the first Saxons settle, they bring in more settlers who are
bought off by supplies 'for a long time' *'multo tempore'* (23:5). Taking the 19 years
already established as 'a long time' in the narrative, and more particularly the sort
of 'long time' for which raids of Picts and Scots persist, that would bring us to a
Saxon revolt in about AD 474.

The revolt itself lasts, irritatingly, 'a time' (25:2) *'tempore ... interveniente aliquanto'*. I take *'aliquanto'* as a smaller measure than *'multo'* from normal usage and
because the description of the horrors of the revolt seem to echo those of the
Great Persecution very closely, a period already clearly established by Gildas as
lasting nine years. So by AD 483 the Saxons return to their homes on the eastern
side of the island. The way is opened for the British resurgence under Ambrosius
leading to the victory at Badon.

How long, then, did this period of resistance take? It must have taken more than
one year, since the *year* of the siege of Badon is significant. A short period would
place Badon at most nine years afterwards, so AD 492. A long period of 19 years
would move this to 502. Gildas is writing 43 years after this point, so between AD
535 and 545, and he considered writing 10 years before that. That would give us
a calculation that Gildas was writing 80–90 years after the arrival of the Saxons,
just over the halfway period of his prophecy that the Saxons would lay the island
waste repeatedly over 150 years. It also squares with the idea that Badon lies halfway between Gildas's writing and the arrival of the Saxons. I believe that Gildas
knows very little about the period preceding the arrival of the Saxons, and that
he imagines this period as taking the same shape as his own time. The period of
attack by Picts and Scots followed by British resistance is modelled on the period
of attacks by Saxons followed by British resistance with which he is more familiar.
For the sake of the argument, I assume that he imagines both to have the same
duration, an average of 19 years.

I am certain that Gildas writes that he was born in the year of the siege of Badon and that this was 43 years and one month ago. This is how Dumville very precisely interprets the passage: 'in the February of a calendar year from which, counting backwards and inclusively, the forty-fourth calendar year was that in the course of which Badon was fought and Gildas was born' (Dumville 1984: 26). The only markers Gildas gives in the sentence are his own age and the siege. Any idea that he is linking to some other date or dating system stretches the grammar past breaking point. Is it too much of a coincidence for him to have been born in that year? Coincidences do happen, and this is hardly the most extreme. The Conspirator Cassius died on his birthday at the Battle of Philippi, Halley's comet seemed to foretell the invasions of 1066. The historian Max Hastings who has written books on the fall of Germany (*Armageddon*) and Japan (*Nemesis*) in 1945 was himself born in 1945. It may even be that Gildas's interest in the history of the wars or his belief that he had a particular calling to preach about them was fostered by the time of his birth. Our perception of the importance of Badon may be distorted anyway. It is neither the first nor the last of the battles in the wars. It is not necessarily even the greatest. Its 'fame' may lie only on the fact that it was the big battle in the year that Gildas was born which, with hindsight, Gildas can see as a turning point in the wars – it is Gildas's birthday which secures Badon's fame for posterity.

Understandably, there is little material which offers clues to dates after the historical section. Constantine put away his lawful wife 'many years before' (28:3), but this is presumably within the time since Gildas's birth, by these calculations say 19 years before writing. Maglocunus killed his first wife after enjoying her 'for some little time' *aliquam diu* (35:3).

I make no claim that these 'dates' are anything but the roughest of rough calculations. On internal evidence a short period can be no longer than 9 years, and on average a long period is 19 years, and no shorter than 10 years. Of course a short period could be even shorter and a long period even longer, but a chronological scheme for Gildas based on dates outside *De Excidio Britanniae* which does not abide by those parameters would be less secure than one which does.

Gildas, a Suggested Chronology

I will turn in a moment to the implications this has for relating *De Excidio Britanniae* to later chronological schemes. In the meantime, it is worth considering the patterns observable in this proposed framework. My rough calculations put Gildas's present 82 years after the Saxon arrival, near enough to the 88 years often deduced by combining Bede's Badon is 44 years after the arrival and Gildas's 44 years after Badon, with Badon literally central to the period. Or, another way of looking at it, the present is just over half way through the 75-year period for which it was prophesied the Saxons will lay waste to Britain. Perhaps it was exactly 75 years 10 years earlier, when Gildas first considered writing.

We could consider the likely impact of the Easter cycle on Gildas's perception of history. 82 years deduced for the time elapsed since the arrival of the Saxons is just an Easter cycle away. This may create a horizon for what Gildas considers to be recent history (within the current Easter cycle) and what he considers further back. Or maybe he is using an Easter cycle pegged to Aetius Consul III, the clearest recent 'date'. This would produce an Easter cycle which ended in 530, between the dates deduced for Gildas thinking of *De Excidio Britanniae* and actually writing it. Perhaps this evoked an 'end times' thinking with Gildas, as such significant calendrical points are prone to do. We should not forget, either, the Metonic cycle which could have created an impression of 19-year building blocks of history, rather than just a coincidence. It could be used, for instance, deliberately to peg Maximus to Aetius even without a common dating system for both men.

I summarise my calculations below. Dates in bold are the only 'real' ones, the others are estimates, to be treated cautiously. I am not suggesting at the moment that any of them should be treated as established. For that we must look at the relationship of *De Excidio Britanniae* to other dating systems.

DATE (AD)	EVENT IN GILDAS	TIME PERIOD GIVEN BY GILDAS
	Britain uninhabited	
	Dreadful tyrants	Long past years
*c.*33	Passion of Christ	Last years of Tiberius
	Roman invasion	
303	Start of nine years of persecution	Tyranny of Diocletian
313	End of Persecution	After nine years
	Church restored	
383	Maximus declared emperor	At length
388	Maximus dies	Without delay
407	Turf wall built	Many years groaning
426	Stone wall built	Year after year of attacks
446 Aetius Consul III	Appeal to Agitius	Agitius ter consul

455	Saxons arrive	A short plague, a little respite, a not long time
474	Start of Saxon revolt	A long time
493	Battle of Badon	A time Gildas born
527	Gildas thinks of writing	A time
537	The Present. Gildas writes	Less than 150 years since Saxons arrive

Dumville (1984: 83) deduces a not greatly different chronology, with the exception that his revolt follows hot on the heels of the first Saxon arrival, which happens in c.480–90, so a revolt c.490, Ambrosius begins fight back in 495, Mount Badon fought in 500, and Gildas writes in 545. I disagree with this specifically on the length of time between the arrival of the Saxons and the revolt. Whatever the estimated durations, Gildas's '*multo tempore*' for the time in which the Saxon settlers are bought off before the revolt must be longer than a year and probably longer than the 10 which is the maximum Dumville allows and the minimum I would estimate.

Archaeology and Chronology

Is this deduced chronology compatible with the archaeological record? Leslie Alcock, formerly the champion of reconciling archaeological and written records, now emphatically rejects it 'I find Dumville's chronology incompatible with the archaeological evidence' (Alcock 1989: 406).

Dating the Arthurian period is a major difficulty, archaeologically. Archaeologists working with Roman sites in Britain are used to having the evidence of coinage to work with. As long as the coins are undisturbed, we know that anything deposited above them must be later than the date the coins were minted. Coins are effectively small inscriptions securely dated to a particular emperor. This is supplemented by inscriptions which may also carry a date or datable material.

None of the British rulers of the early Dark Ages issued their own coins. Although we know coins were in use (we are told so by Gildas) they must have been very old ones, primarily from the last time garrisons in Britain were paid. We can see this moment archaeologically. In AD 403 the Mint of Rome produced a bronze coin with the inscription VRBS ROMA FELIX 'Happy City of Rome' replacing the earlier SALVS REIPVBLICAE 'the safety of the state'. It never reached Britain (Gerrard 2004: 66). Not surprisingly, the non-arrival of the 403 coinage was followed by several revolts in quick succession. Later coins did find their way to Britain, up to a Gallic tremissis of either Severus III or Zeno (480–93) but not on a scale to suggest large imperial shipments (Snyder 1998: 241).

Another convenient dating tool is the pottery sequence. Changing tastes in design and construction can be traced through the incredibly durable material of pottery. The sequences can be constructed and, better still, cross-referenced with other contemporary finds, such as coins. This is the reason for the huge significance of the Tintagel ware. It is pottery which can be dated precisely because it is found in association with coins and other datable evidence from the Eastern Roman Empire. As the storage jars contained relatively perishable commodities, we can be reasonably sure that their fragments in British sites correspond well with their dating in the Mediterranean area. They are thus rather more useful for establishing absolute dates than coins which had a very long period of use.

Modern British token coinage has no intrinsic value and has been changed many times in my lifetime. Yet I am still carrying in my wallet pennies from the early 1970s, which show Elizabeth II as a young woman and describe the decimalised currency as 'new'. Imagine the difficulties if these were the only datable objects found in my house or on my body. This can be tested archaeologically. Coin hoards with fourth-century coins in them were analysed. By comparing the latest dated coin in a deposit with the other coins from the same context, it was found that a fourth-century minted coin was on average 43.6 years +/-10.9 years older than the date of its minting (Gerard 2004: 66). Obviously trying to combine late Roman coins with pottery sequencing thus is very problematical. It has the inevitable result of shifting 'datable Roman' material earlier, to before 403 and consequently 'foreshortened the use of Romano-British pottery and brought material culture falsely in line with the historical record', as Gerrard puts it (2004: 71). It is for this reason, just as much as the drying up of written sources, that the period 400–600 is seen as an archaeological 'Dark Age', with datable coins at one end and pottery at the other and a wasteland without secure dates between.

Archaeologists working with prehistoric periods have scientific dating, primarily radiocarbon dating, to support them. Radiocarbon dates have been taken for Dark Age sites, but unfortunately they lack the precision needed for historical dates. An accuracy of 95 per cent plus or minus 80 years is perfect for determining whether sites are Neolithic, Bronze Age, Iron Age or Dark Age. They are useless for finding out if Saxons arrived in the 420s or the 450s, whether the Ambrosian/Arthurian wars lasted more or less than a generation or whether an earthwork was erected to defend against rival Britons in 500 or encroaching Saxons in 550. As Arnold writes (1984: 3) 'it is unusual in archaeological research for there to be much concern over the accuracy of dating within a 50-year period, but it is obviously crucial to the resulting interpretation of this particular period.'

Archaeologists therefore have to fall back on dates gleaned from history which are in many cases problematic. The date AD 410 (supposedly when the Romans 'left Britain') is often used unthinkingly. A grave discovered in the area of Trafalgar Square, in London, was confidently described by the Museum of London team as 'dating back to about 410 AD' (*Metro*, Friday 1 December 2006). They have not yet been published but I am prepared to bet that nothing in the burials (a date to the eighth consulship of Honorius or a coin of 409 sealed beneath them, a date of the ninth consulship or a coin of 411 sealed above) gives this date. The archaeologists have either taken the burials to be at the extreme late range of 'Roman' or the extreme early range of 'post-Roman', taken absurdly as dividing on the year 410, as if all the undertakers in London had packed up and gone home when they heard the Honorian rescript.

In earlier studies, the works of Bede, a master chronographer who wrote extensively on time and dating issues, were seen as providing very secure dates. *Historia Brittonum*, the Anglo-Saxon Chronicle and the *Annales Cambriae* following in the Bedan tradition, had their dates incorporated in a resulting chronological scheme which mapped out the events 410–590. Sims-Williams (1983b: 2) spelled out the problem: 'historians of the early Anglo-Saxon period were more interested in showing how the narrative, usually constructed from Bede and the Chronicle might be confirmed, amplified or qualified by archaeological or place name data than in investigating the reliability of the primary historical sources.'

Answering this question is absolutely vital but has added to the general confusion and obscurity of the period, rather than illuminating it. Unfortunately, Sims-Williams then proceeded to attack Gildas's chronology. No-one would doubt that Gildas's knowledge of the past beyond living memory was very limited. He himself notes the destruction of historical records in the country which hampers his research. We can be reasonably sure that the impression he gives that there were no Saxons in Britain before the arrival of the three boatloads settled by the Proud Tyrant is as mistaken as his view that there were no Picts in the Island until after the end of continuous Roman rule. This in contrast to Zosimus, Constantius and the Gallic Chronicler of 452, who refer to Saxon invasion events in 408 or 9, 429 or 430 and *c*.441 (Sims-William 1983b: 9). Gildas does not in fact say that the three boatloads of Saxons are the first to settle in or menace the Britons. They are already feared, which indicates some form of previous contact. The importance of the three boatloads is not 'first contact' but the start of the chain of events leading to the situation in Gildas's own time.

Dates in *Historia Brittonum*

By way of contrast, *Historia Brittonum* is positively awash with dates, from every conceivable dating system. The author uses AD dates, dates after the Passion, consular dates, dates from the creation of the world, regnal lengths, dates by 19-year cycles and calculations of intervals between particular significant events. It seems likely that he has used several different sources, each with their own dating systems, and has tried to reconcile them by cross-referencing on occasion. It has to be said, though, that these calculations seldom match perfectly and that either the author was inept at mathematics or the manuscripts we have are almost hopelessly corrupt.

Once again we await Dumville's full publication for the best impression of what the best figures are likely to be, and whether a lengthy section preceding the *Annales Cambriae* in the Harleian manuscript properly belongs to the *Historia*. They point to an arrival date of the Saxons early in the fifth century, in the 420s. Archaeologists have been happy to consider this, in spite of reservations on the quality of *Historia Brittonum*'s sources, as it harmonises with the earlier Saxon presence suggested by archaeology and other written sources. It confirms the chronological unreliability of Gildas and allows the synchronism with the appeal to Agitius to be dropped or redefined.

Unfortunately, the motive for the *Historia*'s redating is clear. Bede's history presents a logical and self-consistent story. The Saxon revolt, confronted by Ambrosius and his successors, leads to a period of British ascendancy. The Britons lapse into the Pelagian heresy and the Church decides to send St Germanus of Auxerre to sort it out. In the course of his mission, Germanus becomes involved in leading a British army against the Saxons and the Picts. He defeats the invaders by encouraging his troops to shout 'Alleluia' with miraculous consequences. The author of *Historia Brittonum* knew this well. Indeed the only source he is specific about possessing is *The Book of the Blessed Germanus*. But the devil is in the details. Although placed in a logical narrative position by Bede, after Ambrosius, the dates will not allow this. St Germanus was operating in Britain in 429, years before the period which Bede claims saw the 'first' Saxon settlements (Sims–Williams 1983b: 6). Prosper of Aquitaine's chronicle (quoted in Snyder 1998:38 and Pace 2008: 339) gives the date and also cites the consulship of Felix and Taurus.

Either *The Book of the Blessed Germanus* itself or his own researches have given the author of *Historia Brittonum* the earlier dates and he attempts to reconcile this discrepancy. He uses Germanus-derived dates to make sure that Vortigern starts his rule, and soon after welcomes the Saxons, in good time to allow both him and the Saxons to interact with Germanus when he arrives.

Ostensibly the dates for Arthur's career are quite simple. He fights against the Saxons 'in those days', previously defined as a growing number of Saxons 'at that time' which immediately follows the death of Patrick. His campaigns end before the arrival of Ida in Bernicia. Beyond that, the picture is immensely complicated. There are 17 dates, which I label A–Q which relate to this period:

	Event	Date as given in *Historia Brittonum*	Deduced AD date
A	The year the Saxons first came to Britain	429 years before the fourth year of King Mermin	
B	The coming of St Patrick to the Irish	405 years after the birth of Jesus	405
C	From the Incarnation of Jesus to the coming of Patrick to Ireland	23 cycles of 19 years, or 438 years	Really 437 years, so either 438 or 437 (assuming the first date is after the Passion and Passion is AD 33. If it is AD 29, then the corrected date should be AD 434
D	From the coming of Patrick to the present	421 years, 22 cycles of 19 years, 2 years in the ogdoad until the present year	418 years + 2 = 420, therefore the present is 825/6 or 857–9
E	Romans rule Britain	409 years, counting from 47 years before the birth of Jesus	Until AD 359
F	The Britons live in fear for 40 years, after which the Saxons arrive	After the killing of Maximus and the end of the Roman Empire in Britain	399, counting up from date E. If the real date of Maximus is used (388) the 40 years of fear takes us to 428, Felix and Taurus

	Event	Date as given in *Historia Brittonum*	Deduced AD date
G	Saxons received by Vortigern	When Gratian ruled for the second time with Equitius, 347 years after the Passion	378 if Passion is AD 29. Gratian II is 371 and Gratian III + Equitius is 374
H	Germanus came to preach in Britain	In the time of Vortigern	
I	Patrick sent to Ireland	In the reign of Theodosius and Valentinian, when Celestine was the Roman Pope	They were consuls in 425 and 426, 430 and 435, Celestine was Pope 422–432
J	Patrick preaches	For 40 years	until 465–475
K	Patrick preaches	For 85 years	until 510–520
L	Constantinus and Rufus	5658 years since the creation of the world	457
M	Stilicho	373 years after the twins, Furius and Rubellius	402
N	Vortigern held the empire of Britain	In the consulship of Theodosius and Valentinian	425–435
O	Saxons came to Britain	Fourth year of the reign of Vortigern, in the consulship of Felix and Taurus, in the 400th year from the Incarnation of Jesus	429–439, but Felix and Taurus is 428. Supporting the idea that 425 is the date being used for Theodosius and Valentinian confuses the Incarnation with the Passion

	Event	Date as given in *Historia Brittonum*	Deduced AD date
P	The quarrel between Vitalinus and Ambrosius, Catguoloph	12 years from the reign of Vortigern	437
Q	Decius and Valerian	69 years from the year when the English first came to Britain and were welcomed by Vortigern	497/8, but Decius is 486, Valerius 521, Decius alone in 529. If the end dates are right them the Saxons arrived in 417, 452 or 460

If we take as a fixed point the fact that Germanus comes to Britain in 429, when he encounters both Vortigern and Saxons, then date N is right 'Vortigern held the empire of Britain in the consulship of Theodosius and Valentinian', presuming this to be their first joint consulship, 425. The Saxons follow four years later (date O), synchronised with the consulship of Felix and Taurus (428) and the 400th year after the Passion, in the year of the consulship of the Twins AD 29, hence AD 429 (the writer wrongly dates this after the 'Incarnation', but the slip is obvious).

There is confusion about the date of Maximus, but after his death the Britons live in fear for 40 years. Taking the real date (AD 388) of his death, this again brings us to 428. The same synchronism is used for St Patrick, connected to St Germanus. So Patrick starts his mission (date I) in the 'reign of Theodosius and Valentian' and that of Pope Celestine (died 432) hence 425, 426 or 430, with the preference to the first one. On these depend dates for the quarrel between Vitalinus and Ambrosius at Guoloph (12 years after the start of Vortigern's reign, hence 437) and the consulship of Decius and Valerian (69 years after the coming of the English, calculated as 497/8).

Various dates are wrong but explicable in this framework. A calculation (B) that Patrick came to the Irish in AD 405 is presumably another example of confusion between Passion and Incarnation dating systems. Assuming this to be so, AD 434 is meant, which is just outside the reign of Celestine and just before the fourth joint consulship of Theodosius and Valentian. If it was actually a 400-year synchronism, then we get 429 again. But it is easy to see that these are simple variations on the same synchronism, a visit of St Germanus in 429 who encounters both Vortigern and Saxons.

A clear indication that these calculations are not right is the Appeal to Agitius. This is the cornerstone of Gildas's chronology. Even if we accept for the moment that he misplaced it or that the appeal concerns Saxons, it has no place in *Historia Brittonum's* historiography. The Romans are gone and it is victorious Britons who fight the Saxons from the time of the revolt onwards.

This raises the questions did Germanus meet Vortigern and did he lead the Britons against the Saxons? We have the *Life of St Germanus* by Constantius of Lyon, a fifth-century contemporary of Sidonius Apollinaris from nearby Clermont Ferrand. Constantius may have seen Germanus, and wrote some time before the 480s. He is thus a better witness than Gildas to the early period, although he himself had not been to Britain. He does not include any dates in his *Life*, which allowed Bede to incorporate the visit, perhaps innocently, after the Battle of Badon. Mostly the Britons Germanus encounters are not named, but it does not seem that there is a single 'Vortigern' ruling the whole country. Specific Vortigern incidents in *Historia Brittonum* have no equivalents in Constantius.

In Gildas's view, a visit after the Saxon revolt would have been a time of chaos, with Saxons ravaging from sea to sea, not a one-off surprise raid such as Germanus encounters. The precise details of the *divortium* are not reproduced. Germanus finds it easy to visit the shrine of St Alban, which is not cut off from the lands of the Britons by Saxon settlements. Everything in the *Life* indicates that this takes place before the Saxon revolt not after it as *Historia Brittonum* suggests. The one point against this is Constantius's claim that Germanus confronts a joint attack by Saxons and Picts. This is unique in the historiography of the period. Gildas makes the Picts and Saxons adversaries, specifically so in the period immediately following their arrival. Constantius uses the phrase, and the word 'Saxons', once. He does not present a Britain either settled by or constantly beset by Saxons. It is my view that here he is simply mistaken. Constantius means 'Picts and Scots', the traditional paring of invaders, well known to be active in the period of Germanus's visit. By the time he writes, it is the Saxons who dominate continental writers' view of Britain. The evidence for this is in the Gallic Chronicles. Sidonius Apollinaris knows Saxons from their raids on France and can describe their distinctive hair styles. They know nothing of the Scots. It is my contention that Germanus neither met Vortigern nor confronted invading Saxons and that *Historia Brittonum's* attempts to incorporate these ideas have resulted in mistakenly early dating for the events.

These are, though, only one set of supporting dates. Use of different sources, updates of the text and miscalculations, either at authorial or scribal stages have resulted in many different dates. The arrival of the Saxons is dated to 429 years before the fourth year of King Mermin. This is such an odd milestone that most commentators have taken it that Year Four of King Mermin is the present and, following Dumville, that he is the patron of the *Historia*. That of course raises the question of when the *Historia's* present was reckoned to be. Using calculations based on multiple 19-year cycles, the author calculates that 23 cycles of 19 years, or 438 years from the Incarnation to the coming of Patrick to Ireland (AD 438). He then calculates that 22 cycles of 19 years plus 2 years of the next cycle (421 years) separate the coming of St Patrick from the present. The present is thus AD 859. This is later than expected for Mermin (Dumville opts for the late 820s, which only works with the erroneous date B).

Date G gives a much earlier idea of the Saxon arrival, claiming that the Saxons were received by Vortigern when Gratian ruled the second time with Equitius. Gratian's second consulship was in 371, but probably the writer means his third consulship, which he did indeed share with Equitius in 374. This is synchronised to 347 years after the Passion, which would really be 378, if the Passion was in AD 29. This would put the end of Roman rule in 334–338, far earlier than even Maximus, so completely unsupported by the rest of the historical construction.

In this morass, there are some dates which could be taken as supporting my suggested chronology of Gildas. The first is the 69 years from the time the English first came to Britain and were welcomed by Vortigern, synchronised to the consulship of Decius and Valerian. A Decius was consul in 486, too early for this to work even with the Germanus date. The real consuls in 497/8 were the Emperor Anastasius in 497 and Joannes Scytha and Paulinus in 498, so a simple scribal error is out of the question. Most likely the author intended either Valerius, consul in 521 or Decius, sole consul in 529 (there was no joint consulship of the two). These would give us an arrival of the Saxons in 452 or 460.

The next area of confusion is the 40 years of fear. The writer is confused as to whether the death of Maximus marks the end of Roman rule (as Gildas thinks) which would give us 428, the consulship of Felix and Taurus as the end of the fear period. However, he also calculates the length of Roman rule in Britain as lasting 409 years, apparently from a start in 47 BC. This would lead to an even earlier date of 359 for the end of Roman rule, and a period of fear ending in 399. This seems far too early, but is supported by another synchronism, the consulship of Stilicho 373 years after the consulship of the twins Furius and Rubellius (AD 29, taken as the year of the Passion), and yielding a date of 402. Stilicho was actually consul in 400. But the 409 figure is suspicious. It appears in Bede, too, as marking the end of Roman rule, as doubtless the writer of *Historia Brittonum* was aware. In Bede, though, it is not the *duration* of Roman rule but instead the AD date of the end of Roman rule, under Constantine III, a calculation which happens to be right. In that case, 40 years of fear would take us to 449 for the start of the Vortigern/Saxon period.

In passing, although *Annales Cambriae* seems entirely independent of *Historia Brittonum's* chronology at this point, its 149-year interval between the two battles of Badon provides an interesting coincidence, if nothing else. The Anglo-Saxon Chronicle records the fall of Bath in 577, which is 149 years after 428.

❀

Bede's Chronology

Although I worked on my chronology of Gildas independent of the later sources, the calculations yield dates which are certainly not unfamiliar. They coincide more or less with the dates given by Bede. This is perhaps hardly surprising, since Bede was working with the same sources, but it is worth looking at what Bede says. In spite of Gildas, he rightly dates the end of Roman rule in Britain to AD 409. He cross-refers the date of Aetius III to 23 years after the start of the reign of Theodosius the younger, thus 446, and this date provides the start of his chronology of the Saxon revolt and British resistance, as it seems to in Gildas. A new imperial date refines this more closely. Marcian became co-emperor with Valentinian in 449 and during their seven-year joint reign (so before 456) the English came to Britain. It may be that Bede has some data linking those two events, but it is equally possible for this to be a deduction, since I arrived at 455 without any need for specific external evidence. The Battle of Badon took place 44 years after the arrival of the English, hence between 493 and 510. This again is a reasonable inference, given that Gildas seems to make the resistance last a generation. Finally the period of British ascendancy effectively ends with the arrival of Ida, who begins his reign in the north in 547. This Bedan chronology is perfectly acceptable with Gildas, on the proviso that the account of Germanus battling the Saxons is an anachronism from the time of Constantius, not an accurate survival of information from Germanus's own time.

Chronology of the Anglo-Saxon Chronicle

Bede was followed by the Anglo-Saxon Chronicle, which used his chronology to construct its account. The historians and archaeologists have a love/hate relationship with this source. While exceedingly inconvenient for the 'peaceful transference of migrants and their ideas' fashion, as a constant litany of inter-ethnic strife, bloodshed and triumphalism, it is nevertheless not treated with the same distain as *Historia Brittonum*. Authors are happy to take named military characters and their battles as convenient hooks on which to hang archaeological contentions and narratives of the development of the Anglo-Saxon kingdoms. As you might expect, the Arthurian double standards are at play.

Cerdic and Cynric are characters who appear for the first time in the Anglo-Saxon Chronicle, complete with lists of battles (five and seven) at often otherwise unknown locations, and absurd over-inflated accounts of their prowess. The two of them kill Welsh king Natanleod and 5000 men with him at the Battle of Natanleag, five times the number Arthur killed at Badon. Their names are automatically suspect. Cerdic has the same British name as Caratacus, the famous enemy of Rome many centuries in the past. He shares a name with characters such as Vortigern's British interpreter in *Historia Brittonum*, the last king of the British enclave of Elmet, a character (possibly the same one) in *Annales Cambriae* who died *c*.616 and several different figures in the Harleian Genealogies, including 'Ceritic guletic' father of 'Cinuit' and supposed ancestor of [R]un son of Arthgal. He is clearly, one might imagine, a composite character founded on a generally famous culture hero and placed arbitrarily in the fifth and sixth centuries to fulfil some 'Hengist' role in the history of the West Saxons.

Cerdic's 'son' Cynric has a British name, meaning 'hound king', obviously cognate with known Celtic deities such as Apollo Cunomaglus 'Hound Prince'. Not a bit of it. Cerdic and Cynric are regularly treated as real characters from the fifth/sixth century, incorporated in more or less distorted accounts of their exploits and genealogies to fit the agendas of later historians. Once again, we can imagine all sorts of reasons why a late ninth-century West Saxon writer might want to invent a glorious invading past for his dynasty, might want to incorporate British names in a kingdom which now had a significant British component in its western lands and might want to stress some kind of link with indigenous Britons in the face of invaders from Scandinavia. Yet they are not relegated to footnotes or dismissed out of hand as legendary. These are figures, remember, who appear without precedent later than King Arthur. They do not even benefit from a mention in Saxon poetry. Gildas never names them, although he is supposedly a neighbour and a contemporary. Neither does Bede, who thinks their claimed stamping ground was in fact colonised by the Jutes, rather than the Saxons and that they were properly called the Gewissae.

Dumville is nothing if not consistent. He does indeed argue (Dumville 1989: 96) that 'Ceawlin is the first of their kings in whom any confidence can be placed', presumably because of his appearance in Bede, and he leads not the West Saxons of Hampshire but the Geuissae in the upper Thames Valley.

The Anglo-Saxon Chronicle places the appeal to Aetius in 443, which is a mistake. The arrival of the Saxons under Hengist and Horsa is noted under AD 449 but, as in Bede, the entry actually dates this to the course of the seven-year joint reign, rather than to the first year. Departing from Bede's and Gildas's concept of the events, the Saxon revolt also breaks out within the same period. In 455 Horsa was killed fighting against Vortigern at Agaelesthrep. Undaunted, Hengist and his son Aesc continue the fight, killing 12 Welsh nobles in battle at Wippedesfleot, and so forth. It gives no time for the Saxons to fight the Picts or to invite new settlers (they only arrive after Hengist's victories have prepared the way), or the amount of time Gildas seems to suggest elapsed. There is no room for peaceful co-operation or British victories in this chronology, and we must find it wanting when compared to Gildas.

The Anglo-Saxon Chronicle produces difficulties at the other end of the proposed chronology. Gildas's premise is that the victory at Badon has brought 40 years of respite from Saxon attacks which have caused the Britons to become blasé about the threat and turn instead to fighting amongst themselves. The chronicle not only has no Badon, it has only a little let up from continuous Saxon invasion and victory. Dumville (1985) shows that the story of Cerdic and the West Saxons includes duplicates of the same events, separated by the 19-year discrepancy. He goes on to demonstrate that is possible neither version is correct. The West Saxon kings list, which survives both independently and as a sort of preface to some versions of the Chronicle, instead offers a calculation based on regnal lengths. Adding the most plausible readings for the reigns yields 104 years from the beginning of Cerdic's reign to the death of Cynegils in 641/2. Thus Cerdic was originally seen as beginning his reign in 537/8.

The significance of Cynegils is that he is the first West Saxon king to be converted (Yorke 1993: 48). There is a conscious decision connect him more closely with the era of the first Anglo-Saxon arrivals found in Bede. As well as clear parallels between the stories of Hengist and Aesc (both named in Bede) and Cerdic and Cynric, the Bretwalda Ceawlin gets the same start date, 560, as Bede gives to his successor as great king, Ethelbert (Yorke 1989: 87).

'In which Arthur and Medraut were slain'

According to Geoffrey of Monmouth, Arthur's last battle was fought in AD 542. This is close enough to the '*Gueith Camlann* [Strife of Camlan, in Welsh], in which Arthur and Medraut were slain', entry in *Annales Cambriae*. There it is dated to year 93, which appears to be somewhere in the region of 537. This is set 21 years after the Battle of Badon and 10 years before the death of Mailcun King of Genedota in the great plague. He is none other than Gildas's Maglocunus. Possibly these dates were intended to be at 10-year intervals. They seem related to each other. The intervening annals are all taken from an original Ulster source and deal with Irish saints.

There are two problems with the dates. The most obvious is that Mailcun is dead 31 years after the Battle of Badon, which contradicts Gildas's assertion that he is still alive 43/44 years after that battle. Dumville does not place much store by the date, pointing out that it is simply a substitution of the entry from the Ulster Annals for 549 '*mortalitas magna in qua isti pausant finnio maccu telduib.*' '*mortalitas magna in qua pausat Mailcun rex Genedotae*' (Dumville 1984: 53). Even so, the date (547 or 549) is actually completely in agreement with his proposed chronology as it is with mine, after the deduced composition of *De Excidio Britanniae*. It may well be that Maglocunus was one of the victims of the Great Plague and this is actually a reliable synchronism. What is wrong is the nearness of this event to the Battle of Badon. Compared with my estimated chronology of Gildas, this *Annales* date is about 20 years later than we would expect it. It is 60 years after the death of St Patrick, which seems a long way from the 'at that time' of *Historia*

Brittonum. I am always wary of simply manipulating dates to get a desired result, but I am convinced this placing is a mistake in the addition of British materials to the Ulster Annals. 'About 20 years later than expected' makes me think that it is misplaced by one Easter cycle of 19 years from an original date of *c.*497.

Was Camlan synchronised to 21 years after Badon or 10 years before the death of Mailcun? I show in *The Reign of Arthur* that the Arthurian entries are likely to be part of a North Welsh phase to the *Annales* extending to not later than the ninth century. Dumville (2007: 31–2), by other means, reaches the same conclusion, that they derive from 'a north British chronicle with some north Welsh material … drawn on to the 770s', as part of a 'Venedotian Easter Chronicle'. The interest in Easter in this section is evidenced by the first entry, the alteration of Easter by Pope Leo, and towards the end (*c.*768) when the Britons changed Easter. In the middle is the first celebration of Easter among the Saxons, in the same year as the second Battle of Badon. This has always been a puzzle. The date *c.*665 does not correspond with anything in Bede, who was interested in nothing so much as the celebration of Easter among the Saxons and who gives detailed material at this point. Neither does it correspond with any dates in the Anglo-Saxon Chronicle.

What, though, if both events were synchronised as 149 (more likely 150) years after the first Battle of Badon, and are in the wrong position now because of misplacing the first battle? What if the true date of the second Battle of Badon and the 'first Saxon Easter' is *c.*646? That, according to the Anglo-Saxon Chronicle, was the year Cenwalh of the West Saxons was baptised. He had just been expelled the previous year by King Penda of Mercia. Bede gives more of the story, explaining that Penda went to war with Coenwalh (as he spells it) when the West Saxon king repudiated his wife, Penda's sister. A war between Mercia and its southern neighbour Wessex would easily encompass most of the suggested sites of Badon. Coenwalh fled to the court of the East Angles, where he was converted to Christianity and baptised.

If Camlan was originally intended to be placed 21 years after Badon, it would be fought in 518. If it was fought in 537, 10 years before the death of Mailcun, that is co-incidentally my deduced date for the writing of *De Excidio Britanniae*. It would be poetic to think that the catastrophic death of the hero of Badon was what actually drove Gildas to write! Unfortunately, my analysis is that the Badon generation had already passed away. Gildas's view is that contemporaries have forgotten this. My conclusion is that Camlan and Badon were a linked pair at the time of their inclusion in the *Annales*. Camlan has no parallel in *Historia Brittonum*. It is an independent piece of evidence for Arthur. It is easy to imagine how such a detail might have been dropped from the *Historia*'s providential narrative.

A chronology, based on a political interpretation of the archaeology, is advanced by Neil Faulkner (2004: 11). He has a period of anarchy *c.*375/425–450/75. This essentially represents the disappearance of stereotypical Roman remains.

✂

Faulkner's interpretation, that the workers and red Christian radicals resist the land lords, land is taken over by the primary producers and so forth, is contentious, as we have seen. His 'age of chieftains', a reactionary age in which military insecurity and threats to property lead to the emergence of competing war lord 'protectors', covers AD 450/75–550/75. These dates are perfectly consonant with my deduced chronology, but it seems that Faulkner has, like me, derived them from historical sources rather than archaeological ones.

BIBLIOGRAPHY

'Arthnou Stone', *British Archaeology* no 37 Sept 1998 www.britarch.ac.uk/BA/ba37/ba37news.html (1 August 2006).

Abrams, L. and Carley, J.P. (eds) (1991). *The Archaeology and History of Glastonbury Abbey: Essays in honour of the ninetieth birthday of C.A.Ralegh Radford* Woodbridge, The Boydell Press.

Adams, J.dQ. (1993) 'Sidonius and Riothamus', *Arthurian Literature 12*.

Alcock, L and Ashe, G. (1968). 'Cadbury: is it Camelot?' in Ashe, G. (ed.) (1968). *The Quest for Arthur's Britain* London, Granada Publishing Ltd pp123-147.

Alcock, L. (1971). *Arthur's Britain: History and Archaeology AD 367–634* London, Allen Lane for Penguin.

Alcock, L. (1972). *'By South Cadbury is that Camelot...': The Excavation of Cadbury Castle 1966-1970* London, Thames and Hudson.

Alcock, L. (1978). 'Her ... Gefeaht with Walas: aspects of the warfare of Saxons and Britons', *Bulletin of the Board of Celtic Studies 27* (1976-8) pp413-24.

Alcock, L. (1982). 'Mortimer Wheeler Archaeological Lecture: Cadbury-Camelot: A fifteen year perspective', *Proceedings of the British Academy 68* pp355–388.

Alcock, L. (1987). *Economy, Society and Warfare among the Britons and Saxons* Cardiff, University of Wales Press

Alcock, L. (1988). 'The activities of potentates in Celtic Britain AD 500–800: a positivist approach' (22–46) in Driscoll, S.T. and Nieke, M.R. (eds) (1988). *Power and Politics in early medieval Britain and Ireland* Edinburgh, Edinburgh University Press pp22-46.

Alcock, L. (1989). *Arthur's Britain, reprinted with revised preface and supplementary bibliography* Harmondsworth, Penguin.

Alcock, L. (1995). *Cadbury Castle, Somerset: The Early Medieval Archaeology* Cardiff, University of Wales Press.

Alcock, L. (2003) *Kings, warriors, craftsmen and priests in northern Britain AD 550-850* Society of Antiquaries of Scotland monograph series, Edinburgh.

Aldhouse-Green, M. and Howell, R. (eds) (2004). *The Gwent County History: volume 1 Gwent in prehistory and early history* Cardiff.

Annales Cambriae (ed. and trans.) Morris, J. (1980). *Nennius: British History and the Welsh Annals* London Phillimore and Co.

Armstrong, K. (2005). *A Short History of Myth* Edinburgh, Canongate Books Ltd.

Arnold, B. (2006). 'Pseudoarchaeology and nationalism: Essentializing difference' in Fagan, G.G. (ed.) (2006). *Archaeological Fantasies: How pseudoarchaeology misrepresents the past and misleads the public* London, Routledge pp154–179.

Arnold, C.J. (1984). *Roman Britain to Saxon England, an archaeological study* Beckenham.

Ashe, G. (ed.) (1968). *The Quest for Arthur's Britain* London, Granada Publishing Ltd.

Ashe, G. (1980). *A Guidebook to Arthurian Britain* London, Longman.

Ashe, G. (1982). *Kings and Queens of Early Britain* London, Methuen.

Ashe, G. (2002). *Mythology of the British Isles, New Edition* London, Methuen.

Ashley, M. (ed.) (1998). *The Mammoth Book of Arthurian Legends*. London, Robinson.

Babelstone http://babelstone.blogspot.com/2009/11/ogham-stones-of-elsewhere.html

Barber, R. (1984). 'Was Modred buried at Glastonbury? An Arthurian tradition at Glastonbury in the Middle Ages' *Arthurian Literature 4*.

Barber, R. (1986). *King Arthur: Hero and Legend* Woodbridge, The Boydell Press.

Barber, R. (1999). *Myths and Legends of the British Isles* Woodbridge, The Boydell Press.

Barber, R. (2004). *The Holy Grail: The History of a legend* London, Penguin.

Barford, P.M., Owen, W.G. and Britnell W.J. (1986). 'Iron spearhead and javelin from Four Crosses, Llandysilio, Powys' in *Medieval Archaeology, Volume 30*, (1986), The Society for Medieval Archaeology, London. pp103-106.

Barrett, J.C., Freeman P.W.M., and Woodward A., (2000). *Cadbury Castle, Somerset: The later prehistoric and early historic archaeology* London, English Heritage.

Barron, W.R.J. (ed.) (2001). *The Arthur of the English, new ed.* Cardiff, the University of Wales Press.

Bassett, S. (ed.) (1989). *The Origins of Anglo-Saxon Kingdoms* Leicester University Press, Leicester.

Batey, C.E., Sharpe, A. and Thorpe, C.M. (1993). 'Tintagel castle: archaeological investigation of the steps area 1989 and 1990' *Cornish Archaeology*, 32, pp47–66.

Bath, B. (1996). 'Audio-tours at Heritage Sites' in McManus, P.M. (ed.) (2000). *Archaeological Displays and the Public: Museology and Interpretation* London, Archetype Publications Ltd. pp157–163.

Bath skyline www.nationaltrust.org.uk/main/w-bath_skyline

BBC News (1998). 'Clue to King Arthur discovered' http://news.bbc.co.uk/1/hi/uk/146511.stm (1 August 2006).

BBC Tintagel, http://www.bbc.co.uk/print/cornwall/attractions/stories/tintagelcastle/images/tintagelcastle.html (1 August 2006).

Bede, *Historia Ecclesiastica*, in Plummer, C. (ed.) (1896). *Venerabilis Bedae Opera Historica*, 2 vols Oxford, Clarendon Press.

Berkhoffer Jr, R.F. (1995). *Beyond the Great Story: History as Text and Discourse* Cambridge, Massachusetts, The Belknapp Press of Harvard University Press.

Biddle, M. (2000). *King Arthur's Round Table: An Archaeological Investigation* Woodbridge, The Boydell Press.

Bradley, M.Z. (1983). *Mists of Avalon* New York, Knopf.

Bromwich, R. (1978). *Trioedd Ynys Prydein: The Welsh Triads* Cardiff, University of Wales Press.

Bromwich, R., Jarman, A.O.H and Roberts, B.F. (eds) (1991). *The Arthur of the Welsh* Cardiff, University of Wales Press.

Brooks, D.A. (1983–84). 'Gildas' De Excidio: Its revolutionary meaning and purpose' *Studia Celtica 18*.

Brooks, N. (1989). 'The creation and early structure of the kingdom of Kent' in Bassett, S. (ed.) (1989). *The Origins of Anglo-Saxon Kingdoms* Leicester University Press, Leicester.

Burrow, I.C.G. (1973). 'Tintagel – some problems' *Scottish Archaeological Forum* V, pp99-103.

Caerleon, www.caerleon.net/history/arthur/page 7 (1 August 2006).

Camden, W., (1610). *Britannia* London.

Camelot (1967). Dir. Logan, J, Warner.

Campbell, A. (1959). *The Chronicle of Aethelweard*, Nelson Medieval Series.

Campbell, E. 'The archaeological evidence for external contacts: imports, trade and economy in Celtic Britain AD 400–800' in Dark, K.R. (ed.) (1996). *External contacts and the economy of Late Roman and Post Roman Britain* Woodbridge, The Boydell Press pp83-96.

Campbell, J. (ed.) (1982). *The Anglo-Saxons* Phaidon.

Camulos, http://www.Camulos.com/arthur/official.htm (1 August 2006).

Carman, J.N. (1973). *A study of the Pseudo-Map Cycle of Arthurian Romance* Lawrence, The University Press of Kansas.

Casey, P.J. and Jones, M.J. (1990). 'The date of the Letter of the Britons to Aetius', *Bulletin of the Board of Celtic Studies 37*.

Castleden, R. (2000). *King Arthur: The Truth behind the Legend* London, Routledge.

Cadwick, H.M. and Chadwick, N.K. (1932). *The Growth of Literature I* Cambridge, Cambridge University Press.

Chambers, E.K. (1927). *Arthur of Britain* London, Sidgwick and Jackson.

Charles-Edwards, T. (1989). 'Early medieval kingships in the British Isles' in Bassett, S. (ed.)(1989). *The Origins of Anglo-Saxon Kingdoms* Leicester, Leicester University Press.

Chrétien de Troyes, Owen, D.D.R. (trans.) (1987). *Arthurian Romances*, London, J.M. Dent.

Coe, J.B. and Young, S. (1995). *The Celtic Sources for the Arthurian Legend* Felinfach, Llanerch.

Colchester Museum, http://www.colchestermuseums.org.uk (27 September 2006).

Collingwood, W.G. (1929). 'Arthur's Battles' *Antiquity 3*.

Collins, R. (2004) 'Before "the end". Hadrian's wall in the 4th century and after. Collins, R. and Gerrard, J. (eds) (2004). *Debating Late Antiquity in Britain AD 300–700*, BAR British series 365, Oxford, Archaeopress.

Collins, R. and Gerrard, J. (eds) (2004). *Debating Late Antiquity in Britain AD 300–700*, BAR British series 365 Oxford, Archaeopress.

Crawford, O.G.S. (1935). 'Arthur and his battles', *Antiquity 9*.

Cunliffe, B. (1984). *Roman Bath Discovered*, London, Routledge.

Dark, K. (1994). *Civitas to Kingdom: British Political Continuity* Leicester, Leicester University Press.

Dark, K. (1994b). 'Review of Thomas, C. 1993 'English Heritage Book of Tintagel, Arthur and Archaeology, London, Batsford/English Heritage' in *Cambrian Medieval Celtic Studies* number 28, Winter 1994, Aberystwyth, University of Wales.

Dark, K. (ed.) (1996a). *External contacts and the economy of Late Roman and Post Roman Britain* Woodbridge, The Boydell Press.

Dark, K. (1996b). 'Pottery and Local production at the end of Roman Britain' in Dark, K. (ed.) (1996). *External contacts and the economy of Late Roman and Post Roman Britain*

Woodbridge, The Boydell Press pp53–65.

Dark, K. (2000). *Britain and the End of the Roman Empire* Stroud, Tempus Publishing Ltd.

Dark, K. (2000b). 'The late Roman transition in the North: a discussion.' In Wilmott, T. and Wilson P. (2000). *The Late Roman Transition in the North, papers from the Roman archaeology conference, Durham 1999*, BAR British series 299, 2000, Oxford, Archaeopress.

Dark, S.P. (1996). 'Palaeoecological evidence for landscape continuity and change in Britain *c.*AD 400-800' in Dark, K.R. (ed.) (1996). *External contacts and the economy of Late Roman and Post Roman Britain* Woodbridge, The Boydell Press pp23–51.

Davey, J. (2004). 'The environs of South Cadbury in the late antique and early medieval periods' in Collins, R. and Gerrard, J. (eds) (2004). *Debating Late Antiquity in Britain AD 300–700*, BAR British series 365 Oxford, Archaeopress.

Davey, J.E. (2005). *The Roman to Medieval transition in the region of South Cadbury Castle, Somerset* BAR British series, 399 2005

Davies, C. (2006). 'Time Team solves the mystery of the Round Table' *The Daily Telegraph* Tuesday 29 August.

Davies, W. (1973). 'Liber Landavensis: Its Construction and Credibility' *English Historical Review*, vol 88 no.347.

Davies, W. (1978). *An Early Welsh Microcosm: Studies in the Llandaff Charters* Royal Historical Society.

Davies, W. (1979). *The Llandaff Charters* Aberystwyth, The National Library of Wales.

Davies, W. (1982). *Wales in the Early Middle Ages* Leicester, Leicester University Press.

Dawes, E. (trans.) (1948). *Three Byzantine Saints: Contemporary Biographies of St Daniel the Stylite, St Theodore of Sykeon and St John the Almsgiver*, London.

Draper, S. (2004). 'Roman estates to English parishes? The legacy of Desmond Bonney reconsidered' in Collins, R. and Gerrard, J. (eds) (2004). *Debating Late Antiquity in Britain AD 300–700*, BAR British series 365 Oxford, Archaeopress.

Driscoll, S.T. (1988). 'The relationship between history and archaeology: artefact, documents and power' in Driscoll, S.T. and Nieke, M.R. (eds) (1988). *Power and Politics in early medieval Britain and Ireland* Edinburgh, Edinburgh University Press, pp162–187.

Driscoll, S.T. and Nieke, M.R. (eds) (1988). *Power and Politics in early medieval Britain and Ireland* Edinburgh, Edinburgh University Press.

Dumville, D.N. (1977). 'Sub-Roman Britain: history and legend' *History* N.S. 62, 1977 pp173–192.

Dumville, D.N. (1984). 'The chronology of *de excidio britanniae*, book 1', in Lapidge, M. and Dumville, D. (eds) (1984). *Gildas, new approaches*, Studies in Celtic History V, Woodbridge, the Boydell Press.

Dumville, D.N. (1984). 'Gildas and Maelgwn, problems of dating', in Lapidge, M. and Dumville, D. (eds) (1984). *Gildas, new approaches* Studies in Celtic History V, Woodbridge, the Boydell Press.

Dumville, D.N. (1985). *The Historia Brittonum: the Vatican Recension* Cambridge, Brewer.

Dumville, D.N. (1985). 'The West Saxon genealogical regnal list and the chronology of early Wessex', in *Peritia*, Journal of the Medieval Academy of Ireland, vol. 4.

Dumville, D.N. (1989). 'The origins of Northumbria: some aspects of the British background.' In Bassett, S. (ed.) (1989). *The Origins of Anglo-Saxon Kingdoms* Leicester University Press, Leicester.

Dumville, D.N. (1990) *Histories and Pseudo-histories of the Insular Middle Ages* Aldershot, Variorum.

Dumville, D.N. (1993). *Britons and Saxons in the Early Middle Ages* Aldershot, Variorum.

Dumville, D.N. (2007) *Celtic essays 2001–2007* vol. I Aberdeen.

Dumville, D.N. (2007). *Celtic essays 2001–2007* vol. II Aberdeen.

Eagles, B. (1989). 'Lindsey' In Bassett, S. (ed.) (1989). *The Origins of Anglo-Saxon Kingdoms* Leicester University Press, Leicester.

Early Kings, http://ww.red4.co.uk/About%2520wales/kings/early/cadfan.jpg (27 September 2006).

Ellis, P.B. (1983). *Celt and Saxon: The struggle for Britain AD 410–937* Constable.

English Heritage events, http://www.english-heritage.org.uk/server/show/ConEvent.339 (1 August 2006).

English Heritage Marketing division (1989). 'Spotlight: visitors to properties in the care of English Heritage 1988/89'.

English Heritage Property, http://www.english-heritage.org.uk/server/show/ConProperty.316 (27 September 2006).

Esmonde Cleary, S. (1993). 'Approaches to the differences between late Romano-British and early Anglo-Saxon archaeology' in Filmer-Sankey, W. (ed.) (1993). *Anglo-Saxon studies in Archaeology and History 6*, Oxford, Oxford University committee for Archaeology.

Esmonde Cleary, S. (2000). 'Summing up' in Wilmott, T. and Wilson P. (2000). *The Late Roman Transition in the North, papers from the Roman archaeology conference, Durham 1999*, BAR British series 299, 2000 Oxford, Archaeopress.

Exxonmobil, http://www.exxonmobil.com/UK-English/operations/UK_OP_OFF_PRODUCTION_SOUTHERN_NORTH.asp (27 September 2006).

Fagan, G.G. (ed.) (2006). *Archaeological Fantasies: How pseudoarchaeology misrepresents the past and misleads the public* London, Routledge.

Fagan, G.G. (2006). 'Diagnosing Pseudoarchaeology' in Fagan, G.G. (ed.) (2006). *Archaeological Fantasies: How pseudoarchaeology misrepresents the past and misleads the public* London, Routledge pp23–46.

Fairbairn, N. (1983). *A Traveller's Guide to the Kingdoms of Arthur* London, Evans Brothers Ltd.

Faulkner, N. (2004). 'The Case for the Dark Ages' in Collins, R. and Gerrard, J. (eds) (2004). *Debating Late Antiquity in Britain AD 300–700, BAR British series 365*, Oxford, Archaeopress.

Fees, C. (1996). 'Tourism and the Politics of authenticity in a North Cotswold town' in Selwyn, T. (ed.) (1996). *The Tourist Image: Myths and Mythmaking in Tourism* Chichester, John Willey and Sons, pp121–146.

Ferris, I. and Jones, R. (2000). 'Transforming an elite: reinterpreting Late Roman Binchester'. Wilmott, T. and Wilson P. (2000). *The Late Roman Transition in the North, papers from the Roman archaeology conference, Durham 1999* BAR British series 299, 2000, Oxford, Archaeopress.

Field, P.J.C. (1999). 'Gildas and the City of the Legions', *The Heroic Age* issue 1, Spring/Summer 1999, http://www.mun.ca/mst/heroidage/issues/1/hagcl.htm

Fields, N. (2003). *Hadrian's Wall AD 122–410* Oxford, Osprey Publishing.

Fields, N. (2006). *Rome's Saxon Shore: Coastal Defences of Roman Britain AD 250–500* Oxford, Osprey Publishing.

Filmer-Sankey, W. (ed.) (1993). *Anglo-Saxon studies in Archaeology and History* 6 Oxford, Oxford University committee for Archaeology.

Fleming, N. (2006). 'The attraction of non-rational archaeological hypotheses: the individual and sociological factors' in Fagan, G.G. (ed.) (2006). *Archaeological Fantasies: How pseudoarchaeology misrepresents the past and misleads the public* London, Routledge pp47-70.

Ford, P.K. (1983). 'On the significance of some Arthurian Names in Welsh', *Bulletin of the Board of Celtic Studies 30*, pp268-73.

Fyfe, R. and Rippon, S. (2004). 'A landscape in transition? Palaeoenvironmental evidence for the end of the 'Romano-British' period in southwest England' in Collins, R. and Gerrard, J. (eds) (2004). *Debating Late Antiquity in Britain AD 300-700*, *BAR British series 365* Oxford, Archaeopress.

Gallen, S. *Myth, mythology and Hidden meaning: Semiotic research in Leisure and tourism – the informed tourist* http://www.arasite.org/sgres.htm/ (1 August 2006).

Gantz, J. (trans.) (1976). *The Mabinogion* Harmondsworth, Penguin Books.

Garmondsway, G.N. (1953). *The Anglo-Saxon Chronicle* London, Everyman.

Garner D. and Wilmott T. 'Chester: Dark Secrets of the arena revealed', *Current Archaeology 224*, November 2008.

Gathercole, P. and Lowenthal, D. (eds) (1990). *The Politics of the Past* London, Routledge.

Gazin-Schwartz, A. and Holtorf, C. (eds) (1999). *Archaeology and Folklore* London, Routledge.

Gazin-Schwartz and Holtorf, C. (1999). '"As long as ever I've known it…": On folklore and archaeology' in Gazin-Schwartz, A. and Holtorf, C. (ed.) (1999). *Archaeology and Folklore* London, Routledge pp3-25.

Gelling, M. (1989). 'The early history of Western Mercia' In Bassett, S. (ed.) (1989). *The Origins of Anglo-Saxon Kingdoms* Leicester University Press, Leicester.

Gelling, M. (1993). 'Why aren't we speaking Welsh?' in Filmer-Sankey, W. (ed.) (1993). *Anglo-Saxon studies in Archaeology and History 6*, Oxford, Oxford University committee for Archaeology.

Geoffrey of Monmouth, *Historia regum Britanniae*, (trans.) Thorpe, L. (1966) London, Penguin Books Ltd.

Geoffrey of Monmouth, *Historia regum Britanniae*, Reeve, M.D. (ed.) and Wright, N. (trans.) (2007) *The History of the Kings of Britain*, Woodbridge, Boydell.

Geoffrey of Monmouth, *Vita Merlini*, (trans.) White, P (2004). *Geoffrey of Monmouth: The Life of Merlin*, Launceston, Bossiney Books.

Gerald of Wales, *De principis instructione*, (ed.) Warner, G.F. (1891), Rolls series, 21, VIII, London.

Gerald of Wales, *Speculum Ecclessiae*, (ed.) Brewer, J.S. (1873), Rolls series, London, Longman and co.

Gerrard, J. (2004).'How late is late? Pottery and the fifth century in southwest Britain.' In Collins, R. and Gerrard, J. (eds) (2004). *Debating Late Antiquity in Britain AD 300-700, BAR British series 365* Oxford, Archaeopress.

Gidlow, C. (2004). *The Reign of Arthur: From History to Legend* Stroud, Sutton Publishing Ltd.

Gilbert, A, Blackett, B. And Wilson, A. (1998). *The Holy Kingdom: the Quest for the Real King Arthur*, Bantam Press.

Gildas, *De Excidio Britanniae*, (ed and trans) Winterbottom, M. (1978). *Gildas: The Ruin of Britain and other works* London, Phillimore and Co. Ltd.

Glastonbury Abbey, www.glastonburyabbey.com (27 September 2006).

Glastonbury Audio guide (2006).

Gransden, A. (1976). 'The growth of the Glastonbury traditions and legends in the twelfth century', *Journal of Ecclesiastical History* 27.4 pp337–58.

Green, M.J. (1997), *Dictionary of Celtic Myth and Legend*. London, Thames and Hudson.

Green, M.J. (1999). 'Back to the future: resonances of the past in myth and material culture' in Gazin-Schwartz, A. and Holtorf, C. (eds) (1999). *Archaeology and Folklore* London, Routledge pp48–66.

Green, T. (2007). *Concepts of Arthur*, Chalford, Tempus.

Green, T. (2007b). 'Lincolnshire and the Arthurian Legend' *Arthurian Notes & Queries 3*, www.arthuriana.co.uk.

Gregory of Tours, *History of the Franks*, trans. Thorpe, L. (1974) Harmondsworth, Penguin.

Hale, C. (2006). 'The Atlantean Box' in Fagan, G.G. (ed.) (2006). *Archaeological Fantasies: How pseudoarchaeology misrepresents the past and misleads the public* London, Routledge pp235 – 258.

Hallam, E. (ed.) (1986). *The Plantagenet Chronicles* London, Weidenfeld and Nicolson.

Hanks, N. www.slaughterbridgedig.blogspot.com)

Harden, D.B. (ed.) (1956). *Dark Age Britain* London, Methuen.

Harke, H. (1998). 'Archaeologists and migrations: a problem of attitude?', *Current Anthropology* vol. 39, number 1, February.

Henig, M. and Lindley, P. (eds) (2001). *Alban and St Albans: Roman and medieval architecture, art and archaeology* The British Archaeological Association Conference transactions xxiv, Leeds.

Henig, M. (2004). 'Remaining Roman in Britain AD 300–700, the evidence of portable art' in Collins, R and Gerrard, J (eds) (2004). *Debating Late Antiquity in Britain AD300–700, BAR British series 365* Oxford, Archaeopress.

Hewison, R. (1987). *The Heritage Industry: Britain in a Climate of Decline* London, Methuen.

Hibbert, C. (1969). *The Search for King Arthur* New York, American Heritage Publishing Co.

Higham, N.J. (1994). *The English Conquest: Gildas and Britain in the Fifth Century* Manchester, Manchester University Press.

Higham, N.J. (2002). *King Arthur: Mythmaking and History* London, Routledge.

Hinton, D.A. (2005). *Gold and Gilt, Pots and Pins: Possessions and People in Medieval Britain* Oxford, Oxford University Press.

Historia Brittonum, Morris, J. (ed. and trans.) (1980). *Nennius: British History and the Welsh Annals* London, Phillimore and Co. Ltd.

Holmes, M. (1996). *King Arthur, a Military History*, Blandford.

Hood, A.B.E. (ed. And trans.) (1978). *St Patrick, his writings and Muirchu's Life* London and Chichester, Phillimore and Co. Ltd.

Howell, R. (2004) 'From the fifth to the seventh century' in Aldhouse-Green Howell and, R, (eds) (2004). *The Gwent County History: vol. 1 Gwent in prehistory and early history* Cardiff

Hughes, K. (1973). 'The Welsh Latin Chronicles: *Annales Cambriae* and related texts', *Proceedings of the British Academy* 59 pp233–58.

Hughes, K. (1980). *Celtic Britain in the Early Middle Ages: Studies in Scottish and Welsh sources*, Woodbridge, Boydell.

Huntley, J.P. (2000). 'Late Roman transition in the North: the palynological evidence' in Wilmott, T. and Wilson P. (2000). *The Late Roman Transition in the North, papers from the Roman archaeology conference, Durham 1999*, BAR British series 299, Oxford, Archaeopress.

Hutton, R. (2003). *Witches, Druids and King Arthur* London, Hambledon Continuum.

Jackson, K.H. (1945). 'Once again Arthur's battles.', *Modern Philology 43*.

Jackson, K.H. (1949). 'Arthur's Battle of Breguoin', *Antiquity 23*.

Jackson K.H. (1959). 'The Arthur of History,' in Loomis, R.S. (1959) *Arthurian Literature in the Middle Ages: a collaborative history* Oxford, Oxford University Press

Jackson, K.H. (1971). *A Celtic Miscellany* Harmondsworth, Penguin.

Jameson Jr, J.H. (1997). *Presenting Archaeology to the Public: Digging for Truths* Walnut Creek, Altamira.

Jenkins, E. (1975). *The Mystery of King Arthur* London, Michael Joseph Limited.

Jones, G.D.B. and Mattingly, D. (1990). *An Atlas of Roman Britain*, Oxford, Basil Blackwell.

Jones, M.E. (1988). 'The appeal to Aetius in Gildas', *Nottingham Medieval Studies 32*.

Jones, S. and Pay, S. (1990). 'The legacy of Eve' in Gathercole, P. and Lowenthal, D. (eds) (1990). *The Politics of the Past* London, Routledge pp160–171.

Kendrick, T.D. (1950). *British Antiquity* London, Methuen and Co. Ltd.

Kirby, D.P. and Williams, J.E.C. (1975-76). 'Review of *The Age of Arthur*, J. Morris', *Studia Celtica 10–11*.

kingstonlacy, www.nationaltrust.org.uk/main/w-kingstonlacy/w-kingstonlacy-estate.htm

Knight, J. (1996). 'Seasoned with salt: Insular-Gallic contacts in the early memorial stones and cross slabs' in Dark, K.R. (ed.) (1996). *External contacts and the economy of Late Roman and Post Roman Britain* Woodbridge, The Boydell Press pp111-112.

Knight J.K. (2001). 'Britain's other martyrs: Julius, Aaron and Alban at Caerleon, 38-45 in Henig, M. and Lindley, P. (eds) (2001). *Alban and St Albans: Roman and medieval architecture, art and archaeology* The British Archaeological Association Conference transactions xxiv, Leeds pp38-45.

Knight, J. (2004). 'Society and religion in the early middle ages' in Aldhouse-Green, M and Howell, R., (eds) (2004). *The Gwent County History: vol. 1 Gwent in prehistory and early history*, Cardiff.

Koch, J.T. (1997). *The Gododdin of Aneirin: text and context from Dark Age North Britain* Cardiff, University of Wales Press.

Konstam, A. (2008). *British Forts in the Age of Arthur* Oxford, Osprey Publishing.

Lacy, N.J. (ed.) (1988). *The Arthurian Encyclopedia* Woodbridge, the Boydell Press.

Lapidge, M. and Dumville, D.N. (eds) (1984). *Gildas, new approaches*, Studies in Celtic History V, Woodbridge, the Boydell Press.

lasovase.blogspot.com/2008/08/dating-battle-of-chester.html

Layamon, *Brut*, Allen, R. (trans.) (1992) *Lawman: Brut* London, Orion Publishing Group.

Laycock, S. (2008). *Britannia, the failed state* Chalford, Tempus.

Layton R. (ed.) (1989a). *Who needs the past? Indigenous Values and Archaeology* London, Unwin Hyman.

Layton, R. (1989b) 'Introduction: Who needs the past?' in Layton R. (ed.) (1989a) *Who needs the past? Indigenous Values and Archaeology* London, Unwin Hyman pp1–20.

Leland. J. *Itinerary in England and Wales Vol 1* Smith, L.T. (ed.) (1964). *The Itinerary of John*

Leland in or about the years 1535–1543 Parts I–III London, Centaur Press.

Lerner, A.J. and Loewe, F. (1960). *Camelot* London, Chapelle.

Levitt, N. (2006). 'The Colonization of the past and the pedagogy of the future', in Fagan, G.G. (ed.) (2006). *Archaeological Fantasies: How pseudoarchaeology misrepresents the past and misleads the public* London, Routledge pp259–285.

Liebeschuetz, W. (1993). 'The end of the Roman army in the Western Empire' in Rich, J. and Shipley G. (eds) (1993). *War and Society in the Roman World* London

Littleton, C.S. and Malcor, L.A. (1994). *From Scythia to Camelot: A radical reassessment of the Legends of King Arthur, the Knights of the Round table and the Holy Grail*, New York, Garland Publishing.

Loomis, R.S. (1927). *Celtic Myth and Arthurian Romance*, Columbia University Press.

Loomis, R.S. (1953). 'Edward I, Arthurian Enthusiast', *Speculum 28*.

Loomis, R.S. (ed.) (1959). *Arthurian Literature in the Middle Ages*, Oxford, Clarendon Press.

Lovegrove, C. (2008a). 'Kings at Tintagel Castle', *Pendragon XXXVI No.1*.

Lovegrove, C. (2008b). 'Finds and Fakes', *Pendragon XXXVI No.1*.

MacDowall, S. (1994). *Late Roman Infantryman 236-565 AD*, London, Osprey.

MacDowall, S. (1995). *Late Roman Cavalryman 236-565 AD*, London, Osprey.

Major, A. (1978). *Early Wars of Wessex*, Poole, Blandford Press.

Malory, *Works*, Vinaver, E. (ed.) (1977). Oxford, Oxford University Press.

Mason D. in www.Lancsarchsoc.org.uk/programmeslisting0708.htm

Mason, D. (2007). Appleby Archaeology Group

Mason, D. (2008). Chester Archaeological Society www.chesterarchaeolsoc.org.uk/heronbridge.html

McManus, P.M. (ed.) (2000). *Archaeological Displays and the Public: Museology and Interpretation* London, Archetype Publications Ltd.

Michlovic M.G. (1990). 'Folk Archaeology in anthropological perspective' *Current Archaeology* 31, pp103–107.

Miller, M. (1975a). 'Bede's use of Gildas', *English Historical Review 90*.

Miller, M. (1975b). 'Historicity and the pedigree of the Northcountrymen', *Bulletin of the Board of Celtic Studies 26*.

Miller, M. (1976–7). 'Starting to write history: Gildas, Bede, and "Nennius"', *Welsh History Review 8*.

Miller, M. (1980). 'Consular years in the Historia Brittonum', *Bulletin of the Board of Celtic Studies 29*.

Miller, M. (1995–6). 'Date-guessing and pedigrees', *Studia Celtica 10–11*.

Monty Python and the Holy Grail (1974). Dir. Terry Gilliam and Terry Jones. Python (Monty) Pictures Ltd.

Morris, C.D., Nowakowski, J., Thomas, C. (1990). 'Tintagel, Cornwall: the 1990 excavations' *Antiquity* vol. 64 no. 245 December pp843-849.

Morris, C.D., Batey, C.E., Brady, K., Harry, R., Johnson, P.G. and Thomas, T. (1999a). 'Recent work at Tintagel' in *Medieval Archaeology, Journal of the Society for Medieval Archaeology* vol. XLIII 1999, London pp206–216.

Morris, C (1999b). 'Tintagel and the Myth of King Arthur' *Institute of Field Archaeologists Yearbook and Directory of members* 1999, Reading, University of Reading pp19–21.

Morris, J, (1973, 1977). *The Age of Arthur: A History of the British Isles from 350 to 650* London Phillimore and Co. Ltd.

Myres, J.N.L. (1969). *Anglo-Saxon Pottery and the Settlement of England* Oxford, Clarendon Press.

Myres, J.N.L. (1986). *The English Settlements* Oxford, Clarendon Press.

Nicolle, D. (1984). *Arthur and the Anglo-Saxon Wars: Anglo-Celtic Warfare, AD 410–1066* London, Osprey Publishing Ltd.

Nowakowski, J.A. and Thomas, C. (1990). *Excavations at Tintagel Parish Churchyard Cornwall, Spring 1990, Interim report* Cornwall Archaeological unit and Institute of Cornish Studies.

O'Brien, E. (1999). *Post-Roman Britain to Anglo-Saxon England: burial practices reviewed* BAR British series 289, Oxford.

Ordnance Survey (1974). *Map of Britain in the Dark Ages*, Southampton, Ordnance Survey.

Ordnance Survey (1994). *Roman Britain, historical map and guide, 5th edition* Southampton, Ordnance Survey.

Pace, E. (2008). *Arthur and the Fall of Roman Britain* Cheltenham, Invermark Books.

Padel, O.J. (1981) 'Tintagel – an alternative view' in Thomas, C. (1981) *A provisional List of Imported Pottery in Post-Roman Western Britain and Ireland* Redruth, Institute of Cornish Studies pp28–29.

Padel, O. (1991). 'Some south-western sites with Arthurian associations' in Bromwich, R., Jarman A.O.H and Roberts, B.F. (eds) (1991). *The Arthur of the Welsh* Cardiff, University of Wales Press.

Pearce, S.M. (ed.) (1982). *The Early Church in Western Britain and Ireland* Oxford: BAR.

Petts, D. (2004). 'Burial in western Britain AD 400–800: Late Antique or Early Medieval?' in Collins, R. and Gerrard, J. (eds) (2004). *Debating Late Antiquity in Britain AD 300–700, BAR British series 365* Oxford, Archaeopress.

Phillips, G. and Keatman. M. (1993) *King Arthur: the True Story* London, Arrow.

Pokotylo, D. and Brass, G. (1997). 'Interpreting Cultural resources: Hatzic Site' in Jameson Jr, J.H. (1997). *Presenting Archaeology to the Public: Digging for Truths* Walnut Creek, Altamira pp156–165.

Prestwich, M. (1988). *Edward I* London, Methuen.

Pretty, K. (1989). 'Defining the Magonsaete' in Bassett, S. (ed.) (1989). *The Origins of Anglo-Saxon Kingdoms* Leicester University Press, Leicester.

Preucel, R. and Hodder, I. (eds) (1996). *Contemporary Archaeology in Theory* Oxford, Blackwell Publishing Ltd.

Radford, C.A.R. (1942). 'Tintagel in History and Legend' in *Journal of the Royal Inst. of Cornwall* 25 (1942) appendix 26-41, pp40–41.

Radford, C.A.R. (1956). 'Imported pottery found at Tintagel, Cornwall' in Harden, D.B. (ed.) (1956). *Dark Age Britain* London, Methuen pp59–70.

Radford, C.A.R. (1968). 'Glastonbury Abbey', in Ashe, G. (ed.) (1968). *The Quest for Arthur's Britain* London, Granada Publishing Ltd pp111–122.

Rahtz, P. (1968). 'Glastonbury Tor' in Ashe, G. (ed.) (1968). *The Quest for Arthur's Britain* London, Granada Publishing Ltd pp111–122.

Radford, C.A. and Swanton, M.J. (1975, revised 2002). *Arthurian sites in the west revised edition* Exeter, University of Exeter Press.

Rahtz, P. (1991) 'Pagan and Christian by the Severn Sea' in Abrams, L. and Carley, J.P. (eds) (1991). *The Archaeology and History of Glastonbury Abbey: Essays in honour of the ninetieth birthday of C.A. Ralegh Radford* Woodbridge, The Boydell Press pp3–37.

✂

Rahtz, P. (1993). *English Heritage Book of Glastonbury* London, B.T. Batsford/English Heritage.

Rahtz, P. and Watts, L. (2003). *Glastonbury: Myth and Archaeology* Stroud, Tempus Publishing Ltd.

Rahtz, P.(2004). 'Foreword' in Collins, R. and Gerrard, J. (eds) (2004). *Debating Late Antiquity in Britain AD 300–700, BAR British series 365* Oxford, Archaeopress.

Rahtz, P., Hirst, S. and Wright, S. M. (2000). *Cannington Cemetery* Britannia Monograph series no. 17, London.

Ralph of Coggeshall, *Chronicon Anglicanum* (ed.) Stevenson, J. (1875). Rolls series 66, London. Longman and Co.

Reader's Digest Association (1973). *Folklore, Myths and Legends of Britain* London, The Reader's Digest Association Ltd.

Renfrew, C. and Bahn, P. (2004). *Archaeology: Theories, Methods and Practice, 4th edition* London, Thames and Hudson.

Rich, J. (ed.) (1992). *The City in Late Antiquity* London, Routledge.

Rich, J. and Shipley G. (eds) (1993). *War and Society in the Roman World* London

Ridley, R.T. (trans.) (1982). *Zosimus: New History*, Sydney, Australian Association for Byzantine Studies.

Rivet, A.L.F. and Smith, C. (1981). *The Place-Names of Roman Britain* London, B.T. Batsford Ltd.

Romer, J. (2000). *Great Excavations* London, Cassell and Co.

Robinson, H.R. (1976). *What the Soldiers wore on Hadrian's Wall* Newcastle upon Tyne, Frank Graham.

Rose, G. (1998). *translations* http://omega.colums.ohio.state.edu/mailing_lists/ LT.ANTIQ/1998/08/0020.php (1 August 2006).

Rüsen, J. (1993). *Studies in Metahistory* Pretoria, Human Sciences Research council.

Sacred Texts, www.sacred-texts.com/neu/eng/ppx/pp05.htm (1 August 2006).

Salway, P. (1981). *Roman Britain* Oxford, Oxford University Press.

Schaffner, P (1984). 'Britain's *Iudices*' in Lapidge, M. and Dumville, D.N. (eds) (1984). *Gildas, new approaches* Studies in Celtic History V, Woodbridge, the Boydell Press. pp151–155.

Scott, J. (1981). *The Early History of Glastonbury* Woodbridge, Boydell and Brewer.

Scull, C. (1993). 'Archaeology, early Anglo-Saxon society and the origins of Anglo Saxon kingdoms' in Filmer-Sankey, W. (ed.) (1993). *Anglo-Saxon studies in Archaeology and History 6* Oxford, Oxford University Committee for Archaeology.

Selwyn, T. (ed.) (1996). *The Tourist Image: Myths and Mythmaking in Tourism* Chichester, John Willey and Sons.

Sherley-Price, L. (trans.) (1955). *Bede: A History of the English Church and People* Harmondsworth, Penguin.

Sidonius Apollinaris. *Poems and Letters*, trans. Anderson, W.B. (1936 vol. 2 1965) London, Loeb Classical Library.

Sims-Williams, P.(1983a) 'Gildas and the Anglo-Saxons' in *Cambridge Medieval Celtic Studies. 6* (1983) pp1–30.

Sims-Williams, P. (1983b). 'The settlement of England in Bede and the Chronicle', in *Anglo Saxon England 12*, (1983) Cambridge, Cambridge University Press pp1–41.

Smiles, S. (1994). *The Image of Antiquity: Ancient Britain and the Romantic Imagination* New Haven, Yale University Press.

Smith, A.D. (1999). *Myths and Memories of the Nation* Oxford, Oxford University Press.

Smith, A.H.W. (1998). 'The names on the stone.', *Ceridwen's Cauldron 39*, Oxford, Oxford Arthurian Society.

Smith, R. (2003). 'When you're in a hole…' *The Guardian*, 16 June.

Snyder, C.A. (1998). *An Age of Tyrants: Britain and the Britons AD 400–600* Stroud, Sutton Publishing.

Snyder, C.A. (2000). *Exploring the World of King Arthur* London, Thames and Hudson Ltd.

Sokal, A.D. (2006). 'Pseudoscience and postmodernism: Antagonists or fellow travellers?' in Fagan, G.G. (ed.) (2006). *Archaeological Fantasies: How pseudoarchaeology misrepresents the past and misleads the public* London, Routledge pp286–261.

Somerset, http://somerset.gov.uk/archives/ASH/Endromanocc.htm (27 September 2006).

South Cadbury Environs Project, http://web.arch.ox.ac.uk/~scep/home.php (26 September 2006).

South Somerset District Council, Museums and Heritage services, http://www.southsomersetmuseums.org.uk/heritage/cadbury.htm (27 September 2006).

South, S. (1997). 'Generalized versus Literal Interpretation' in Jameson Jr, J.H. (1997). *Presenting Archaeology to the Public: Digging for Truths* Walnut Creek, Altamira pp54–62.

Spector, J.D. (1996). 'What this Awl Means: Towards a Feminist Archaeology' in Preucel, R. and Hodder, I. (eds) (1996). *Contemporary Archaeology in Theory* Oxford, Blackwell Publishing Ltd pp485–500.

Stallibrass, S. (2000). 'How little we know, and how much there is to learn: what can animal and human bones tell us about the late Roman transition in Northern England?' in Wilmott, T. and Wilson P. (2000). *The Late Roman Transition in the North, papers from the Roman archaeology conference, Durham 1999*, BAR British series 299, 2000 Oxford, Archaeopress.

Stewart, M. (1979). *The Last Enchantment* London, Hodder.

Stoneman, R. (trans.) (1991). *The Greek Alexander Romance* London, Penguin Books Ltd.

Sutcliff, R. (1963). *Sword at Sunset* London, Hodder.

Thomas, C. (1968). 'Are these the walls of Camelot?' *Antiquity* 43 (1969).

Thomas, C. (1981). *A provisional list of Imported Pottery in Post-Roman Western Britain and Ireland* Redruth, Institute of Cornish Studies.

Thomas, C. (1982). 'East and West: Tintagel, Mediterranean imports and the early insular church', in Pearce, S.M. (ed.) (1982). *The Early Church in Western Britain and Ireland* Oxford, BAR, pp17–34.

Thomas, C. (1993). *English Heritage Book of Tintagel, Arthur and Archaeology* London, B.T. Basford Ltd/English Heritage.

Thompson, E.A. (1979). 'Gildas and the history of Britain', *Britannia 10*.

Thompson, E.A. (1984). *Saint Germanus of Auxerre and the End of Roman Britain* Woodbridge, Boydell Press.

Thompson, P. (1988). *The Voice of the Past: oral history, second edition* Oxford, Oxford University Press.

Time Team, www.channel4.com/history/timeteam/archive/2000arthur.html (1 August 2006).

Tintagel Web, www.tintagelweb.co.uk (27 September 2006).

Todd, M. *Anglo-Saxon Origins: The Reality of the Myth*, http://www.intellectbooks.com/nation/html/anglos.htm (27 September 2006).

Treharne, R.F. (1971). *The Glastonbury Legends* London, Sphere Books Limited.

Truro Museum (2006). Inscribed slate caption.

Turner, S. (2004). 'Coast and Countryside in 'late antique' southwest England *c.*AD 400-600' in Collins, R. and Gerrard, J. (eds) (2004). *Debating Late Antiquity in Britain AD 300–700, BAR British series 365* Oxford, Archaeopress.

University of Glasgow (1998). *Tintagel excavation report* http://www.gla.ac.uk/archaeology/projects/tintagel/index.html (27 September 2006).

Vatican Recension, (ed.) Dumville, D.N. (1985). *The Historia Brittonum 3 The 'Vatican' Recension* Cambridge, D.S. Brewer Ltd.

Visit Winchester, brief history, http://www.visitwinchester.co.uk/site/about-winchester/brief-history (1 August 2006).

Visit Winchester, literary connections, http://www.visitwinchester.co.uk/site/about-winchester/literary-connections (1 August 2006).

Wacher, J.S. (1995). *The Towns of Roman Britain*, London, Routledge.

Wade-Evans, A.W. (trans.) (1938). *Nennius's 'History of the Britons' together with 'The Annals of the Britons' and 'Court Pedigrees of Hywel the Good'* London, Society for Promoting Christian Knowledge.

Wade-Evans, A.W. (1944). *Vitae Sanctorum Britanniae et Genealogiae* Cardiff, University of Wales Press.

Ward, D.J. (1969). *The Divine Twins: an Indo-European myth in Germanic tradition* University of California Folklore Studies vol. 19.

Ward-Perkins, B. (2005). *The Fall of Rome and the End of Civilization* Oxford, Oxford University Press.

Welch, M. (1989). 'The kingdom of the South Saxons: the origins' In Bassett, S. (ed.) (1989). *The Origins of Anglo-Saxon Kingdoms* Leicester University Press, Leicester.

Wheeler, M. (1972). 'General Editor's preface' in Alcock, L. (1972). '*By South Cadbury is that Camelot…': The Excavation of Cadbury Castle 1966–1970* London, Thames and Hudson pp7–8.

White, H. (1973). *Metahistory, The Historical Imagination in Nineteenth-Century Europe* London, The Johns Hopkins University Press.

White, P. (2002). *King Arthur's Footsteps* Launceston, Bossiney Books.

White, R. (ed.) (1997). *King Arthur in Legend and History* London, J.M. Dent.

White, R. (2007). *Britannia Prima: Britain's last Roman province.* Chalford, Tempus Publishing Ltd.

Whitelock, D. (ed.) (1955). *English Historical Documents c.500–1042*, Eyre and Spottiswoode.

Whittaker, D. (1993). 'Landlords and warlords in the later Roman Empire' in Rich, J. and Shipley G. (eds) (1993). *War and Society in the Roman World* London

Williams, H. (1899). *Two Lives of Gildas by a Monk of Ruys and Caradoc of Llancarfan* Cymmrodorion Record Series.

Williams, H (2004). 'Artefacts in early medieval graves: a new perspective' in Collins, R. and Gerrard, J. (eds) (2004). *Debating Late Antiquity in Britain AD 300–700, BAR British series 365* Oxford, Archaeopress.

Williams, I (ed.) and Williams, J.E. Caerwyn (trans.) (1968). *The Poems of Taliesin*, Dublin, Institute of Advanced Studies.

Wilmott, T. and Wilson P. (2000). *The Late Roman Transition in the North, papers from the Roman archaeology conference, Durham 1999*, BAR British series 299, 2000, Oxford, Archaeopress.

Wilmott, T. (2000). 'The late Roman transition at Birdoswald and on Hadrian's Wall' in Wilmott, T. and Wilson P. (2000). *The Late Roman Transition in the North, papers from the Roman archaeology conference, Durham 1999*, BAR British series 299, 2000, Oxford, Archaeopress.

Wilson, P. (2000). 'Cataractonium (Catterick): the end of a Roman town?' in Wilmott, T. and Wilson P. (2000). *The Late Roman Transition in the North, papers from the Roman archaeology conference, Durham 1999*, BAR British series 299, 2000, Oxford, Archaeopress.

Wiseman, H.M. (2007). 'The historicity and historiography of Arthur: A critical review of *King Arthur: Myth-making and History* by N. Higham and *The Reign of Arthur: From History to Legend* by C. Gidlow', *The Heroic Age*, issue 10, http://www.mun.ca/mst/heroicage/issues/10/forum.html

Wood, C.T. (1991). 'Fraud and its consequences: Savaric of Bath and the reform of Glastonbury', in Abrams, L and Carley, J.P. (eds) (1991). *The Archaeology and History of Glastonbury Abbey: Essays in honour of the ninetieth birthday of C.A. Ralegh Radford* Woodbridge, The Boydell Press, pp273–283.

Wood, I. (1984). 'The end of Roman Britain: continental evidence and parallels' pp1-25 in Lapidge, M. and Dumville, D.N. (eds) (1984). *Gildas, new approaches*, Studies in Celtic History V, Woodbridge, the Boydell Press pp1–25.

Wood, J. (2004). 'Caerleon restaurata: the narrative world of early medieval Gwent' in Aldhouse-Green, M. and Howell, R. (eds) (2004). *The Gwent County History: volume 1 Gwent in prehistory and early history* Cardiff.

Wood, M. (1981). 'In Search of the Dark Ages' BBC.

Wood-Langford, E. (2008). *Looking for Camelot (A New Hypothesis)* Guildford, Grosvenor House.

Wright, N. (1985). 'Did Gildas read Orosius?', *Cambridge Medieval Celtic Studies 9*.

www.cityofbath.co.uk/tours/body_thingstoseeinbath.html

www.guardian.co.uk/environment/gallery/2009/Feb/09/solsbury-hill-protest-anniversary)

www.Leeds.ac.uk/ims/fieldsofconflict/fieldsofconflictabstracts.htm

www.resurgence.org/magazine/article2931-Solsbury-Hill.html

www.solsburyhill.org/explainationsolsbury.html

Yorke, B. (1989). 'The Jutes of Hampshire and Wight and the origins of Wessex' in Bassett, S. (ed.) (1989). *The Origins of Anglo-Saxon Kingdoms* Leicester, University Press, Leicester.

Yorke, B. (1993). 'Fact or fiction? The written evidence for the fifth and sixth centuries AD' in Filmer-Sankey, W. (ed.) (1993). *Anglo-Saxon studies in Archaeology and History 6*, Oxford, Oxford University committee for Archaeology.

INDEX

✄